Time To Be Rational

Darwin, Demons and Sex

Also by Geoff Simons

Time To Be Rational

Darwin, Demons and Sex

Geoff Simons

METHUEN

306 .
6
Sim

First published in Great Britain 2009 by
Methuen Publishing Ltd
8 Artillery Row
London
SW1P 1RZ

10 9 8 7 6 5 4 3 2 1

A CIP catalogue record for this book is available from the British Library.

ISBN 978-0-413-77683-9

Set in Bembo by SX Composing DTP, Rayleigh, Essex
Printed and bound in Great Britain by TJ International Ltd, Padstow

Contents

Jesus didn't know his kerb drill and he was killed on the crossing.

Quotations from children, *Times Educational Supplement*, 28 July 1972

An Islamist rebel administration in Somalia has had a thirteen-year-old girl stoned to death for adultery after the child's father reported that she was raped by three men . . . A lorry load of stones was brought . . . for the killing . . . Nurses were instructed to check whether Aisha Ibrahim Duhulow was still alive when buried in the ground. They removed her from the ground, declared that she was, and she was replaced in the hole where she had been buried for the stoning to continue.

The Guardian, 3 November 2008

Aisha was crying when dragged to the hole to be buried with only her head protruding . . . As the stoning proceeded, her face and head were bleeding copiously. 'It is the command of Allah,' said a man.

Testimony of anonymous eyewitness, *Today*, BBC Radio 4,
4 November 2008

Acknowledgements

I am grateful to Christine Simons, who helped enormously with this book, as always.

Particular thanks are due to Jonathan Wadman, Methuen editor, whose patience and diligent efforts made an invaluable contribution to this work.

I also thank 'God', without which this book would not have been written.

Geoff Simons
February 2009

Preface

I, as an atheist, hold these truths to be self-evident.

Today, in the light of modern physics, we are bound to conclude that matter/energy is all there is, though our view of it constantly changes and develops. It seems that physics and chemistry alone constitute all the phenomena of the world, including human beings with their remarkable brains capable of generating creativity, compassion and love. There are no substances other than matter/energy that might constitute the fabric of supernatural entities.

Despite all the efforts of philosophers and theologians over millennia it is impossible to give the symbol 'god' any intelligible meaning that serves religious belief. Attempts to cloak 'god' with mystery do no more than signal its vacuous nature.

What philosophers have called the 'standard arguments' (teleological, cosmological, ontological, moral etc.) for God's existence are all invalid, sometimes sharing flaws and sometimes individually exhibiting unique fallacies.

No-one can doubt that the long process of biological evolution has been rooted in misery, disease, blood letting and pain. The suffering of animals began before *Homo sapiens* emerged on the earth and has continued ever since. The extent of this suffering alone, before we even address the suffering of human beings, has led philosophers and theologians to consider the 'problem of evil'. The suffering of animate creatures on earth rules out the Christian and Islamic deities, said to be 'omnipotent' and 'compassionate', as manifest absurdities.

It is easy to see that no imagined divinity can provide a ground for morality. To claim 'God is good' – and to avoid tautology – implies that there is an independent concept of good prior to its application to a deity. Similarly, there are no grounds for believing that a celestial tyrant watches our every move and insists that we behave according to its moral prejudices. We derive our concept of good from rational social considerations, without help from imaginary supernatural forces.

God does not exist, just as Zeus, Ra and Baal do not exist. The term 'God' was born in ancient times, in a pre-scientific world. Today it is sustained mainly by self-interested social forces, such as political hierarchies and misogynistic imams. It is widely propagated by creating terror through the brutal indoctrination of children.

We are bound to conclude also, however regretfully for some, that heaven, hell, demons, angels, fairies, elves, hobgoblins, vampires and werewolves do not exist. All are imaginary creations that embellish our fictions, but have no reality in the world.

What we call 'free will' is a meaningless symbol, often paraded by sadistic moralists as an excuse to inflict pain. ('He had free will. He could have behaved differently.') Free will, rationally viewed, is nothing more than conditioned choice – of which electronic computers are also capable. There is nothing free about it.

Research into brain functions suggest that mysticism and revelation say nothing whatever about realities outside the person. They do, however, provide interesting data for psychologists and psychiatrists.

Faith, the last resort of the dogmatic believer, is the blind determination to embrace attractive notions, in the absence of reason or evidence. Where reason and evidence support a belief, there is no talk of faith. 'It's not a matter of reason, it's a matter of faith.' In short, faith makes the believer infinitely gullible: *anything* that is emotionally appealing can be believed.

The character of the human body suggests that there is no afterlife, no survival beyond death. Personality and mind decay totally with the brain. 'Spirit' and 'soul' are symbols invented in the vain attempt to allow believers to escape mortality. It signals mainly the fear of extinction, but the symbol denotes nothing about the nature of human beings.

Alternatives to reason cannot stand. To argue – using logic? – against logic is an absurd enterprise.

If anyone suggests that these truths are mere polemics I would quote David Pears: 'Philosophic theories are usually developed polemically.'[1] *It is just that some polemics are more polemical than others.*

Geoff Simons
February 2009

Introduction

Advocates of mainstream religion have always been keen to propagate their beliefs: for example, through the indoctrination of children. This has nothing to do with teaching children to think, but rather the reverse – to encourage the blind acceptance of doctrine in the absence of critical scrutiny. For example, in madrasas and other religious schools in Pakistan, India, Saudi Arabia, Britain and other countries, children who cannot read or speak Arabic are often taught to memorise Arabic verses from the Koran, as if being able to recite particular passages without comprehension is the essence of piety. Students who manage to memorise the entire Koran are regarded as especially devout, while their less diligent classmates, compelled to study the Koran and nothing else, struggle to memorise as much as they can. This narrow approach to education has been regarded as a form of child abuse, not least because on occasions the religious devotion of the mullahs runs to excess.

In May 2008 a blind seven-year-old, Mohammed Atif, was beaten to death in a Pakistani madrasa for failing to memorise the Koran. The boy was first hung by his feet from a ceiling fan for an hour by his religious teacher, Qari Ziauddin, before being beaten. The boy died of severe head injuries, and marks of physical torture were found on his body. Ziauddin, arrested by the police, said: 'We punish students who don't learn their lessons. We used to get similar beatings when we were studying in the schools. It is not uncommon.'[1]

There are now 1,600 unregulated madrasas in Britain, and evidence of serious child abuse in many of them. An unpublished report by an imam, Irfan Chishti, based on interviews with Muslim victims and others, revealed the extent of the abuse. One child was 'picked up by one leg and spun around' by his madrasa teacher, while another said that a teacher was 'kicking in my head – like a football'. One madrasa teacher slapped a seven-year-old girl so hard on her ear that she needed emergency hospital treatment; a twelve-year-old girl was hit whenever she mispronounced a word or forgot a verse of the Koran. Some Muslim teachers punish children by using the 'Hen', in which a child is forced to hold his ears while squatting with his arms fed through his legs. A number of mainstream primary teachers, having become aware of such abuses, have informed social services of the child protection issues involved. Here problems arise because the beating of children is regarded as normal practice in many Muslim communities.[2]

This harsh approach to education has inevitable consequences for legislation and social attitudes in Islamic countries. For example, in July 2008 eight women and one man in Iran were sentenced to death by stoning after being convicted of adultery in verdicts blamed on a resurgence of hardline Islamic funda-mentalism. The hearings were held in private in the absence of witnesses and defence lawyers. The female defendants claimed they had been raped and forced into prostitution, and asserted that they did not understand interrogations conducted in Farsi, not the defendants' language. Proposed laws before the Iranian parliament were intended to allow execution for witchcraft and to sanction punishments such as blinding and amputation, measures supported by hardline religious groups.[3]

At the same time Christian cults in the United States were implementing practices to protect polygamy and to break up the family. For example, up to 1,000 teenage boys, some as young as thirteen, had been separated from their parents and thrown out of their communities by the leaders of the Fundamentalist Church of Jesus Christ of Latter-Day Saints to make more young women available for older men. The boys, some dumped on the side of the road in Arizona and Utah, were told that they would never see their families again or go to heaven.[4] The sect believes that no man can go to heaven if he has fewer than three wives; reckons that black people, the descendants of Cain, are inferior; and teaches that America, first colonised by a lost tribe of Israelites, was visited by Jesus after his resurrection.

Elsewhere superstitious communities were intent on persecuting people thought to be violating holy teachings. Thus albinos in Tanzania, believed to possess evil magic powers, were being burnt to death, while homosexuals in the Anglican communion were receiving death threats for allegedly ignoring the Word of God. The Pope, driven to acknowledge the scale of sexual abuse by priests, was issuing further apologies (see Chapter 5). Christianity and Islam, supposedly inspired by one true divinity, continue to face various schismatic pressures deriving from politics, culture and the growing secularism of the modern world.

Today it is obvious that irrational creeds, whether embodied in mainstream religion or in extremist cults, lack independent protocols for the settling of internal disputes and controversies. The inevitable result is superstition, manifest throughout faith groups around the world and countered only by the objective criteria provided by rational enquiry. Charles Darwin offers the supreme example of how empirical evidence can be used to counter irrational beliefs and social repression.

Chapter 1, 'The Law of Evolution', profiles the unique contribution made by Darwin in charting the process that yielded all the richness of the biological world and in consequence the place of humankind within it. The word 'law' is carefully chosen. Opponents of Darwin make great play of the *theory* of evolution: 'It's only a theory.' It is time we gave the law of evolution its proper designation. Today evolution is as securely established as any other biological fact. Hence we never talk about the theory of the circulation of the blood or the theory of DNA. Today the law of evolution is properly regarded as a crucial part of objective biological knowledge.

Chapter 2, by way of contrast, charts the superstitious world that generated the mainstream religions. Here we argue that there is no logical difference between religion and cult. Both rely on the irrational adoption of superstitious notions that gain no support in reason. Both discourage rational enquiry, urge blind acceptance and propagate fear. Both derive from a more ignorant phase of human development. The religious believer who criticises cults should note that the same strictures apply equally to mainstream religious doctrines, which, through accident of politics and history, have come to enjoy a measure of social respectability.

Chapter 3 focuses on the matter of interpretation. Today religious belief is beset by problems. Sacred texts are criticised from within and outside the faith; the morality of religious figures is often questioned; there is no sure authority; 'scholars' work hard to suggest ways in which the doctrine can be reworked for the modern age – which in turn breeds more dissension and disagreement. And fresh interpretation has its own unique problems. By what authority can a human scholar recast the words of a divinity?

Chapters 4 and 5 indicate something of the social and human impact of mainstream religion – here, in the realm of sexual behaviour. It is no accident that sexual repression, at times amounting to a psychopathology, has borne most heavily on women. Men have made the rules, written the texts, imposed the doctrines. Women in consequence have been disparaged, commodified and abused. The disreputable social impact of religion is multifaceted, but to focus solely on how religion has distorted the status of women is one ample indictment among many.

The atheist has no need to square the circle. There is no requirement to make sense out of religious nonsense. The atheist is not troubled by interpretation since the sacred texts can be discarded as largely unhelpful in addressing human problems in society. Instead the development of mainstream religion can be studied like any other social phenomenon – which in turn forces us to acknowledge its confused and repressive role throughout the long pre-scientific phase of human society. It is high time we learnt to outgrow the religious superstitions that continue to dominate the social attitudes of much of the world. It is high time we learnt to be rational.

1
The law of evolution

It is . . . easy to see why the churches have always fought science and persecuted its devotees.

Albert Einstein, *The World as I See It* (1935)

Since the time of Darwin we understand much better why living creatures are adapted to their environment . . . There is no evidence of design about it.

Bertrand Russell, *Why I Am Not a Christian* (1927)

The Babylonians believed that all things were created from the body parts of a dismembered goddess. The Greeks believed that the bird Nyx, at first alone in the void, sat on a golden egg for ages until Eros broke out and made Uranus and Gaia fall in love. The Japanese believed that an original germ of life stirred things around until a muddy sea yielded a green shoot that grew into a lonely god. The African Bushmen believed that people and animals lived peacefully together under the earth until a god dug a hole to let them out. The Australian aborigines believed that the supreme god awoke a sleeping sun goddess and told her to turn the sleeping spirits into forms. The Iroquois believed that a man pushed his wife through a hole in their island home in the sky to fall into the waters beneath. In these and countless other creation myths there are common themes such as birth, the origins of life and the arrival of sin in the world.

The myth makers, keen to embellish burgeoning cults and religions, never shrank from attempts to fill the vast void in human knowledge. They were eager to deal with the central questions that have plagued people from the earliest times. Our question is: do we believe their answers? Do we believe the Hebrew/ Christian myth that insists that God created day and night on the

first day and the sun on the fourth day?[1] Do we believe the
Muslim myth that God created man from blood clots?[2] Or, since
the myth maker Mohammed could not make up his mind, from
dried clay?[3] Of course Muslims are here presented with a problem
since they are expected to believe the Koran in its entirety – an
obligation deriving from the supposed unique authority of
Mohammed, sometimes signalled in unusual ways. The atheist
Bertrand Russell tells us that after Mohammed's death his son-in-
law, who was preparing the body, exclaimed: '*O propheta, certe
poenis tuus coelum versus erectus est!*' ('O prophet, undoubtedly your
penis, now that it is erect, is pointed to heaven!')[4] Whether or not
this detail will help to persuade doubting Muslims to embrace the
prophet I cannot say.

The central question is whether we are to attempt a rational
enquiry into the origins and development of humankind or
whether we simply accept fanciful tales that purport to provide an
explanation. Put simply, is our allegiance to science or superstition? Of course there are plenty of people, including some
scientists, who heroically struggle to marry the two. The vast and
growing authority of science cannot be dismissed or ignored, and
yet the appeal of the supernatural persists. There are psychological
factors at work here that sometimes lead people into absurd
realms, even people who should know better. The faith of the
religious cosmologist or biologist would not survive for an instant
if the tools of scientific enquiry and analysis were robustly applied
to supernatural beliefs that remain rooted in a pre-scientific age.

The tension between science and religion has been apparent
over the millennia, and to hope, as some do, that they will marry
and live happily ever after is a gross delusion. Science has evolved
as a cautious endeavour, propelled by self-corrective mechanisms
that discard unsatisfactory hypotheses and build upon what can
be consensually grounded in experiment and reason. Scientific
failures, frauds, controversies and subversion by political establish-
ments do nothing to dilute the power of scientific method.
Religion, by contrast, plucks notions, often ridiculous, out of the
imagination and has no regard for consistency or the progressive
accumulation of verifiable knowledge. The massive libraries of

biochemistry, nuclear physics and computer science represent treasure houses of consensual knowledge, dazzling tributes to human accomplishment. Where is the equivalent in the world of religion? Scientists in New York and Beijing, in Moscow and Manchester, in Leipzig and Sydney agree on the structure of the DNA double helix and the nuclear mechanisms at the centre of stars. Where is the equivalent vast consensual knowledge, at once coherent and rationally evolving, in the world of religion?

Galileo Galilei (1564–1642) represents the much-rehearsed archetype of the enduring conflict between science and super-naturalism. A founder of the experimental method, he published his *Dialogue Concerning the Two Chief World Systems*, openly supporting Nicholas Copernicus (1473–1543), who had established through his observations and calculations that the earth and the planets revolved around the sun.[5] The Roman Catholic Church responded to Galileo, having dragged him in chains before the Inquisition, with a sentence denouncing him

> for holding as true a false doctrine . . . namely that the sun is immovable in the centre of the world, and that the earth moves . . . for having pupils whom you instructed in the same opinions . . . for maintaining a correspondence on the same with some German mathematicians . . . for publishing certain letters on the sunspots . . . and for [contesting] the Holy Scriptures.[6]

Galileo's views were denounced as 'heretical', representing a doctrine that was 'so pernicious' that it had to 'be altogether rooted out, not [to] insinuate itself further to the heavy detriment of the Catholic truth . . . altogether contrary to the Holy and Divine Scripture'. The church banned the *Dialogue* and punished Galileo for his 'grievous and pernicious error': 'We condemn you to the formal prison of this Holy Office for a period determinable at our pleasure . . . We order you during the next three years to recite, once a week, the seven penitential psalms.'[7] Galileo – seventy years old, very ill and going blind, and facing the possibility of horrendous torment – was forced to 'abjure, curse and detest the said errors and heresies, and generally every other error and sect contrary to said Holy Church'. He would subject himself to 'all the pains and punishments decreed' and acknowledged himself a 'delinquent'.[8] Galileo was rumoured to have whispered, after the abjuration, '*Eppur si muove*' ('Nevertheless it does move').

Even today, despite papal commentaries, the attitude of the Roman Catholic Church to Galileo is ambivalent. Perhaps, some clerics have suggested, it was not what Galileo said that mattered but the way he said it: he was too abrupt. Heretics must be punished for their polemical tone. Later an attempt was made to salvage the authority of the papacy by arguing that it was a 'commission', not the Pope, that condemned Galileo, and the church even claimed credit for the way it had handled the matter: 'It will be found that the Galileo case furnishes splendid evidence of the Church's truly scientific attitude and procedure.'[9] In the same fashion the creationist Stephen C. Meyer, citing O. Gingerich, argued in 1999 that it was Galileo's defective logic, failing to meet the church's high standards, that got him into hot water: much of the reason for his trouble with the Vatican 'stemmed from Galileo's inability to meet scholastic standards of deductive certainty – a standard that he regarded as neither relevant to nor attainable by scientific reasoning'.[10] So a sick old man had to be dragged before the inquisitors for punishment because of a methodological difference of opinion. In early March 2008 the Vatican, eager to demonstrate that it was at last catching up with the sixteenth century, was reportedly planning to erect a statue of Galileo in the Vatican garden near the apartment in which he was incarcerated while waiting trial.[11]

The fate of Galileo was far from isolated. The church constantly campaigned against science, dragging heretics before the Inquisition to be sentenced to torture and execution. Examples could be given from the fields of astronomy, biology, physics, psychology and so on. Here it is enough to cite a few examples of religious obscurantism in the field of medicine, given by Bertrand Russell in *Religion and Science* (1935). In the eighteenth century inoculation against smallpox aroused a storm of protest among clerics, and the Sorbonne pronounced against it on theological grounds. One Anglican clergyman published a sermon in which he declared that Job's boils were doubtless due to inoculation by

the Devil, and many Scottish ministers signed a manifesto saying
that the new medical practice of inoculation was an attempt 'to
baffle a Divine judgement'. In the same fashion theologians railed
against vaccination in the nineteenth century, regarding it as
'bidding defiance to Heaven itself, even to the will of God'. In
1885, when there was a severe outbreak of smallpox in Montreal,
the Roman Catholics were urged by the clergy to resist
vaccination. One priest stated: 'If we are afflicted with smallpox,
it is because we had a carnival last winter, feasting the flesh, which
has offended the Lord.' For the same reasons worthy clerics
opposed anaesthetics for women in childbirth because of Genesis
3: 16 ('In sorrow shalt thou bring forth children') – but it was
acceptable to give them to men because God had put Adam into
a deep sleep when he extracted his rib. Compare all this with the
modern theological opposition to artificial contraception, artificial
insemination by donor and stem cell research. In earlier times the
works of the scientists were placed on the *Index Librorum
Prohibitorum* (Index of Forbidden Books), still operative well into
the second half of the twentieth century, in a vain attempt to stem
the growing avalanche of unwelcome philosophy and rational
ideas. Today, under the pressures of growing secularisation, the
clerical authorities are increasingly forced to bow under the sheer
weight of scientific progress. But the legacy of the medieval
conflict between reason and faith remains manifest – particularly
in the field of evolutionary science.

The Jesuit Martin J. Scott declared that it 'is historically certain
that from the beginning of Christianity to the present day the
Catholic Church has been the greatest friend and supporter of
science'. But it remains the case that *divine* truth, shaped by a
presumed infallibility, reserves the right to modify or reject *human*
truth. Pope Pius XI described how this worked. The sciences
could be allowed to continue using their own principles and
methods, but the church 'takes every precaution to prevent them
from falling into error by opposition to divine doctrine, or from
overstepping their proper limits, and thus invading and disturbing
the domain of faith'.[12] One purpose of this attitude is to enable the
church to exploit some gullible Christian communities by

sustaining their belief in superstitious practices – for example, pertaining to miracles and relics – that would be rejected in any other context.

The writer Paul Blanshard has drawn attention to a four-page circular carrying the official imprimatur of Archbishop (later Cardinal) Francis Spellman and issued during the Second World War by the Carmelite National Shrine of Our Lady of the Scapular in New York. The scapular, a small cloth tied about the neck, was guaranteed to work miracles if Catholic soldiers wearing it came under fire – as happened with Franco's soldiers in the Spanish Civil War. And if by chance a soldier were to die, presumably on an off day for the scapular, he would be saved from hell in the afterlife: each garment bore the comforting words 'WHOSOEVER DIES CLOTHED IN THIS SCAPULAR SHALL NOT SUFFER ETERNAL FIRE'. The scapular was offered free but donations 'will be gratefully accepted'. At the same time, declared the pamphlet, a scapular was 'not a talisman . . . a rabbit's foot . . . [but] the sign of devotedness to the Blessed Virgin'.[13] So what was the truth about the scapular? Did it work magic or did it not? Only a religion or a cult could invite such a question in the modern age.

As with the scapular, so with relics, particularly those of Jesus and the saints. The church is too cautious to 'guarantee' the genuineness of any particular relics but maintains they should be venerated if properly approved (Canon 1283), and 'episcopal authentication' has been given to thousands of them. In the early days of Christianity the supposed bones of the martyrs and splinters from the true cross were sold for large sums, and the market was well served by fresh relics that appeared miraculously. More than one commentator has remarked that the wooden relics from the cross would amount to a large forest.[14] In Geneva, John Calvin was disappointed to learn that he had been kissing a stag's bone when he thought he was kissing the arm of St Anthony, and that St Peter's supposed brain was actually a pumice stone. He was driven to remark on how the world had been cheated: 'I can mention three foreskins of our Saviour's circumcision, fourteen nails exhibited from the three driven into the cross, three robes for Christ's seamless garment . . . three spears by which our Saviour's side was pierced, and five sets of linen cloth' in which his body was wrapped.[15] It helps when popes create fresh saints because the relics of new ones are just as effective in working miracles, some of which are associated with hallucinations conjuring the Virgin Mary.

In the historical context of magic, relics, miracles, visions and other superstitions it is hardly surprising that the church has long been deeply unhappy about the law of biological evolution. In 1909, half a century after the first publication of Darwin's *Origin of Species*, Pope Pius X directed all Catholics to accept the Hebrew/Christian creation myth and the account of Adam's fall as historical. Later the *Catholic Almanac* stated that 'no system even of mitigated evolution has been scientifically proved'; while the Jewish convert David Goldstein declared that, while people could speculate about the evolution of the human body, 'there is no substantial scientific data to sustain' the hypothesis.[16] As late as 1940 Father Paul Carroll, a Jesuit biologist, stressed that good Catholic teaching must include 'a single pair of progenitors of the human race', and he quoted with approval the statement: 'The truth is you are a heretic in a dozen ways if you admit what the world is calling evolution . . . The evolutionists have an answer . . . an irritating, erroneous, unproved and unprovable one – and one condemned by the Church.'[17]

This religious disquiet about science in general and evolution in particular continues to feature in the modern world. In July 2003 Tom Vail, who conducted 'Christ-centred tours' through the Grand Canyon, edited a glossy coffee table book, *Grand Canyon: A Different View*, for sale to tourists in the Canyon National Park. Geologists estimate that the rocks deep in the canyon date back two billion years, while the canyon itself was caused by river erosion six million years ago. By contrast, Vail's *Grand Canyon* reckons that the canyon was forged a few thousand years ago by the flood that carried Noah's ark. In this context it is significant that the canyon's bookshop is subject to a congressional mandate to promote scientific understanding, and Vail's book was the only one of twenty-six documents submitted over a two-year period to be approved for sale.[18] On 22 July 2003 the park's chief of interpretation declined to tick a box on the product evaluation form to say whether the book was accurate or not but scrawled on the document: 'Interpretation of the canyon from a different perspective – interesting timing in the light of recent events!'[19] Here she is referring to the earlier decision by Donald Murphy, deputy director of the National Park Service, to restore brass plaques bearing Bible verses that the superintendent had removed on first-amendment grounds.[20]

The Murphy decision and the adoption of the Vail book, 'aggressively attacking modern science',[21] accorded with Christian beliefs expressed over the years. The origins of the Grand Canyon had nothing to do with science but had been revealed in the Old Testament. Thus one international Christian ministry, Answers in Genesis, declared that the canyon's rock formations 'dramatically demonstrate the reality of the catastrophic global Flood of Noah's day'; and the creationist Steven Austin claimed to identify canyon tectonics 'associated with the formation of an ocean basin midway through Creation Week [as revealed in Genesis]' and 'ocean deposits from the post-Creation, but pre-Flood world'.[22] The Alliance Defense Fund, founded by members of the Christian right, has pledged to take legal action, if necessary, to ensure that the Vail book remains in Park Service shops.

This was all part of a pattern. In February 2007 the Texas Higher Education Coordinating Board considered an application by the Institute for Creation Research (ICR), which accepts the Bible as literal truth on all topics, to grant online master's degrees in science education – in which, we may presume, students would be taught that vegetarian dinosaurs frolicked happily with human beings until man's fall into sin. An advisory panel to the board recommended that Texas should accept the application but prominent scientists, including Nobel laureate Steven Weinberg, urged the board to deny accreditation.

The argument over creationism was fuelled by the manifest sympathy in the Bush White House and the Department of the Interior to Christian fundamentalism. George W. Bush himself had told a *New York Times* reporter that 'the jury is still out on creationism', and in consequence the National Park Service had been forced to keep an open mind on the controversy. And this was part of a more general conflict between religious convictions and scientific work in such areas as global warming, lead poisoning, AIDS, stem cells and pregnancy prevention. In February 2004 more than sixty leading scientists, including twenty Nobel Prize winners, wrote a public letter expressing their outrage at what was happening under the Bush administration. Specialists were being replaced by unqualified people; scientific advisory committees were being disbanded; scientific reports were being censored and suppressed; scientific knowledge was being misrepresented. 'The distortion of scientific knowledge for partisan political ends must cease.'[23] And it was plain that this distortion was intimately linked to the religious beliefs of the US President.

Today it is equally obvious that Islam too has immense problems with many aspects of scientific research. We all know of the remarkable and enduring contributions to science, mathematics, philosophy and literature made by the early Muslims under the Abbasid caliphate, most famously during the rule of Harun al-Rashid and his intellectually brilliant son al-Mamun,[24] who arranged for the preservation and translation of much of the classical scholarship that was being pillaged and destroyed during the Dark Ages of Christianity.[25] But these glory days existed a millennium and more ago. The long centuries of the Ottoman empire, the major Muslim successor to the Abbasids, boasted no equivalent contribution to human intellectual achievement; and today, like the Bush White House and fervent Christians around the world, Muslims have trouble squaring the superstitions of their sacred works with the philosophical implications of modern science. The researcher Yoginder Sikand notes that the prominent Deoband madrasa in India still insists that the sun revolves around the earth[26] – no *eppur si muove* here – and there are probably many more that teach the same doctrine. Sikand himself says that 'much of what the madrasas taught was simply outdated' (for example, maintaining special seating arrangements for invisible *jinn*).[27]

Of course the text of the sacred Koran is one of the principal difficulties facing progressive Muslims struggling to drag their faith

into the twenty-first century. For example, the Turkish authorities are heroically tackling the tasks of recasting the Koran and
Hadith in an attempt to make Islam more relevant to the modern
world (see Chapter 3). It is difficult to avoid the conclusion that
this is a hopeless task.

Mohammed – or whoever wrote Surah 4: 82 – was keen to
emphasise that there were no contradictions in the Koran, to him
a sign of its divine authorship (less than a compelling argument to
the modern reader). But was he right? Perhaps the canonical
Koran that eventually emerged contained items that Mohammed
had not himself recited, or perhaps they were wrongly transcribed
into the final text. In any event there are many problems in
assuming the scientific accuracy of the Koran. We have mentioned blood clots and clay. There is more to wonder about.

For example, simple numerical consistency would seem to be a
requirement in any rational view of the world. Various verses,
borrowing from Genesis, state that God created the heavens and
the earth in six days.[28] But another verse (Surah 41: 8) says that he
created the earth in two days. Are we to conclude that he spent
two days fashioning the earth and four days creating all the rest,
including the heavens (I would have thought that Saturn and its
rings alone would have taken more than two days)? Or he created
the earth in two days and apparently spent four days putting
mountains and food ('sustenance for all alike') on the earth (Surah
41: 9) – so that takes the specified six days but it leaves out the rest
of the solar system, the billions of galaxies and the heavens. In
addition, Surah 41: 11 tells us that God spent two days making
seven heavens. So perhaps it all took eight days to create the earth
(two days), the mountains (four) and the heavens (two), and that
leaves out the gases of Neptune and the Great Red Spot of Jupiter
(unless such things are part of the heavens). It all seems a bit
confusing, suggesting that God – or Mohammed – was baffled by
simple arithmetic.

There are plenty of other examples of numerical inconsistency.
In Surah 4: 12–14 and 176, Mohammed details numerical
inheritance laws in the event of a man's death, but it can be shown
that if a man dies and leaves behind his mother, his wife and two
sisters, the sum of the various entitlements add up to more than

the available property.[29] It is easy to construct other examples of this sort, suggesting that Mohammed had not thought the issue through properly. And he had other confusions of a different type. Is one of God's days equivalent to a thousand human years (Surah 22: 46) or fifty thousand (Surah 70: 4)? Is there one garden in Paradise (Surah 79: 41) or several (Surah 18: 31)? The Koran, like the Bible, could have done with a decent copy editor.

In fact there are other clues, this time from the Old Testament, that the Almighty, or the human chroniclers of the texts, were not interested in numerical consistency. Genesis 7: 2 states that some animals would be taken into Noah's ark 'by sevens'; whereas Genesis 6: 19 reckons that two animals of every species would be taken in for salvation. Creationists have struggled to argue that a 550-foot-long ark would be big enough for all animal species, which they reckoned amounted to not more than 25,000 – and this builds nonsense upon absurdity. We already know, to note only one type of animal, more than 350,000 species of beetle. And would every type of virus be catered for? Presumably some of the animals would be rabid in order to host some of the life-forms that would populate the postdiluvian world.

The Koran and the Genesis of the Torah contain many obvious examples of arithmetic confusion, and also evidence of scientific ignorance. We have hinted at the sheer silliness of the ark story, which requires millions of species to live harmoniously on a small boat, with adequate food supplies and ways of coping with abundant waste products. Would *Tyrannosaurus rex* really be content with munching vegetables (and where did they come from)? Would the lion, possibly rabid, and the antelope really be bosom pals? And the Koran does no better when it ventures into areas of scientific truth.

Again it is significant how blood clots are dealt with, already mentioned, in explaining the origin of a human being. Surah 23: 14 states that clotted blood is made into a piece of flesh which is then made into bones. The bones are then clothed with flesh and a man (never a woman first?) is brought forth: 'Blessed therefore be God, the most excellent of makers.' But the description is not one that would be recognised by modern science. It seems that God and Mohammed did not know much about embryology at the time. And the prophet was equally ignorant about plate tectonics. Various verses in the Koran suggest that the mountains were created in order to stop the earth shaking when earthquakes took place.[30] Mohammed, seeing that mountains were large and heavy, was beguiled into inventing a fanciful reason for their existence. It seems surprising that he did not notice that earthquakes did take place, invalidating the supposed *raison d'être* of mountains. Again Mohammed obviously had no clue about the geological reason why mountains were formed.

The stars, we learn, were created to serve as missiles – in effect, cosmic hand grenades – to be thrown at demons to stop them eavesdropping on heavenly affairs. Mohammed, obviously ignorant about the nature of stars, could never have written as he did if he had known that each star was akin to our sun, vast flaming orbs, that could never be used like stones 'to pelt the devils with'.[31] He suggested also that the moon was an independent illumination for the earth,[32] evidently not knowing that it shone only through reflected light.

We cannot avoid the conclusion that Mohammed was ignorant about embryology, geology and cosmology – which helps to explain the crude and superstitious doctrines that are propagated in madrasas throughout the world. For example, Yoginder Sikand notes that many of the *ulama* (authorities on Islam and Muslim law) he encountered were 'fiercely narrow-minded', teaching 'outdated' ideas; that the acquisition of 'knowledge' is equated with 'understanding the will of God'; that Western science challenges 'deeply held Muslim beliefs and assumptions'; that many *ulama* regard a house containing an English book 'to have been rendered impure'; and that a term, *zeheni irtidad* (intellectual apostasy), has been invented to denote any attempts to introduce Western rational ideas into the madrasas.[33] A dialogue with a typical modern Muslim thinker gives further clues about how science – in particular, evolution – is regarded by believers. Here we are not surprised to find close accord with the Christian creationists:

> This [Darwinian] theory erred when it established evolution on the basis of haphazard mutations and mistakes. It totally overlooked any element of planning or creativity. Chance mutations can never be

valid bases for an explanation of the inventiveness, accuracy, and precision we observe in everything around us . . . All that science has ventured so far are guesses.[34]

It is time to consider more directly the law of evolution.

The arguments for biological evolution did not begin with Charles Darwin, nor did they begin with his grandfather Erasmus Darwin, Alfred Russel Wallace or Robert Chambers – all of whom published evolutionary ideas before Darwin's great work. They began, as did many other purportedly modern ideas, in the ancient world. For example, the Mayan culture, which began around 1800 BC, managed to combine a 'streamlined evolution' with a strong religious commitment – a nice model for today's hapless progressive believers. The Mayans believed that the rain-god constructed human beings by modifying his previous creations. There was no sign here of evolution working through hereditary descent and random mutations but suggestions of a gradually evolving biological world, albeit under the hand of a creative deity who first made the rivers, then fish, next serpents and finally human beings. Here the members of a totem clan believed themselves to be descendants from a common non-human ancestor – particular species progressively changing to yield men and women. Thus the Turtle clan of the Iroquois reckoned that their turtle ancestors gradually shed their cumbersome shells and thereby developed into human beings. The crayfish ancestors of the Choctaws came onto the land, learnt to walk on two legs and duly formed the Crayfish clan. The Osages believed they were descended from a male snail and a female beaver.[35] It is clear that totemism, unlike the Darwinian law of evolution, held that every tribe of people was descended from a separate species of animal unrelated to other hereditary lines, but the idea of biological descent was widespread. Humankind was not created by magic at the whim of a deity but had kinship with pre-existing species. The biological laws of descent were not understood – no hint of mutant genes here – but human beings owed their origin to shaping forces, sometimes divine, working on the rest of the biological world.

The Ionian philosopher Thales of Miletus (c.624–c.546 BC) suggested, like the Mayans, that life first began in water, with chance alone 'responsible for the entire process' of the evolution of humankind from simple matter.[36] In the same fashion Anaximander (610–546 BC) reckoned that man evolved from fish or fishlike forms that cast off their scaly skins and moved to live on the land, at the same time positing a pre-fish primal substance (*apeiron*) that 'encompasses all the worlds'[37] – suggesting here the sort of multiple universe theory that is so beguiling to modern physicists. These worlds were not created but developed through conditions of eternal motion that stimulated also the evolution of biological species on earth. Life arose from evaporating moisture and again humankind, like every other animal, was descended from fishes. And here there is a sweet piece of logic – human beings must have evolved from animals of a different sort because, owing to their long infancy, they could not have survived as an original form.

The Greek thinker Empedocles of Acragas in Sicily (c.490–430 BC), often dubbed the father of evolutionary naturalism, argued that chance alone was responsible for the entire process of development from simple matter to human beings, and went so far as to teach that *all living organism types evolved from trial-and-error recombinations of animal parts*.[38] He judged also, anticipating Darwin by more than two millennia, that natural selection was the primary mechanism of biological evolution, the fittest being most likely to survive to pass on their traits to their offspring.

In the sixth century BC Xenophanes of Colophone, a disciple of Anaximander, observed fossil fishes and shells, and concluded that they had been underwater for some time and were involved in the evolutionary process – so becoming the first known person to use fossils as evidence for a theory of natural development; the Greek historian Herodotus (c.484–c.425 BC) also observed fossil shells in Egypt and speculated about their history; and the Greek physician Hippocrates of Cos (c.460–c.357 BC) is known to have collected fossils. Aristotle (384–322 BC), destined to provide a congenially supernatural platform for the Catholic schoolmen, is associated with an idea that religious believers were not keen to promote – the notion that human beings are the highest point of one long, continuous 'ascent with modification' of life.[39]

The Roman philosopher Titus Lucretius Carus (c.99–c.55 BC), author of the six-volume hexameter poem *De Rerum Natura* (On the Nature of Things), was equally determined to interpret the world in naturalistic terms. In Book I he observes that 'nothing from nothing ever yet was born',[40] and that people are fearful of nature because they are ignorant and so are forced to believe that gods are busy in the universe.[41] Hence a Roman in the first century BC was able to discern the conservation laws that feature so prominently in modern physics, denouncing the eager gap fillers who were as active in the ancient world as they are today. Lucretius perceived that patterns were discernible in nature, that certain imagined events were excluded by natural law. Otherwise chaos would rule: fruit trees, for example, would stop producing the same fruit year by year.[42] So here we even have the hints of DNA, the notion that biological templates can ensure the identity of the hereditary line. Every species carries '*a secret [hereditary] power of its own* [emphasis added]'.[43]

The 'secret power' – seen as essential by Lucretius, and identified as coded DNA in the modern world – resides in all animate things. It ensures that successive generations are able to embody their characteristic features: people breed people, apes apes, spiders spiders (until, as so exhaustively described by Darwin, the progressive accumulation of chance genetic mutations allows the gradual emergence of new life forms). In this context Lucretius was even able to speculate about the 'primal germs' that the theory demanded – the gametes of the modern age. That the agents of the 'secret power' could not be detected by the primitive technology of the ancient world did nothing to discourage him ('doubt not my words, because our eyes no primal germs perceive'). Was it not obvious that many powerful forces, such as the winds and the clouds, shape in a thoroughly naturalistic way the world and yet remain invisible?[44] We infer existent things, if they are not perceived, from their evident effects. Winds, primal germs – for Lucretius the evidence for their existence was everywhere. And he also taught that nothing exists except atoms and the void, just as the modern materialist insists that there is nothing in the world except matter and energy (or the space-time continuum).

Lucretius seems to give a hostage to the creationists, remarking that eyes were made that we might see, that thighs and knees were designed to enable human beings to walk, but he quickly refutes any divine involvement. Any such divine interpretation was getting the reasoning back to front: the eyes, the tongue and the ears had to arrive *before* sight, speech and hearing were possible: 'No seeing ere the lights of eyes were born / No speaking ere the tongue created was . . . ears created were / Much earlier than any sound was heard.'[45] In modern terms, the incidence of fortuitous mutations enabled animal and plant species to exploit new powers, and so enabled new species to evolve.

To those who insisted on believing in a celestial designer, Lucretius proclaimed that the manifest products of such a 'power divine' told not of omnipotence but of gross incompetence because there were so many obvious faults in creation.[46] It is easy to list our own items, the faults – plagues, earthquakes, tsunami, volcanic eruptions etc. – in what religious believers tell us is a product of the Almighty. Lucretius had his own suggestions: 'intolerable heat' and 'a perpetual fall of frost', and what is left would quickly be overrun with brambles if human beings did not 'groan and sweat' to till the land. Here he remarks that the crops would not spontaneously grow, and that even with the 'sternest toil' all man's labour can be destroyed by the weather ('Why do the seasons bring distempers with them?'). Lucretius, struggling against the mood of his time, saw what can so easily be proclaimed today – that there is no transcendent design, that where design *appears* to exist it can be explained by naturalistic laws that shape the evolution of living species.

We did not have to wait for Darwin to see that a 'secret power' could sustain hereditary biological lines. The notion is clear in the ancient naturalists and philosophers – in such Greeks as Empedocles and Epicurus, and in Lucretius. H. F. Osborn concluded: 'Darwin owes even more to the Greeks than we have ever recognised.'[47] And he might have added at least one Roman. Even before the birth of Christ ancient thinkers were suggesting that naturalistic mechanisms were able to shape the course of biological evolution, with the corollary that a divine designer was an unnecessary hypothesis.

The doctrine that design in nature required a celestial designer rested on the argument from analogy, an approach explored in detail by the Scottish philosopher David Hume (1711–76) in a seminal work *Dialogues Concerning Natural Religion*.[48] Here he conveyed his thoughts in imaginary conversations between three disputants exploring questions of philosophy that were 'so obscure and uncertain, that human reason can reach no fixed determination' with regard to them. This is a diffident approach which may surprise those who have been led to regard Hume as an atheist. In fact he states that the 'being of a God' is an 'obvious and important truth', which 'the most ignorant ages have acknowledged [and] for which the most refined geniuses have ambitiously striven to produce new proofs and arguments'.[49] Perhaps it is a trick, a beguiling device to divert the reader from Hume's actual beliefs for it is certainly the case that, as Cleanthes, Philo and Demea bat the points to and fro, the best arguments are the sceptical ones.[50]

At one stage the world is seen as 'one great machine, subdivided into an infinite number of lesser machines, which again admit of subdivisions, to a degree beyond which human senses and faculties can trace and explain' – which is all so remarkable that we may conclude that 'the Author of Nature is somewhat similar to the mind of man'. The argument is quickly dismissed. We may conclude that a house has an architect or builder but since a house does not resemble the universe we can scarcely infer similar minds at work in its creation.[51] Such arguments are used to show that the mind of God cannot be inferred from observed phenomena – which renders the mystics at one with the sceptics: 'How do you mystics, who maintain the absolute incomprehensibility of the Deity, differ from Sceptics or Atheists, who assert that the first cause of all is unknown and unintelligible?'[52] So, it seems, we can say nothing about the nature of God – which presents all sorts of problems for believers who insist that God is interested in human affairs. And the point about analogy is pressed further.

How can the unity of the Deity be established? Since 'a great number of men join in building a house or a ship, in rearing a city, in framing a commonwealth, why may not several deities combine in contriving and framing a world?'[53] The point is easy to make for the modern world: an expert in designing car batteries is unlikely to be an expert in engine design, just as an expert in tyre materials will leave silicon chip design to someone else. In Hume's language, a great number of men (and women) join in building a modern motor vehicle.

Believers will protest that God is Omnipotent and One, even though in the Koran he does not know much about blood or stars, but their objection is in any case premature. The design argument relies upon analogy and that is what we are using. Hume might have said that there is one god for designing dragonflies, another for giraffes; perhaps one goddess knows all about the octopus, while another is keen on framing oak trees. Perhaps there is a celestial trade union for retired deities, pension schemes for the divine needy. Hume does suggest that since the world is 'very faulty and imperfect' it may be 'only the first rude essay of some infant deity, who afterwards abandoned it, ashamed of his lame performance'; or perhaps 'it is the production of old age and dotage in some superannuated deity; and ever since his death, has run on at adventures, from the first impulse and active force, which it received from him'.[54] Approaching from another direction, Hume might also have said that, with proper design demarcations in the framing of the human body, there is a liver god, a heart god, a brain god etc. – much in line with the specialisms of modern medicine. In any event the use of analogy that the creationists rely on seems to conduct them to an unambiguous polytheism. Do they intend such a conclusion?

Another pre-Darwinian thinker, Immanuel Kant (1724-1804), encapsulates in his book *Critique of Pure Reason* what he calls the physico-theological argument, a version of the design argument, in four statements:

1. We observe in the world manifest signs of an arrangement full of purpose, executed with great wisdom . . .
2. This arrangement of means and ends is entirely foreign to the things existing in the world . . . the nature of different things could not of itself . . . harmoniously tend towards certain purposes, were they not chosen . . . by a rational and disposing principle . . .

3. There exists therefore a sublime and wise cause (or several)
. . . a free and intelligent cause of the world . . .
4. The unity of this cause may be inferred . . .[55]

Like Hume, Kant makes a number of criticisms of this argument.
For instance, it is quickly pointed out that the argument at best
only establishes an *architect*, not a *creator*, of the world. (The point
that a *designer* does not necessarily *make* things is discussed below in
connection with the modern incarnation of the design argument –
intelligent design.) It is also interesting to note Kant's parenthetical
'or several' in point 3 (above). Perhaps, he implies, there is a
committee of divine architects – as with Hume's clear implication
that the design argument leads to polytheism. Other criticisms are
included, some of which apply to all supposed proofs for God's
existence (see Chapter 8), until Kant ultimately embraces the weak
'moral imperative' as a reason for belief in God.

Such thinkers as Hume and Kant were worthy opponents of
clerical absurdities (despite Kant's lapse into fallacy). But how
vastly their scepticism would have been strengthened had they had
lived in the age of Darwin.

We have seen that Darwin owed much to the Greeks (and to
Lucretius). He also owed much to his grandfather, since Erasmus
(1731–1802) expounded many evolutionary ideas – including the
notion of natural selection – with enthusiasm, not least in
Zoonomia, or the Laws of Organic Life (1794), which was translated
into German, French and Italian. Charles was generous enough to
concede that he probably derived much of his evolutionary theory
from Erasmus. And at least one commentator, Desmond King-
Hele, has argued that Erasmus Darwin's theory was more accurate
than even the later editions of *The Origin of Species*,[56] where Charles
was seemingly willing to entertain, albeit briefly, elements of the
erroneous Lamarckian speculations on the transmission of acquired
characteristics, before crushing the idea.[57] Charles Darwin admitted
also that without Robert Chambers's book *Vestiges of the Natural
History of Creation* (1844) he may never have written the *Origin*,[58]
and in addition acknowledged the priority of Patrick Matthew,
who 'anticipated all Darwin's main conclusions by 28 years'.[59]

Erasmus, a robust secularist, had none of the seeming philosophical caution that Charles would later display. Charles's other
grandfather, the pottery patriarch Josiah Wedgwood, held
Unitarian beliefs, roundly denounced by Erasmus as 'a featherbed
to catch a falling Christian'.[60] Wedgwood, it was hinted, had
abandoned so much of Christianity – such as Christ's alleged
divinity and the doctrine of the Trinity – that he was not far from
being an atheist. Darwin himself was destined to follow a similar
route, gradually being driven *by science* to abandon the faith which
as a young man he had taken for granted. But he would never be
so bold as to call himself an atheist. His father, Robert, had wanted
him to go into medicine but this did not appeal, and so the best
remaining option was . . . the Church of England. There was
much religion in the family and it seemed inevitable that Charles
would end up preaching gentle sermons to country congregations.

In the early days Darwin had occasional doubts about his faith
but these were quickly set aside under the impact of appropriate
reading. He found various Christian texts persuasive, and in
particular *Evidence of Christianity* (1824) by the Reverend John
Bird Sumner (1780–1862), which was overwhelmingly
convincing, not least in its posing of the proposition that 'either
Jesus did not exist, or if he actually lived, but was not the son of
God, hence an impostor'.[61] Neither option was possible, and so
Christianity remained 'wonderfully suitable . . . to our ideas of
happiness in this world & the next world . . . [There was] no other
way except by [Jesus's] divinity of explaining the series of
evidence and probability.'[62] But this simple faith would gradually
dissolve, unable to withstand the great pile of naturalistic evidence
that Darwin would accumulate and which told an entirely
different story.

For a while the believers held him in thrall. He was very
impressed with the books of William Paley (1743–1805),
archdeacon of Carlisle, who wrote various apologetic works,
including *View of the Evidences of Christianity* (1794) and *Natural
Theology* (1802). How reasonable Paley made the design argument
seem! Of course he is best known for his 'watch example': how,
Paley asks, should the observer react to finding a watch upon the
ground? We can quickly see that 'its several parts are framed and

put together for a purpose' – and for a full page of *Natural Theology* the watch's intricacies are explored. We cannot doubt that its design suggests a responsible 'artist', the intelligent cause of the watch's intricacy. And yes, we know that the watch sometimes goes wrong – as do animal species – but that obvious truth never makes us doubt that there is nonetheless an intelligence behind the design. These and other points are made to show that a deity, an intelligent designer, must exist as a source of the complexities of nature.

Darwin studied Paley's *Principles of Moral and Political Philosophy* (1785) and the *Evidences* for his Cambridge BA examination, which he passed in 1831. The work of Paley was generally seen as providing an accurate description of the nature of the world; its premises and arguments were accepted in all right-thinking circles; every Cambridge ordinand swore by its conclusions.[63] At first Darwin was so impressed with Paley's 'logic' that he learnt it by heart.[64]

It is argued that Darwin owed a debt to Paley, though Christianity was not saved. Both men were interested in the biological eye as a key consideration in the development of species; both devoted particular chapters to the instincts of birds and insects; both considered the significant relationships between wax, honey and bee stings; and both used similar language in discussing instinct and emotion. Both men felt immense wonder at the prospect of the natural world. Biological complexity required explanation and, whereas Paley lacked the necessary scientific instinct, Darwin set about the task with immense labour and a rare capacity to marshal prodigious amounts of data. It was Paley's misfortune to be born at the beginning of the Darwinian age. Earlier exponents of the design argument had only to cope with the relatively unscientific efforts of Lucretius and Hume, but the disciples of Paley were to find the *Origin of Species* a difficulty of an entirely different order.

In 1830, as Paris faced revolution, the infidel missionary Robert Taylor began performing in the Rotunda, a ramshackle building on the south bank of the Thames. Here, several times a week, he staged impious melodramas and bombastic atheist sermons. 'God and the Devil', he roundly and mischievously declared, were 'one and the self-same being . . . Hell and Hell-fire . . . are, in the original, nothing more than names and titles of the Supreme God.'[65] Darwin was aware of all this. Taylor's sobriquet, 'The Devil's Chaplain', stuck in his mind (and was borrowed by Richard Dawkins as a book title).[66] But he was not about to abandon his Christian beliefs. In 1831, aged twenty-two and his faith intact, Darwin began his voyage on the HMS *Beagle*, which would last for five years and come to be recognised as an episode of revolutionary significance in the history of human thought. While Captain Robert FitzRoy was charting and recharting rivers and harbours, Darwin was intently studying animals, plants, fossils and geology in preparation for writing one of the greatest books in world scientific literature. Thus he begins the introduction to the *Origin of Species* with the words: 'When on board HMS *Beagle*, as naturalist, I was much struck with certain facts in the distribution of the organic beings inhabiting South America.'[67]

The first edition of the *Origin* was published on 24 November 1859, more than twenty years after the conclusion of the *Beagle* voyage – a delay occasioned as much by Darwin's concern at the likely impact of publication as by the progressive amassing and analysis of ever more empirical data. On the day of publication the first print run of 1,250 copies sold out. The novelist and Christian socialist Charles Kingsley enthused: 'It *awes* me. If you be right then I must give up much of what I have believed.'[68] Darwin, amazed at the scale of the response to the book, at once began preparing a second edition, which the publisher, John Murray, decided would run to 3,000 copies. Charles Lyell, whose immensely influential *Principles of Geology* (1830) Darwin had read on the *Beagle*, was reportedly 'absolutely gloating' over the book, and the biologist T. H. Huxley lavished 'such tremendous praise' that Darwin was embarrassed. Already Huxley, later to be dubbed Darwin's 'bulldog', was 'sharpening his beak and claws' to rend 'the curs [mostly theologians] who will bark and yelp'.[69] Atheists everywhere, not bothered by the swelling mixed metaphor, were enthralled.

It is not always remarked that FitzRoy also published an account of the voyage of the *Beagle*, fit in some ways to rival Darwin's own description.[70] He touched on many of the topics that Darwin was considering, cited some of the same fossil data, read some geology and proposed some of the same ideas. However, in his concluding chapters, one on 'the origin and migration of the human race' and the other on the 'Deluge', FitzRoy was determined to uphold a literal interpretation of the Bible, including a Creation in six 24-hour days, the flood and the ark, and the subsequent dispersal of the survivors to repopulate the earth. FitzRoy, like Paley, was intrigued by the complexities of biological systems; like Paley, he was up against an intellectual giant. It is interesting to note that Darwin's copy of Lyell's *Principles of Geology*, a volume that was so influential in shaping Darwin's thought, carried a pencilled notation inside the front cover: 'Given me by Capt. F.R. [FitzRoy] – C. Darwin'.[71] A fundamentalist Christian had supplied Darwin with one of the tools that would enable the great biologist to shatter the theoretical foundation of Christianity.

At first Darwin, still carrying the baggage of residual religious belief, was willing to entertain the notion of a divine creator who had been busy with more than one creation: 'The one hand has surely worked throughout the universe. A Geologist would perhaps suggest that the periods of Creation have been distinct & remote the one from the other, that the Creator rested in his labour.'[72] But such silliness would not last long. Lyell had charted through geology a route to evolution but needed Darwin to convince him. Darwin himself already knew about theories of evolution, and perceived that the major facts he had discovered about biological extinctions, taxonomy and geographical distributions suggested that the development of the organic world had to be interpreted in a fresh way. But throughout the entire *Beagle* voyage he had not yet sufficiently ordered his thoughts to proclaim the law of evolution. Howard E. Gruber (1922–2005), a professor of natural science at Michigan University, charted in detail Darwin's 'First Theoretical Model' (dating to July 1837), the framework of speculation that would in due course yield the universally accepted law.[73] At the end of the *Beagle* voyage Darwin was far from ready to offer the *Origin of Species* to the world.

The long intellectual journey faced many problems and complications, but in essence the law of evolution, like many theoretical insights, proved to be astoundingly simple. Huxley exclaimed after reading the *Origin*: 'How extremely stupid not to have thought of that!' And the biologist and atheist Richard Dawkins, praising Darwin, noted the character of this simplicity.[74] The beauty of the concept of natural selection is that 'it assumes little to explain much . . . Its Explanation Ratio – what it explains, divided by what it needs to assume in order to do the explaining – is large'.[75]

Darwin is doing no less than explaining the whole of life – and this is genuine explanation, not the pseudo-explanation that relies on mystery and magic. Countless religious believers have invented fanciful 'explanations' for the whole of reality, but if we dignify these by calling them hypotheses, how many have been systematically scrutinised under the microscope of reason, dissected in the laboratory of experimental science? In fact, all of them – and what remains? The 'explanations' explain nothing, the hypotheses blow away on the wind of transparent analysis. The denominator in Dawkins's explanatory equation is 'spectacularly small and simple: natural selection: the non-random survival of genes in gene pools' or, putting the matter another way: 'Given sufficient time, the non-random survival of hereditary entities . . . will generate complexity, diversity, beauty, and an illusion of design so persuasive that it is almost impossible to distinguish from deliberate intelligent design.'[76] Darwin's work embodies the paradox of a seemingly diffident and cautious character cohabiting with an audacious intellect, a mind so prodigious in its capacity for labour and speculation that Darwin dwarfed the brilliant men in his circle and with whom he corresponded. When he was preparing to publish the *Origin* he suspected that it would be regarded as a lengthy blasphemy: he had already experienced something of this from members of his family and he was about to scandalise a nation, the world even. He wrote that perhaps he should never have completed the work, but was soon cheered by the responses of such men as Hooker, Lyell, Wallace and Huxley: 'You may think me presumptuous [he wrote to Sir Joseph Hooker] but I think my book will be popular to a certain extent . . . among scientific and semi-scientific men; why I think so is, because I have found in conversation so great and surprising an interest among such men.'[77]

The simplicity and power of two basic ideas – 'descent with modification' and 'natural selection' – define the scope of Darwin's discovery of the law of evolution. He begins in the *Origin* with a description of the selection of animals in domestication and compares this with the endless struggle for existence in the wild. In Chapter 4, 'Natural Selection; or the Survival of the Fittest', Darwin asks: 'Can the principle of selection, which we have seen as so potent in the hands of man, apply under nature?' and we already guess what the answer will be: '*I think we shall see that it can act most efficiently* [emphasis added].'[78] Already Darwin is anticipating theological misrepresentations, since some people have said that he speaks of natural selection 'as an active power or Deity; but who objects to an author speaking of the attractive power of gravity ruling the movements of the planets? Everyone knows what is meant and is implied by *such metaphorical expressions* [emphasis added].'[79]

In Chapter 13 of the *Origin* Darwin presents substantial data to support his conclusion that all life forms are connected via their descent from common ancestors, and that during this process crucial modifications take place to facilitate the astonishing variety and richness of the biological world. Alfred Russel Wallace had reached similar conclusions following his research in South America and the Malay archipelago, but he could not match Darwin's masses of evidence and the two decades spent in organising irrefutable arguments. Darwin knew that people would have problems in admitting that one species had given birth to another, not least because the sheer scale of geological time – say, 100 million years – was difficult to imagine. And he went so far as to address some of the 'difficulties of the theory', knowing that not only theologians but scientists of the day would find it hard to accept his conclusions.

In Chapter 6 Darwin admitted that some of the difficulties were 'so serious' that he could 'hardly reflect on them without being in some degree staggered'.[80] He classified them under four heads: Why were there not innumerable transitional forms with 'all nature in confusion'? Could natural selection produce organs of trifling importance, such as the tail of a giraffe used as a fly flapper as well as an organ 'so wonderful as the eye'? Can instincts be acquired through natural selection, even to the extent that a bee making cells 'has practically anticipated the discoveries of profound mathematicians'? How can the theory account for species, 'when crossed, being sterile', producing sterile offspring, whereas 'when varieties are crossed, their fertility is unimpaired'?[81] But this is not sufficient: in a further chapter Darwin considers 'miscellaneous objections to the theory of natural selection', and addresses all these problems with meticulous attention to detail and persuasive argument.[82] It is significant that there is no mention of the theologians in all this. The question of how life developed was seen as a purely scientific matter: the gods had nothing to do with it.

Outraged theologians and faith-leaning scientists disagreed. It would be possible, as Captain FitzRoy had heralded, to create a congenial amalgam of religion and evolution – in our terms, between superstition and science. This strategy was attempted in many ways. For example, the Anglican clergyman George Henslow (1835–1925) adopted what would become a commonplace ploy: the world required a creator but one that would step back, miracles apart, and let biological evolution run its course. Here simple protoplasm was assigned remarkable powers of adaptation in changing environments, powers that were invested the mysterious force of 'directivity' above and beyond the laws of physics and chemistry. It was by means of directivity, Henslow suggested, that the creator provided the first blob of protoplasm with 'practical omnipotence'. This remarkable blob was the ancestor of all life, plants and animals alike. In his *Present-day Rationalism Critically Examined* (1904), Henslow declared: 'If the Argument from Design be not restored, that under *Adaption* under *Directivity* takes its place; and William Paley's argument, readapted to evolution, becomes as sound as before; and indeed, far strengthened, as being strictly in accordance with facts.' And there were many variations on the basic theme. Darwin was too mighty a figure to be totally ignored by the Bible thumpers – a course which they would all have preferred.

George Douglas Campbell (1823–1900), the eighth Duke of Argyll, supposed that several creations were as likely as one, and reckoned that all the major biological orders originated in special and characteristic germs, each with its own 'internal directing

agency'. St George Mivart (1827–1900) wanted a theory of
evolution that 'accepts, distributes and harmonises' the three
elements of the organic universe ('the teleological, the typical, and
the transmutationist'). And the American philosopher John
Bascom (1827–1911) proposed a theory of evolution in which
mechanical and material causes are transformed by a spiritual
agency: here, with yet another semantic twist, a 'plastic power' is
assigned to life by a designing divinity.[83] Directivity, internal
directing agencies, plastic power and suchlike were no explanation at all. They were simple labels for theological ignorance,
lacking all the vast elucidatory power of descent with modification and natural selection. They showed as always the
theological instinct to use nonsense to simulate profundity.

This approach is well represented in the work of Francis Howe
Johnson (1835–1920), a celebrated Massachusetts Congregational
minister, who argued that the radical defect in a purely naturalistic
theory of evolution was the absence of any 'intelligent guidance',
the means whereby the evolutionary process could be rendered
purposeful according to some divine plan. The answer was simple:
in Johnson's teleology there was posited a 'new and totally unknown principle' outside the reach of the experimental scientist.
But how do we know that this important principle exists? How
do we detect it? What grounds are there for believing in it? There
is no evidence, there are no grounds – a state of affairs that
Johnson would have conceded: 'The fact that we can nowhere
detect the points at which intelligence exerts its shaping influence
is no argument against the reality of such influence.' In short, we
don't know what we're talking about but we'll believe it anyway.
This was a good example of blind faith at its best.

To some clerics the emergence of a coherent theory of
evolution seemed a godsend. Now it was possible to show how
humankind could develop from brute matter through the various
stages of animal nature to the sublime maturation of the spirit.
Perhaps Darwin had shown how the perfection of the soul might
be achieved. Perhaps 'spiritual evolution' was what mattered. It
seemed to the clerics, eager to dispense with secondary physical
matters, that biological evolution was little more than a metaphor
for the real focus of evolution, that of the spirit. Henry Ward

Beecher, another nineteenth-century cleric, argued that the theory of evolution was

> but a slow decree of God . . . in that waiting experiment which was to run through the ages of the world, God had a plan by which the race should steadily ascend, and the weakest become the strongest and the invisible become more and more visible, and the finer and nobler at last transcend and absolutely control its controllers, and the good in men become mightier than the animal in them.[84]

In this context it was inevitable that Christian Darwinism, a term first used in 1867, should have appeared as the overarching attempt to square the circle. The Scottish theologian James Averach (1839–1922) argued that the Darwinian theory 'may be held in such a form as to have no dangerous consequences for philosophy or theology', though he was quick to suggest that the theory was 'attended with many difficulties'. It was possible, Averach argued, that the theory of evolution could be seen as both a scientific doctrine and a teleological idea, with biological research employed to fortify the traditional notion that God was the supreme maker of all things: science could only reveal the means that were adopted to achieve the creative ends. In the same fashion the clergyman Aubrey Lackington Moore (1848–1890) struggled to break down the obvious conflict between Darwinism and the church ('For the Christian theologian the facts of nature are the acts of God').

Darwin himself was not comfortable with the science–religion controversy. Radical secularists embraced him as their own (Karl Marx sent him a new edition of *Das Kapital,* inscribed from a 'sincere admirer'), but he was not eager to consummate the relationship. He saw the possibility of speaking out on religion as a 'frightfully difficult' moral problem about which he had 'never been able to make up [his] mind'. He had used theological language freely in the *Origin* as a metaphorical device and had discussed the evolution of religion in *The Descent of Man*, but he was reluctant to express his own views in public. On one occasion he commented that the question of God's existence was 'beyond the scope of man's intellect'.[85] Adrian Desmond and James Moore, biographers of Darwin, head one of their chapters 'Never an Atheist' and indicate that Darwin's Christian faith had withered gradually. He was not prepared to join atheists such as Robert Carlile and Robert Taylor in denouncing religious belief, but was horrified at the seeming cruelty of Christian doctrine: it seemed 'to show that the men who do not believe, and this would include my Father, Brother and almost all my best friends, will be everlastingly punished. And this is a damnable doctrine.'[86] He later commented, when pressed, that a man could be 'an ardent Theist and an evolutionist', and he had never sought to deny the existence of a deity. Finally he opted for the term *agnostic*, coined by T. H. Huxley, to denote his view of the matter: 'In my most extreme fluctuations I have never been an Atheist in the sense of denying the existence of a God. I think that generally (and more and more as I grow older), but not always, that an Agnostic would be the more correct description of my state of mind.'[87]

When Charles Bradlaugh, a campaigning atheist and parliamentarian, and his co-publisher Annie Besant were arrested and committed for trial for publishing do-it-yourself contraceptive advice, Darwin was subpoenaed for the defence. He was horrified, not least for what such an appearance would do for his reputation, and he immediately cited years of illness, his consequent withdrawal from society and public meetings, and the 'great suffering' that a court appearance would entail.[88] In addition he sent an extract from his book *The Descent of Man* (1871) to express his opposition to any form of artificial contraception.[89] Darwin, the biological revolutionary, was a social reactionary. At the same time there was much in his writing, quite apart from the law of evolution through natural selection, that the atheists welcomed as ammunition.

In the *Descent* Darwin notes that belief in God has been advanced as 'the most complete' distinction between man and the lower animals, but argues that this belief is not innate or instinctive in human beings. However, belief in ubiquitous 'spiritual agencies' seems to be universal. Hence to argue from *belief* to *existence* is a hazardous affair, a 'rash argument', since we would be compelled to accept the existence of 'many cruel and malignant spirits, only a little more powerful than man'.[90] At the same time he acknowledged that his conclusions will be denounced by some as 'highly irreligious'.[91]

Francis, Darwin's son, emphasised that his father regarded a man's religious beliefs as a private matter, concerning him alone, and he notes his agnosticism. Darwin was sensitive to the feelings of others and reluctant to publish in a field which he had not subjected to continuous study. (We can only speculate on how religious belief would have been crushed by the weight of empirical evidence that Darwin would have produced.) When invited in November 1871 to publish his religious views he again cited his poor health ('I *never* pass twenty-four hours without many hours of discomfort'), adding that 'at no time' was he a 'quick thinker or writer' ('whatever I have done in science has solely been by long pondering, patience and industry').[92] In a reply to an enquiry from a German student, Darwin commented that science had nothing to do with Christ, except in so far as scientific research encourages caution in admitting evidence.

However, it is obvious that Darwin was often preoccupied with religious topics, despite his disclaimers. Thus Francis Darwin includes extracts from the *Autobiography* in which his father comments on many aspects of religious belief. He notes that he was laughed at on the *Beagle* by several of the officers for quoting the Bible as a moral authority; that he found divine revelation incredible; that the writing of the gospels could not be proved to be contemporaneous with the described events; and that his disbelief [in Christianity] crept over him at a very slow rate – 'but was at last complete'.[93] It was inevitable that he would see 'the law of natural selection' as undermining William Paley's design argument.[94] He concluded that *all* organic systems, physical and mental, had been generated through natural selection. There was no room in this scheme for a supernatural consciousness, a soul or a teleological plan hatched in some celestial mind.

Moreover, it could scarcely be argued that the suffering in the world was occasioned by man's sin and imposed for his moral improvement, since countless non-human sentient beings suffered greatly without any moral improvement: 'This very old argument from the existence of suffering against the existence of an intelligent First Cause seems to me a strong one.'[95] People believe in

God through deep inward convictions and feelings, but Darwin could not see that these 'are of any weight as evidence of what really exists'. And in the same fashion the human commitment to the immortality of the soul, a strong and almost instinctive belief, brings a certain comfort in a physical world where the planets will in time grow too old to support life. Darwin's belief in some first cause having an intelligent mind 'has very gradually, with many fluctuations, become weaker' – and again the diffident disclaimer: 'I cannot pretend to throw light on such abstruse problems. The mystery of the beginning of all things is insoluble by us, and I for one must be content to remain an Agnostic.'[96]

Huxley's agnosticism was an altogether more robust affair. He relished public meetings, welcomed any opportunity to harangue believers and, had it not been for his own choice in terminology, would have been widely regarded as an atheist. His pious opponents did not hesitate to advertise his heresies. The biographer Adrian Desmond, picking up on the nineteenth-century attitudes to the great Apostle of Science, used the subtitle 'The Devil's Disciple' on the first volume of his work on Huxley.[97] Darwin engaged only reluctantly in the great dispute between science and religion; Huxley rejoiced in the chance to ram scientific philosophy down the throats of ignorant believers. Devil's disciple, high priest or the pope of science – Huxley, celebrating his role, knew where he stood.

On one occasion a group of evangelical chemists, led by a Plymouth Brethren paint manufacturer, delivered an indignant petition to the British Association for the Advancement of Science (BAAS). The worthy believers demanded – as if it were within their discretion to do so – that the association 'maintain a harmonious alliance between Physical Science and Revealed Religion'. The trouble was that Huxley and his enthusiastic disciples, his 'dangerous clique', were baiting parsons – the poor things! – with the glee 'a small boy feels when he is tying a kettle to a dog's tail'.[98] There was much priest baiting about and one clash of civilisations is remembered more than the rest.

On 30 June 1860, six months after Darwin's Origin burst upon the world, evolution was the inevitable topic of a meeting of the BAAS. Some 700 people turned up, and a number of churchmen

– and Huxley – were on the platform. The American Dr John Draper spoke for an hour on 'The Intellectual Development of Europe Considered with Reference to the Views of Mr Darwin', and other speakers addressed the theme. Then Samuel 'Soapy Sam' Wilberforce, Bishop of Oxford, coached for the occasion by the great anatomist Sir Richard Owen, rose to speak. He was not well grounded in the sciences but was about to confront Huxley, an experimental biologist with an international reputation.

The bishop poured scorn on the theory of evolution, to the great delight of the audience, and then turned to address Huxley: 'Was it through his grandfather or grandmother that he claimed descent from a monkey?' Not a bad line, even though it was totally bereft of any knowledge of evolution. Huxley whispered the words 'The Lord hath delivered him into mine hands' – which may not have pleased his ardent atheist disciples – and then rose to respond. At first he explained Darwin's key ideas, exposing Wilberforce's ignorance and error. And then he declared, to the bishop's complete humiliation, that he would not be ashamed to be descended from a monkey but *would* be ashamed to be 'connected with a man who used great gifts to obscure the truth'. The crowd loved it.

There were some consolations to be found in religious belief, but Huxley proclaimed that 'truth is better than much profit . . . If wife and child and name and fame were all to be lost to me one after the other, still I will not lie.' The first duty is to seek truth and to say and to feel, as 'the most sacred act of a man's life', that 'I believe such and such to be true'. For example, he was not impressed with the biblical tale of demons being transferred to the Gadarene swine, the sort of superstition that was common to all barbarous people. In general he refused to regard blind faith as a reasonable substitute for knowledge, and endlessly urged the doctrine of science: 'I cannot believe that the great mysteries of existence will be laid open to me on other terms.'[99] Huxley perceived in all this a peculiar resemblance to the Christian posture of entire surrender to the will of God: reason and science demanded entire surrender to 'the fact', the only basis on which secure beliefs could rest: 'I have only begun to learn content and peace of mind since I have resolved at all risks to do this.'[100] There is no security in mystery and magic, in explanations that explain nothing, in doctrines of eternal torment, in fantastical inventions that swirl through the night. There is security only in the patient accumulation of empirical data and the cautious framing of hypotheses that in due course may contribute to the swelling body of human knowledge.

Huxley went so far as to equate 'Divine Government' with 'the sum of the customs of matter', but emphasised equally the importance of an ethical dimension: 'The rewards in life are contingent upon obedience to the *whole* law – physical as well as moral – and that moral obedience will not atone for physical sin, or *vice versa*.'[101] It is a touching faith – that virtue will bring its own reward.[102] Huxley, like his hero, Darwin, had undergone his own intellectual and 'spiritual' journey, though becoming a more evangelical figure than his mentor.

The law of evolution, demonstrated so boldly in the *Origin*, is essentially a scientific matter but it had abundant ethical consequences. It undermined central religious beliefs about the unique status of human beings and inevitably raised ethical questions. If God, as a discredited source of morality, was tottering – and with It (*sic*) the church – what was the basis for proper social behaviour? Some of the ethical offshoots of the freshly advertised doctrine were unfortunate; for example, the brutal competitiveness espoused in elements of social Darwinism. But the problem was not a new one. Faith had not solved it, since priests and propagandists had always made of religion what they wanted. Any evolution-fuelled attack on faith did not make morality a purely subjective business. There was an important sense in which moral sensitivities had always been subjective in essence. In exposing the law of evolution beyond informed criticism, Darwin had simply forced human beings to view their nature in a realistic way. Religious believers found the encounter with scientific truth deeply traumatic, and many of them continue to suffer many of the symptoms of psychological disturbance.

It was not the first time that freethinking minds had confronted widespread superstition – Lucretius, Hume and Hypatia[103] would not want us to say that – but Darwin and his supporters had shaken the foundations to an unprecedented degree, and they have not yet settled. The battle between biology and bibles (not only the Judeo-Christian texts, but those of Islam and other religions) continued in the post-*Origin* nineteenth century, throughout the twentieth, and carries on in feverish turmoil today.

In the second half of the nineteenth century most biology textbooks still reflected the pre-Darwinian view of humankind's place on earth. One exception was a leading text – Asa Gray's *First Lessons in Botany*, later renamed *The Elements of Botany*.[104] It is interesting to note that Gray, a Harvard professor of botany, was the only American that Darwin took into his confidence before the publication of the *Origin*. But Gray, like Darwin himself, was forced to travel the arduous intellectual journey. His book *First Lessons in Botany and Vegetable Physiology* (1857) carried the statement that 'the Creator established a number of species at the beginning, which have continued by propagation, each after its kind'. But a later edition, entitled *Elements of Botany for Beginners and for Schools* (1887), omitted this religious affirmation; and Gray made various other changes to his texts in the light of Darwin. At the same time Gray, an orthodox Christian, managed to accept evolution by merely giving God a different role. Whereas originally a supreme deity had functioned as the immediate reason for diverse species, now God still had plans but was perceived as 'lying behind nature', whatever that meant. This ploy was to become increasingly familiar in the twentieth century, as progressive Christians fought to preserve some niche, however mysterious and obscure, for the ailing deity. However, the creationists, invariably protected by crude dogma, continued in their innocent faith.

The mid-nineteenth-century zoologist Louis Agassiz, unlike his Harvard colleague Gray, never managed to embrace the law of evolution; and so, with the like-minded A. A. Gould, wrote biology textbooks proclaiming that man and the animals 'were created by the word of God . . . [a] truth . . . confirmed by the revelations of science, which unequivocally indicate the direct intervention of creative power.'[105] Still, Agassiz was not happy with Genesis, reckoning that the richness of the biological world had come about through separate divine acts of creation. Pre-

Darwinist ideas survived also in geology textbooks, though the impact of biological evolution was beginning to impact on books in all the related disciplines. In the 1880s scientists in America and elsewhere, trained in a post-*Origin* world, were beginning to write high-school textbooks that invariably dealt sympathetically with evolution. For example, Charles E. Bessey, who had studied botany under Gray at Harvard, emphasised the importance of laboratory methods and prairie-related ecological concepts. A later edition of his *Botany for High Schools and Colleges* (1880) included both the introduction, distribution and extinction of species over the great course of geological time and a chapter dealing with the evolution of angiosperms. And Bessey was determined to convert people: 'The mission of the true teacher is to burn the thoughts in, brand his students for life.'[106]

Joseph LeConte was yet another liberal Christian struggling to square the circle. He worried about how long man had been on the earth. Was it 100,000 years or only 10,000, as some people maintained? Able to live with a Lamarckian brand of evolution, he refrained from mentioning divine creation but was not keen to discuss natural selection either. Darwin had driven LeConte to consider evolution but he was no Darwinist. It was obvious that religious believers were being dragged along by the chariot of science but not many were able to complete the journey. Faith as a route to truth about the origins of *Homo sapiens* was being increasingly marginalised by the day, and a nod was given to the ancient thinkers who plainly had more wisdom than modern Christians and their ilk. In 1911 the eugenicist Charles Davenport, director of the Carnegie Institution's Department of Experimental Evolution, wrote in a textbook:

> We have seen how the Greeks regarded the evolution of the organic world as a part of cosmic philosophy. Through a narrow interpretation of the Mosaic account of creation, the Christian church was led away from those broad views . . . It was the great service of Charles Darwin to offer such a theory, accompanied by proofs so numerous and presented in a fashion so judicial as to win acceptance by all.[107]

This was the prevailing mood among scientists at the start of the twentieth century. George W. Hunter's *A Civic Biology* (1914) defined evolution, proved by a fossil record spanning 'millions of years', as 'the belief that simple forms of life on earth slowly and gradually gave rise to those more complex and that thus ultimately the most complex form came into existence'. Hunter declared of Darwin: 'He gave the world the proofs of the theory on which we today base the progress of the world. Man is presented as a product of this evolution, with the Caucasian race being "finally, the highest type of all".'[108] It is easy to see that, while Darwin's science was largely unassailable, the theory of natural selection could be used as a fascist apology for the political creeds destined to emerge through the twentieth century.

In 1918 Clifton F. Hodge and Jean Dawson published *Civic Biology* (not to be confused with the Hunter volume). Here there was yet more praise for what Darwin had accomplished. After explaining the law of evolution the two authors declaim: 'Charles Darwin, by lifelong application and sacrifice, marked the greatest advance in discovery of the laws of life that the world has known.' *Civic Biology* affirmed that it was 'as impossible now to take the ideas of descent and of natural selection out of the world as to take a star out of the sky.' *School Science*, a professional journal for science teachers in America, had no doubt in 1902 that the teaching of zoology had progressed 'from the narrow ideal of religious and memory training to the broader conceptions of mental, moral and physical development' according to the most recent scientific advances. A decade later the journal was urging that zoology be taught through science and not religion, and lamented that certain rural areas were 'holding out' against evolution, as though a beleaguered military contingent. In 1916 *School Science* was continuing to campaign for the inclusion of evolution in high-school biology – a call endorsed by the National Education Association. It seemed that Darwin had won the battle – by sheer weight of evidence and argument. A few primitive enclaves were refusing to surrender but, the evolutionists assumed, history would leave them behind. In fact, in the scientific communities this was largely the case. But the Christian soldiers were not about to surrender. There were skirmishes and more yet to come.

Immediately after the First World War, with everyone horrified at what had transpired in the trenches of mainland Europe, an anti-evolution crusade began in America and caused many superstitious ripples beyond. Beset by growing religious and political concerns, people readily responded to the call of the Christian activist William Jennings Bryan, later to become famous through the 'Tennessee monkey trial' (see below), to 'drive Darwinism from our schools';[109] and he rejoiced that but for the fact that only a small percentage of children had gone to high school and college in the past, Darwinism could have 'done more harm'.[110] Bryan, William Bell Riley, head of the World Christian Fundamentals Association (WCFA) and John Roach Straton, a prominent Baptist minister, were the leaders of the anti-evolution crusade. Bryan, like any good Muslim, saw no distinction between religion and politics, and campaigned for both throughout his life. A cartoonist depicted him as a big-game hunter using one shotgun barrel to fire at a [Republican Party] elephant as he tries to enter the Treasury and another to fire at Darwinism – the monkey – as he tries to enter the school room. At the time of his death Bryan was planning to run for the Senate.

In 1919 the eighteenth amendment to the US constitution, banning the sale of alcoholic beverages, was decisively ratified (ushering in prohibition and a massive boost to organised crime). Could the same be done with Darwinism? Could the teaching of biological evolution through natural selection be prohibited in American schools? The Christian crusader T. T. Martin suggested that it would be better to poison the nation's children than to teach them about Darwinism: 'Ramming poison down the throats of our children is nothing compared with damning their souls with the teaching of evolution, that robs them of a revelation from God and a real Redeemer.'[111] The historian George Marsden commented that after 1920 the fundamentalists, then dominating the conservative evangelical councils, were engaged in holy warfare 'to drive the scourge of modernism out of church and culture'.[112] Before long the teaching of evolution would become a target of the new crusade. Bryan was continuing, with little relevant knowledge, to attack the scientific and moral standing of evolution. At first his standard speech was 'The Menace of Darwinism', but then he added 'The Bible and Its Enemies', in which evolution featured prominently, to his repertoire. Both speeches were printed as pamphlets and were widely circulated to provide pious activists with ammunition to attack the infidel evolutionists. Bryan declaimed, with staggering ignorance, that because science was 'the explanation of facts . . . *Darwinism is not science at all. Darwin does not use facts*' (emphasis added).[113] Moreover, Darwin served to 'lay the foundations for the bloodiest war in history'.[114]

On 24 March 1923 America's first anti-evolution law was passed in Oklahoma, following the efforts of the anti-evolution crusaders and a call by the state Baptist general session for legislation banning 'the teaching of evolution in our school system'. One legislator told his colleagues that if he had a chance 'to down this hellish Darwin here' he would do it; another legislator urged the state to leave 'the hellish teachings' of Darwin out. In April the Florida State Assembly unanimously approved a Bryan proposition declaring it improper for any public-school teacher 'to teach or to permit to be taught Atheism, or Agnosticism, or to teach as true Darwinism or any other hypothesis that links man in blood relation to any form of lower life'; and on 25 May the measure became effective, though with minimal impact on teaching policies. In January 1925 bills outlawing the teaching of evolution appeared in both houses of the Tennessee legislature, with the lower house quickly passing the bill: 'It shall be unlawful for any teacher to teach any theory that denies the Story of Divine Creation of man as taught in the Bible; and to teach instead that man has descended from a lower order of animal.'[115] Teachers who violated the prohibition would be fined. But by now the pro-evolution activists were beginning to marshal their forces for yet another bout between science and superstition.

In response to the Tennessee legislation, the American Civil Liberties Union announced that it was looking for a Tennessee teacher who was willing to help it test the law in the courts. The willing teacher was John T. Scopes, who had erred in using George W. Hunter's *A Civic Biology*, highly sympathetic to

evolution, to conduct a review for the final biology examination
in a school in the city of Dayton. By coincidence the annual
convention of the WCFA, assembled in Memphis, was then
formally commending the governor and legislature of Tennessee
for 'prohibiting the teaching of the unscientific, anti-Christian,
atheistic, anarchistic, pagan, rationalistic evolutionary theory'.

The WCFA leadership then asked Bryan to represent the
association at the trial. He agreed to do so, 'without compen-
sation', and resolved to take on the 'so-called scientists' in a 'battle
royal' for the Christian people of Tennessee. Clarence Darrow,
the most famous defence attorney in the country, and Dudley
Field Malone agreed to appear for the defence. Darrow himself,
prepared to support Bryan's presidential campaigns, had rejected
Christianity, doubted the existence of a god and was an enthusiastic supporter of evolution. Malone, another political supporter
of Bryan, had worked widely for radical causes, defending the civil
rights of women, blacks and political reformers.[116] Scopes was
convicted and paid a derisory fine, and history judged that
evolution was the moral victor.[117]

The nominal Bryan victory encouraged other Christian
legislators in their struggle to achieve anti-evolution statutes. In
Mississippi T. T. Martin claimed that 'every man, woman and
child in the place wants an anti-evolution law passed', and packed
the House of Representatives gallery with Christian zealots. A co-
sponsor of an anti-evolution bill declared that its defeat would be
'a compromise with the devil'; and another proponent echoed the
words of Martin: 'We don't want evolution theory rammed down
the throats of our children.'[118] The bill was adopted on a vote of
seventy-six to thirty-two, and the drama made its way to the state
Senate. A supporter declared that scientists see things as material
and often lose sight of the spiritual: 'I'd rather have the leadership
of one Christian mother than of all the scientists in the world.'[119]
And, in the event, the anti-evolution bill was adopted, encourag-
ing zealous efforts elsewhere. In Arkansas a petition succeeded in
placing a similar measure on a 1928 ballot to test public attitudes
to evolution, but here national attention was diverted by
presidential campaigning. The measure against evolution succeeded in winning almost two thirds of the statewide vote,

suggesting that hostility to Darwin extended far beyond the
stereotypical Bible thumpers to a solid majority of the people.
There was then a lull in the doctrinal war until fresh campaigners
found new ways of fighting the old battles.

After the diversions of the Second World War the Christian
fundamentalists were clearly on the defensive. There was mounting
pressure for the repeal of the few anti-evolution measures on the
statute, and the 1960s represented a 'decade of legal triumph for
evolutionary teaching',[120] forcing the creationists to regroup. In
1982 the historian George Marsden commented that the fundamentalists were using a literal reading of the Bible in times of
uncertainty, just as they had done in reaction to the 'barbarism' of
the First World War, which they attributed to a Nietzschean
evolutionary philosophy. Creationist legal challenges, agitated by
the growing secularism in society, were widespread in the 1970s
and early 1980s, whereupon the evolutionists responded with their
own missionary zeal.

The upshot was an uneasy compromise. Scientists were
virtually unanimous on the irrelevance of creationism to science
teaching but legislators were forced to heed a public opinion that
spoke with a much more divided voice. This meant that
creationism was gradually creeping into public schools, with
fundamentalists claiming successes in converting the young now
that they were no longer indoctrinated solely in Darwinian
evolution. In 1988 the popular fundamentalist journal *Moody
Monthly* noted that the Supreme Court had approved the teaching
of 'any and all facets' of the origin of humankind, but cautioned
against teaching anything called 'creation science' as science,
because the court had classified it as a religious doctrine.[121] By the
1990s the religious zealots had largely abandoned any campaigns
to evict the teaching of evolution from the schools. The most they
could attempt was to force creation science onto the syllabuses and
to find reasons why the term should not be derided as an obvious
oxymoron. The fresh creationist strategy, developing through the
1990s and beyond, was called 'intelligent design'. The battle was
far from over.

In May 2005 the Kansas Board of Education, true to form, was
hearing evidence from anti-evolutionists trying to ensure that

pupils learnt 'alternatives to evolution' that require a guiding hand
in the origin of life. Mainstream scientists – for example, as
represented by the American Association for the Advancement of
Science – were boycotting the meetings and holding protests. Jack
Krebs, vice-president of Kansas Citizens for Science, commented:
'They [the anti-evolutionists] have hijacked science and education.'[122] In November, Lord May of Oxford gave a valedictory
speech at the end of his five-year presidency of the Royal Society
to denounce the impact of religious fundamentalism on pressing
issues facing humanity.[123]

At the same time a federal judge in Pennsylvania ruled, in a 123-
page decision, that it was unconstitutional to teach intelligent
design in a biology class – a significant victory for evolution.[124] But
in Britain a significant number of science students on campuses or
in sixth-form colleges were challenging the theory of evolution
and arguing that Darwin had got it wrong, while an examinations
board admitted that 'creationism' would be introduced into a
biology course in September 2006.[125] Nevertheless, Rowan
Williams, the Archbishop of Canterbury, was saying that creationism should not be taught in schools:

> I think creationism is . . . a kind of category mistake, as if the Bible
> were a theory like other theories . . . if creationism is presented as a
> stark alternative theory alongside other theories I think there's just
> been a jarring of categories . . . My worry is that creationism can end
> up reducing the doctrine of creation rather than enhancing it.[126]

In short, creationism can't compete with evolution so let's keep
the religious categories so slippery that they are beyond denial.

The archbishop knew the problems. Creationism was not just a
'category' mistake, it was a mistake, and that was the upshot of the
matter. In April 2006 the geneticist Steve Jones delivered a Royal
Society lecture, 'Why Creationism Is Wrong and Evolution Is
Right', in which he compared creationism to the theory that
babies are brought by storks.[127] And in June a statement signed by
national science academies from sixty-seven countries called for
'evidence-based' teaching of the origins of life, and denounced
some faith-based schools for not teaching evolution:

We urge decision-makers, teachers and parents to educate all children about the methods and discoveries of science . . . Within science courses taught in certain public systems of education, scientific evidence, data, and testable theories about the origins and evolution of life on earth are being concealed, denied or confused with theories not testable by science.[128]

In November 2006 *The Guardian* revealed that some fifty-nine schools in England were using creationist teaching materials condemned by the government as 'not appropriate to support the science curriculum'.[129] The following month the government was reportedly planning to write to schools to tell them not to use creationist materials in science lessons, but by 2008 there were ample signs that 'evolution denial' was growing in British society.[130]

In America, fundamentalists in Kentucky were happy to celebrate the opening of the world's first creationist museum, in which animatronic children and tyrannosaurs frolic happily together by a waterfall. In this Garden of Eden all the dinosaurs are vegetarians, and were created only 6,000 years ago. Ken Ham, the head of Answers in Genesis, a 'Young Earth' creationist ministry, explains that people knew all about dragons, which were probably dinosaurs, and scientists should never be trusted on dating the fossil record:

When we look at a fossil it doesn't have a label on it. There is no absolute dating method you can use to absolutely age-date anything . . . you can't have millions of years of fossils because, in the fossil record, you have evidence of animals eating each other. And the Bible makes it clear that originally, animals were vegetarians, as man was vegetarian.

And Noah did not swamp the ark with dinosaurs because he only took *young* dinosaurs on board.[131]

The history of religion and philosophy is littered with variants of the notion that God, or gods and (occasionally) goddesses, had a celestial hand in the creation of the world. The idea has been frequently rebranded, as if to indicate that it had not been selling well under its familiar name, sobriquet or image. So during this lengthy historical process we moved from descriptions of creative acts by this or that deity to more sophisticated attempts to present the design argument; from matters of teleology (a good word for philosophers) to creationism; from Aristotle and Aquinas and Kant's (refuted) physico-theological argument to Henri Berson's 'vitalism'; and from frantic nineteenth-century abuse of Darwinism to the twentieth century birth of intelligent design (ID). These are all the same misbegotten animal. It just dyes its hair from time to time.

The supporters of ID are largely motivated by desperation. They see how Darwinism is accepted by the vast bulk of the world's scientific community, with the corollary that the gods have been evicted from the process of biological development on earth (and elsewhere?). If supposed divine acts of creation are to be protected this cannot be achieved by substituting funda-mentalist rhetoric for scientific enquiry, and so creationism has to be shown to be *scientific*. This would be a neat trick if it could be managed, but it is easy to spot the magician's moves.

The first tactic of the ID activists is to keep theology out of the picture – which in itself is a victory for science. What would William Jennings Bryan have thought about that? Here an attempt is made to present arguments, some philosophical and some empirical, to demonstrate that the idea of intelligent design is a purely rational enterprise, unrelated to any creationist nonsense of the past. As in most stage productions, there is a leading man or woman. We soon learn that the ID lead is played by a character called 'irreducible complexity' (IC), which has an imposing ring to it. Put simply, there are complex systems in the biological world that could not have originated through the progressive accumulation of modifications, as specified by the evolutionists. Darwin himself was worried by the complexity of the eye: how could such a complex organ have occurred through chance mutations? For a while the creationists seized on the eye but then it slipped through their fingers. Many eyes were being discovered in the zoological world, some much more primitive than others, and gradually it became possible to chart one or more evolu-tionary routes. Hence the creationist and more recently the ID brigades were forced to hunt for complex systems that lay beyond the reach of the evolutionists. And here, in one respect at least, the biologists were propping up the IDers (not to be confused with *ideas*) as they limped along in their endless quest for the Holy Grail. For science itself was revealing systems in nature which it could not explain in evolutionary terms. This of course was inevitable: it is impossible to search for an explanation for something until you have discovered it. But the IDers were delighted to learn that scientists were not infallible. Perhaps the gaps in their knowledge signalled IC. And perhaps this in turn meant that God existed, that Mary was a virgin, that you should not eat meat on Fridays but should hang homosexuals any day of the week.

The current ID favourite signalling IC is the bacterial flagellum, which would never have been discovered but for the painstaking efforts of skilled scientists traditionally derided by superstitious fools.[132] It has to be said at the outset that the flagellum is truly remarkable, comprising a rotary device that propels a bacterium through a liquid. Its tail, working as a propeller, is attached to a drive shaft which uses a flow of acid from the outside of the bacterium to power the turning motion, while an effective stator stabilises the structure. Some forty different types of protein are necessary for the activity of the flagellum, and if any one of these is absent the mechanism does not work.

The IDers are very impressed, and immediately declare that the flagellum is an example – there are others, such as the blood-clotting cascade – of IC.[133] This is, alas, a hazardous enterprise. Tell the scientists that something cannot be explained in their evolutionary terms and they are quickly on the case. In the seventeenth century Thomas Burnet (c.1635–1715) declared: 'It is a dangerous thing to engage the authority of Scripture in disputes about the natural world, in opposition to reason lest Time, which brings all things to light, should discover that to be false which we had made Scripture to assert.'[134] In short, if today we do not have an explanation it is likely that tomorrow we will. And in fact the flagellum was quickly being targeted.

Richard Dawkins has pointed out the IDer Michael Behe's confusion on this matter when testifying in court on behalf of

creationists trying to impose ID creationism on a school syllabus –
which the presiding judge, John E. Jones, described as a move of
'breathtaking inanity'.[135] Behe alleged in court that the biological
literature had ignored the issue of the bacterial flagellum – a claim
that was manifestly untrue. The literature had focused on many of
the issues raised by Behe and other IDers,[136] and Kenneth R. Miller
of Brown University, in Providence, Rhode Island, had addressed
the flagellum in detail in an article nicely entitled 'The Flagellum
Unspun: The Collapse of "Irreducible Complexity"'.[137] Here
Miller focused on a 'nasty little device', the Type III secretory
system (T3SS), which allows bacteria to inject toxins through the
cell membranes of victim hosts. While at first sight unrelated to the
flagellum, it has been found that the proteins of the T3SS are
directly homologous to the proteins in its basal portion.[138] This
suggests that one evolved function, that of the T3SS, had been
incorporated in a larger biological system, the bacterial flagellum,
to facilitate other modes of behaviour: 'From an evolutionary point
of view, this relationship is hardly surprising. In fact, it's to be
expected that the opportunism of evolutionary processes would
mix and match proteins to produce new and novel functions.'[139]

Today there is debate about whether the T3SS evolved first and
was then incorporated into the flagellum, whether the flagellum
evolved first, or whether the two systems evolved in parallel. One
important consideration is that bacteria would have needed a
means of propulsion before they needed a T3SS, and flagella are
found in a more diverse range of bacterial species than is the T3SS.
Howard Ochman, of the University of Arizona, has commented:
'The most parsimonious explanation is that the T3SS arose later
[than the flagellum].'[140] It is also significant that the bacterial
flagellum has many different forms, all with similar features that
suggest a common ancestor. The science writer Dan Jones has
pointed out that the proteins in two flagella – *Escherichia coli* K12
and *Salmonella enterica* LT2 – have proteins in common with other
bacterial species, again suggesting evolutionary links with other
organisms. This research suggests in turn that just two ancestral
proteins – a proto-flagellin and a proto-red/hook protein – were
probably components of a putative flagellum 'that is ancestral to
all flagella, dubbed the "ur-flagellum"'.[141] Hence we may conclude

that there is 'incontrovertible evidence' showing that bacterial flagella are 'cobbled together from recycled components of other systems – and vice versa – through gene duplication and diversification. In other words, they evolved.'[142]

In short, there are already ample clues as to how the flagellum, relatively new to science, emerged as part of the evolutionary process: it certainly cannot be assumed to be irreducibly complex. And this of course is the IDers' problem: clutch at something that today is little understood and rest an entire case on the assumption that in principle scientists will never be able to offer an explanation. It's a dodgy approach, roundly and copiously ridiculed by Dawkins in *The God Delusion*[143] and more succinctly elsewhere in an imaginary conversation between A. L. Hodgkin and A. F. Huxley, who in real life won the Nobel Prize for their model of the nerve impulse:

> *Hodgkin:* I say, Huxley, this is a terribly difficult problem. I can't see how the nerve impulse works, can you?
>
> *Huxley:* No, Hodgkin, I can't, and these differential equations are fiendishly hard to solve. Why don't we just give up and say the nerve impulse propagates by Nervous Energy?
>
> *Hodgkin:* Excellent idea, Huxley, let's write the letter to *Nature* now, it'll only take one line, then we can turn to something easier.[144]

This is analogous to a commentary in a book extract by the famous biochemist Joseph Needham (1900–1995) discussing vitalism, the idea that a 'vital essence' distinguishes living systems from brute matter. He emphasises that the arguments of the modern vitalists, akin to the creationists, are not 'sufficient to sustain the weight placed on them'; and that there is another objection to the doctrine – namely, that it discourages further research: 'Whereas the mechanistic hypothesis [akin to evolutionary biology] does at least provide definite theories which can be proved or disproved, vitalism simply *fills up the gaps* in mechanistic descriptions after the fashion of Columbus's map maker, "Where Unknown, there place Terrors" [emphasis added].'[145]

Professor Behe does not stop at the flagellum. He reckons also that the complexity of the immune system will never be explicable in evolutionary terms – an argument that did not impress Judge Jones: 'He [Behe] was presented with fifty-eight peer-reviewed publications, nine books, and several immunology text-book chapters about the evolution of the immune system . . . he simply insisted that this was simply not sufficient evidence for evolution . . . that it was not "good enough".' When cross-examined by Eric Rothschild, chief counsel for the plaintiffs, Behe admitted that he had not read most of the fifty-eight documents, causing Rothschild to say that, thankfully, there *were* scientists who toiled to help us combat disease: 'By contrast, Professor Behe and the entire intelligent design movement are doing nothing to advance scientific or medical knowledge and are telling future generations of scientists, don't bother.'[146]

The IDers' tactic of trying to keep religion out of the debate, to insist that ID is a scientific matter, is patently absurd. Moreover, this approach is totally discredited when, as it must, the decrepit figure of theology stumbles onto the stage. It was there all along. The flagellum and the immune system were held up to hide the embarrassment of the confused actor on the boards but, as a once-powerful performer, he still insists on uttering a few halting lines. Thus, on the old fellow's behalf, the IDer William Dembski argues for intelligent design and is keen also – as well as focusing on the usual ID concerns – to consider prayer, Moses and Pharaoh, the Philistines and the ark, the sign of the resurrection, core commitments of Christianity, miracles, the Christology of Chalcedon and so on.[147] This nicely illustrates a peculiar feature of IC: it conveniently affirms the religion of the advocate. It is quite remarkable how a scrutiny of complexity in nature conducts a Christian to the Bible and a Muslim to the Koran. The unsuspecting flagellum has a lot to answer for.

There is one important consideration, age old but irrefutable, that finally buries the IDers with little trace, but before mentioning it we should note the *anthropic principle*. This suggests that because the earth in particular and the universe in general are 'finely tuned' to allow the emergence of life there must be a celestial Fine Tuner twiddling the knobs. The knobs in question are the physical properties of matter, realised through half a dozen fundamental constants holding all around the universe, that allow the growth of, for example, hydrocarbon molecules able to support life. Already there is a prodigious literature exploring this argument. It originated in 1974 with the British mathematician Brandon Carter, was expanded by the physicists John Barrow and Frank Tipler,[148] and was made available to a wider audience in such books as Paul Davies's *The Goldilocks Enigma*.[149]

There are various possible responses to the anthropic principle. The universe is so vast that an unimaginable number of possibilities will be realised through all the immensity of space and time – so perhaps we have won a sort of cosmic lottery. Or perhaps, to add to the confusion and the available range of possibilities, there are many universes existing in a 'multiverse' or 'megaverse'. We happen to have emerged in one (probably of many) that is propitious for life. At the same time our luck will not hold out indefinitely. Apart from such man-made threats as nuclear war and global warming, there are hazards on an altogether vaster scale – such as the ultimate explosion of the sun to form a red giant star, destroying the solar system in the process. It will not be long, in cosmological terms, before the anthropic principle is overthrown by the unfriendly behaviour of atoms at the heart of stars.

Our age-old and irrefutable consideration is the familiar one, mentioned earlier, that positing God to explain IC, even allowing that it exists, or the anthropic principle, at best a temporary set of circumstances, explains nothing – simply because it requires the invention of a further vast complexity that is without explanation. There is no religious believer that would deny that God is unimaginably complex – to the point that it is often depicted as 'transcendent', 'incomprehensible', 'beyond all human under-standing' and suchlike, but with the endearing paradox that we still know it wants us to avoid adultery, never to eat pigs and always to shudder at divine wrath. To struggle to entertain an entity that is so immense and so self-contradictory is evidence for one thing only – human foolishness mired in the dark night of an ignorant age.

Charles Darwin provided massively overwhelming evidence – from the fossil record, the geographical distribution of species, embryology, morphology, comparative anatomy, the extinctions of species, behavioural characteristics etc. – to establish the law of evolution through natural selection.[150] In addition to the best-known texts, such as the *Origin* and the *Descent*, he also wrote in detail about the building of coral reefs, the importance of sexual selection and the biology of birds, orchids, barnacles and much more. Darwin represented a staggering project that dwarfed the efforts of his many brilliant colleagues and correspondents. But despite all this he knew nothing about the biochemical mechanism of heredity. He surmised that such must exist but he had no means of probing the innermost workings of the biological cell. A new scientific revolution – destined to immeasurably strengthen Darwin's central postulates – began almost a century after the first publication of *The Origin of Species*.

On 25 April 1953 the biochemists James Watson and Francis Crick, working at Cambridge in collaboration with King's College, London, published a devastating article, 'A Structure for Deoxyribose Nucleic Acid', in *Nature*, one of the most prestigious scientific journals in the world. It began with the elegantly understated and historic words 'We wish to suggest a structure for the salt of deoxyribose nucleic acid (D.N.A.). This structure has novel features which are of considerable biological interest.'

Towards the end of this brief (two-page) article Watson and Crick commented: 'It has not escaped our notice that the specific pairing we have postulated immediately suggests a possible copying mechanism for the genetic material.'[151] This statement rested on the discovery that the base pairing in DNA (adenine links to thymine and guanine to cytosine, the bases referred to as A, T, G and C) provides the mechanism by which genetic information carried in the double helix could be precisely copied – a dramatic scientific insight that started a revolution in molecular biology destined to facilitate, for example, the manipulation of DNA for genetic engineering and medical research, and the decoding of the genome of human beings and those of such research organisms as the mouse, yeast and the fruit fly. In addition, and highly significant for our purposes, the discovery of the double helix yielded further overwhelming evidence in support of Darwin's postulate of evolution through natural selection. Just as geological fossils continue to provide substantial support for evolutionary biology, so 'fossil genes' help to demonstrate that life forms have evolved from earlier biological systems.[152]

The DNA of every animal and plant carries the specific coded instructions for the building of proteins that perform all the necessary tasks in the organism, from carrying oxygen to building tissue. The two helical strands of DNA are composed of four distinct bases, chemical building blocks represented by A, T, G and C, as noted. It is the order of bases in a sequence of DNA (for example, ACGTCGATAA) that forms the unique instructions for building the characteristic proteins for all life forms. However, the copying mechanism sometimes generates mistakes in the base sequence – a mutation – which may equip the organism to cope better than its rivals in a changing environment. Or, alternatively, a biological function that is no longer required causes the related genes to decay over time: 'Fossil genes reside in DNA much in the same way that fossils reside in sedimentary rock . . . these broken pieces of yesterday's code reflect the adaptation of species, including humans, to new ways of life.'[153]

In short, the advances in molecular biology based on an understanding of the role of the DNA double helix in heredity provide overwhelming evidence of Darwinian evolution. The creationists and IDers are eager to accept the role of DNA in crime detection. If they fully understood its character they would acknowledge that any ideas of special creation or ID have been finally crushed under the irresistible weight of scientific knowledge, with the corollary that any claims to the contrary are a mixture of farce and absurdity.[154]

Today evidence for the law of evolution continues to accumulate. That *Homo sapiens* has kinship with the rest of the biological world is being made increasingly obvious, not least through studies of non-human animal behaviour. Frans de Waal, professor of primate behaviour at Emory University in Atlanta, Georgia, has provided important examples of empathy in rhesus monkeys, where, for example, a monkey will refuse to pull a chain that delivers food to itself if this gives an electric shock to a companion (one monkey starved itself for twelve days in these circumstances) – clear evidence for the existence of a moral faculty

(we may wonder about the moral sensitivities of the experimenters).[155] Other work at Emory suggests that capuchin
monkeys resent unfair reward schemes, as when companions are
suddenly given grapes instead of cucumbers for similar work.[156]
Elsewhere de Waal has provided abundant evidence from
chimpanzees – for example an abused individual being comforted
by another, expressions of gratitude for grooming, the use of
punishment to impose social rules – to show that human morality
has evolutionary roots in the animal world.[157]

There are countless other examples showing the manifest
continuity between human and non-human mental capacities. For
example, baboons have been shown able to plan ahead for
expeditions to find food; a dolphin, nursed back to health by a
dedicated trainer, was reportedly 'dying of a broken heart' after her
death; archaeologists have found evidence – primitive anvils and
stone hammers – demonstrating that chimpanzees experienced their
own 'stone age'; gorillas use plant leaves to clean their faces and
hands after a meal; and research has shown that chimpanzees are
capable of altruistic behaviour, helping each other in difficult tasks.
Researchers have demonstrated that fish can count up to four. (I
will not encourage a crude and excessive anthropomorphism by
asking pet owners to supply their own examples.)

In the same fashion, scientific research continues to fill in the
gaps in our evolutionary knowledge. Many religious believers –
Christians, Muslims and others – refuse to acknowledge the
weight of scientific evidence. Instead they prefer to peddle lies
about evolution – which demonstrates only their abysmal
ignorance. In February 2008 Donald Prothero, a professor of
geology at Occidental College, Los Angeles, pointed out in *New
Scientist* that the creationists were ignoring a wealth of transitional
fossils found since Darwin's era, which provide proof of the
evolutionary process:

> Foremost among their tactics is to distort or ignore the evidence for
> evolution; a favourite lie is 'there are no transitional fossils'. This is
> manifestly untrue. We now have abundant evidence for how all the
> major groups of animals are related, much of it in the form of excellent
> transitional fossils.[158]

We are accustomed to the creationists and IDers spreading falsehoods about the fossil record, but they have not yet begun to dissemble about fossil genes. Do they understand this branch of molecular biology? Have they even heard of fossil genes? We must await the likely plethora of misleading and ignorant commentary with bated breath. The following examples, culled from the general and technical press, and which could be vastly extended, are typical of scientific work bearing directly on the course of evolution:

> Geology remains a rich source of fresh information, providing fossil data that enables biologists to uncover one 'missing link' after another: findings that have provided crucial clues about the evolution of whales are a good example.[159]

> Researchers at Trinity College, Dublin, have used DNA evidence to chart the history of Scottish polar bears.

> Scientists working on fossilised feathers found in 100-million-year-old amber in Charente-Maritime, western France, have noted a key missing link – 'an intermediate and critical stage' – in the evolution of birds.

> Researchers from the University of Oslo Natural History Museum have discovered the fossilised remains of a pliosaur, helping to explain the evolution of marine predators.

> Scientists at the University of Edinburgh have managed to recreate the evolutionary steps that may have produced *Heliconius heurippa*, a hybrid butterfly.

> Researchers at the J. Craig Venter Institute, Rockville, Maryland, and the University of Rochester, New York, have discovered copies of the genome of the *Wolbachia* bacterium lurking within the genetic code of fruit flies, wasps and nematode worms, suggesting that genes can transfer from bacteria to multicellular organisms and so speed up the evolutionary process.

> Fossilised remains found in Georgia, the former Soviet republic, have a peculiar mix of physical features suggesting a missing link between hominid species.

Remains of *Homo floresiensis*, measuring 3 feet tall, have been found in the Malay archipelago, again suggesting links in the human evolutionary chain.

Scientists at the University of Chicago examining the DNA of humans, rats, macaques and mice concluded that humans developed their cognitive abilities through a large number of mutations in a short time, unlike the normal course of evolutionary change.

Studies of fossilised chimpanzees' teeth in east Africa have filled in one of the greatest gaps in the evolutionary record.

Scientists studying the human genome have spotted signs of recent evolution in the genetic code as humans migrated from equatorial regions.

Researchers working in the Canadian Arctic have discovered the fossilised remains of *Tiktaalik roseae*, a fish that 'walked on land' – yet another missing link.

Scientists at the University of Auckland, studying the number of genetic mutations in closely related plants, have explained the rich variety of life forms in the tropics.

Today it is easy to see that one of the main battles between science and superstition was comprehensively won in 1859, and that the defeated candidate refused to acknowledge his abject humiliation. The contest continues, often descending to the levels of ludicrous farce – but in essence the choice is a simple one. In considering the nature of life in general and *Homo sapiens* in particular, do we prefer to be guided by Charles Darwin and the molecular biologists or by William Jennings Bryan, Bishop 'Soapy Sam' Wilberforce, and Bishop James Ussher and Sir John Lightfoot, who insisted that the world was created on 23 October 4004 BC at nine o'clock in the morning?

The religious response to evolution is only one example of the hostility that many believers show towards science. In the United States this attitude surfaced grotesquely during the hideous Bush years, when Christian fundamentalism was perpetually on display. Here there was an inevitable conflict between, on the one hand, reason and the progressive accumulation of empirical evidence and, on the other, ancient garbled texts and subjective feelings that admit no scrutiny. Absurd claims were made for holy works, and social damage was wrought through bigotry. In these particulars Christianity and Islam are equally culpable.

The inauguration of Barack Obama on 20 January 2009 was a seismic social and political event. Throughout his two-year campaign he said little or nothing about how scientific principles should guide policy in crucial areas, though he was clearly sympathetic to what scientists were saying about global warming and stem cell research. Perhaps significantly, he recorded words that seemed to convey agnosticism. Thus, describing his experience of a multi-faith rally, he said: 'With our eyes closed, we uttered the same words . . . in our hearts we each prayed to our own masters . . . we all clung to our own foolish magic.'[160] However, during the election campaign he was manifestly 'comfortable with the language of the Bible'[161] and was prepared to talk about his own conversion and the notion of sin, but elsewhere we find a more ambiguous message. In *The Audacity of Hope* Obama comments on his baptism in the Trinity United Church on the South Side of Chicago: 'I felt God's spirit beckoning me. I submitted myself to His will, and dedicated myself to discovering His truth.'[162] At this stage he clearly believed that God was a fellow but did now know what 'His truth' was.

In that same chapter Obama has no hesitation in criticising the Bible:

> Should we go with Leviticus, which suggests that slavery is all right and eating shellfish is an abomination? How about Deuteronomy, which suggests stoning your child if he strays from the faith? Or should we just stick to the Sermon on the Mount – a passage so radical that it's doubtful that our Defense Department would survive its application?[163]

At the end of the chapter he admits that he is not sure what happens when we die or where the 'soul' resides.[164] It is likely that President Obama is a burgeoning agnostic who sees some good social effects of Christianity but is reluctant – for obvious political reasons – to apply his critical intelligence to the supernatural foundations of his faith.

We remember how his predecessor 'trampled science'[165] in the interests of the Christian right. Religious commitment is an obvious prerequisite for any political candidate in America but, hopefully, this manifest piety will not be allowed to shape Obama's policy as it did with George W. Bush.[166] The forty-third President's clear sympathy with Christian fundamentalism went far beyond a facile belief that creationism should be taught in schools as a legitimate alternative to biological evolution. The writer Esther Kaplan summarises how Christian commitment impacted on the behaviour of the Bush administration:

> From global warming to lead poisoning, from AIDS research to pregnancy prevention, the Bush administration has chosen to sacrifice science whenever it conflicts with the needs of Bush's corporate patrons or his evangelical base. Administration officials have attacked and investigated scientists and public health experts working in fields that offend Christian right sensibilities; stacked scientific committees with believers who filter data through a religious prism; censored government science when its conclusions are inconvenient to the family values agenda; and based policy decisions on unsound science.[167]

Scientists at the National Institutes of Health noticed that their applications for research grants were being scrutinised by Republican congressional staffers to ensure that money would not be spent on research into subjects such as homosexuality or prostitution in ways that offended the Christian right. In one trivial example, a researcher paying a $5 fee to enter a bathhouse to investigate risky homosexual behaviour relevant to AIDS was construed as using taxpayer money to support same-sex practices. This meant that scientific researchers were increasingly forced to couch their grant applications in euphemistic language to circumvent Christian sensitivities.

One consequence of this pious scene was that research into AIDS was thrown into jeopardy. More than one million Americans are HIV infected, twenty-two million are drug addicts, and around 300,000 American teenagers become pregnant each year,[168] but the government showed reluctance to support public health research in these areas. Funding for research into AIDS, for example, was attacked since it was about 'queers, junkies and whores'.[169] Christian fundamentalists, obsessed with moral bigotry, worked to influence government attitudes to research into public health concerns.

Early in the Bush presidency public health providers in the fields of HIV, sexually transmitted diseases and pregnancy prevention, harassed with a seemingly endless series of audits, were charged with perpetrating obscenity, financial impropriety and unsound science. At the same time the National Association for the Research and Theory of Homosexuality (NARTH) and the Medical Institute for Sexual Health (MISH), both organs of the Christian right, were working to influence government policy. NARTH claimed to have found scientific evidence for the absurd notion that homosexuality is a mental disease that can be cured through therapy, while using 'shoddy survey data to associate gay sexuality with pedophilia, extreme promiscuity and suicide', offering 'a veneer of scientific legitimacy for anti-gay measures in Colorado and Oregon'.[170] The shoddy data was presented by NARTH on behalf of Gale Norton, then Bush's secretary of the interior. MISH, a widely acknowledged peddler of fake science, proclaimed that condoms do not help to prevent the spread of sexually transmitted diseases and that only sexual abstinence, beloved by the Christian right, was the answer. Debra Hauser, vice-president of Advocates for Youth, a sex education organisation, commented that the efforts of MISH, lacking peer review, were 'pretty insidious'.[171]

David Hager, a member of the Christian right who submitted material to a sympathetic Bush administration, has urged people to rely on prayer rather than medical treatment. He applauded a woman who asked her pastor to pray for her instead of accepting treatment for heavy menstrual bleeding; and in a popular book, *Stress and the Woman's Body* (written with his wife), he offers prayers, instead of medical treatment, as cures for headaches, premenstrual stress and cancer. Bush responded to such efforts by placing Hager on the government's Advisory Committee for Reproductive Health Drugs. Other Bush appointees, Joseph Stanford and Susan Crockett, relying on what *Scientific American* called 'faithbased reasoning',[172] were reliably opposed to abortion and were sceptical of all forms of contraception. Their task, applauded by Bush, was to guarantee that the committee would make no recommendations to government that would upset the Christian right.

Bush evinced no interest in science, evidently regarding it as a seeming obstacle to those who were committed to following God's path. This led to funding restrictions on 'questionable' research projects, the stacking of government committees with Christian activists, the censoring of public health information, opposition to stem-cell research, and the propagation of false information – for example, that abortion makes breast cancer more likely.[173] The Bush administration also misrepresented scientific findings – a conclusion of the Union of Concerned Scientists in a 2004 investigation into the behaviour of the government:

> There is significant evidence that the scope and scale of the manipulation, suppression, and misrepresentation of science by the Bush administration is unprecedented . . . World-renowned scientific institutions such as the CDC [the Centers for Disease Control] and the National Institutes of Health take decades to build a team of world-class scientific expertise and talent. But they can be severely damaged in short order by the scientifically unethical behaviour such as that displayed by the current administration.[174]

It is plain that Bush used executive power to impose religious beliefs on the work of public health scientists during the period of his tenure. Consequently, social problems were not addressed as effectively as they deserved to be, and many scientists became demoralised and impatient for a change of regime.

It is hard to believe that President Obama will show a similar obeisance to the Christian right. Bush helped to display the nonsense in fundamentalist Christianity. The claims in some brands of Islam are equally absurd.

A primary difficulty faced by Muslims is the alleged divine status of the Koran – an increasingly problematic notion in the modern world. We can imagine the scenario: an illiterate Arab, thought by some to have epilepsy, is spoken to by an invisible deity. Did Mohammed ever have an off day? Did he ever forget items that were dictated to him? Did God edit his errors? Mohammed, albeit a 'prophet', was only a human being prone to error. It is certainly true that it took time for an official version of the Koran to emerge.[175] And it was left to many later Muslims to use the Koran to propagate absurdities – for example, that it contains 'scientific miracles', an idea highly relevant to the Muslim attitude to science.[176]

We know that the Koran urges believers to reflect on the wonders of the world,[177] but it is an enormous leap of faith to proclaim that such bland statements convey scientific information. However, some Muslims make such a claim, as conveyed in the popular literature known as *ijaz*, or 'scientific miracles of the Quran'.[178] Today *ijaz* literature clogs Islamic bookshops, and the *ijaz* concept is propagated widely through television and websites in many countries. And this modern nonsense is not confined to untutored believers. Nidhal Guessoum, professor of astrophysics at the American University of Sharjah, proclaims: 'Almost everything, from relativity, quantum mechanics, Big Bang theory, black holes and pulsars, genetics, embryology, modern geology, thermodynamics, even the laser and hydrogen fuel cells, have [*sic*] been "found " in the Quran.'[179] This is far removed from the time when Koranic verses were quoted to 'prove' that manned space flight would never happen.[180]

Maurice Bucaille, physician to the Saudi royal family, commented in his book *The Bible, the Quran, and Science* (1976) that 'it is impossible not to admit the existence of scientific errors in the Bible', but by contrast 'the Quran most definitely did not contain a single proposition at variance with the most firmly established modern knowledge'. This inevitably boosted *ijaz* confidence and encouraged the propagation of many absurdities – not least the notion that Surah 23: 12–14 ('We first created man from the essence of clay: then placed him, a living germ, in a secure enclosure. The germ We made a clot of blood, and the clot a lump of flesh. This We fashioned into bones, then clothed the bones with flesh, thus bringing forth another creation . . .') is a perfect depiction of embryonic development. In this context it has been claimed – for example by Bucaille and the Canadian professor of anatomy Keith Moore – that the Koran is a scientific treatise. Hence Surah 84: 18–19 ('[I swear by] the moon in her full protection: that you shall march onwards from state to state') is an accurate depiction of space travel. In the same fashion, Surah 36: 36 ('Glory be to Him who made all things in pairs') is claimed to predict anti-matter. Such 'inanities'[181] are widely held by Muslim professors – for example, by 70 per cent of the science professors in Guessoum's university, who believe that the Koran is rich in scientific facts and theories. Thus P. A. Wahid, the former dean of the Faculty of Agriculture at Kerala Agricultural University, proposes in *The Computer Universe: A Scientific Rendering of the Holy Koran* a model of Koranic science that explains the existence of angels, the Divine Master Plan, and how the Koran predicted the advent of chemistry and biology. Sardar concludes: 'The underlying message in these books is that all the science you need is in the Koran – no need to get your hands dirty in a lab or work within mainstream theories.'[182]

We are not surprised in this context that *ijaz* literature is firmly opposed to the Darwinist interpretation of biological evolution (Guessoum: 'Muslim scientists are "scientists by day and creationists by night"'). Here Christian fundamentalists and Muslim scientists operate hand in hand. Both classes of propagandist have been seduced by ancient texts into promoting absurdities – for example, that Noah's ark contained dinosaurs co-existing happily with 350,000 species of beetle and that Einstein's general theory of relativity can be found in the Koran. Where? Where?

We are driven to share George Monbiot's comment that 'religion – in particular fundamentalist religion – makes you stupid'.[183] Anyone who doubts this should look around, and read more widely, whether daily reportage or the abundant literature describing today's witch burnings in Africa, the occult groups that underlay the worst Nazi excesses, the exclusion of women from mosques, Sikh hostility to adult theatre, the traditional Roman Catholic hatred of gays and women, and the Christian fundamentalist pro-life lust for capital punishment and war. We remember also how, during the presidential election campaign, it emerged that the publicly pious Sarah Palin thought that Africa was a country rather than a continent and that she could not name the three countries in North America. This was a graphic example of the general ignorance in one of the most religious countries of the world. Recent surveys revealed that nearly a third of young Americans, keen to proclaim their faith, could not find the Pacific Ocean on a map; more than 10 per cent could not find the United States;[184] two thirds could not find Iraq; and a fifth believed that the sun revolves around the earth.[185] In religious America, among the mass of the population, there is a clear preference for magic and myth rather than reason and knowledge.

In this context evolutionary science, and much else in science, fares badly. Religion, keen religion, is silly, dogmatic, bigoted and cruel. Religion, fervent religion throughout the world, makes people stupid – and dangerous. It took two devout Christians, highly susceptible to the influence of faith, to cause the deaths of one million Iraqis.[186] And, as I write in mid-January 2009, the Israeli armed forces are perpetrating an escalating massacre of Palestinians – helpless men, women and children – in Gaza, where there are already thousands of casualties. What does this say about the values of Judaism?

2

Superstitious roots

> Prodigies, omens, oracles, judgements . . . there is nothing
> mysterious or supernatural . . . all proceeds from the usual propensity
> of mankind towards the marvellous . . . though this inclination may
> at intervals receive a check from sense and learning, it can never be
> thoroughly extirpated from human nature.
>
> David Hume, *An Enquiry Concerning Human Understanding* (1748)

There is no doubt that mankind has a 'propensity towards the
marvellous',[1] and that this characteristic of human nature has
yielded foolishness, gross irrationality and consequent impediments to social and intellectual progress.[2] Put another way, the
spiritual history of human society has been marked at best by silly
and amusing doctrines, and at worst by primitive superstitions that
have led to torture, murder and war. It is possible to argue
that superstition and religion are not the same thing: that whereas
the one may be criticised on rational grounds, the other represents
a mature attitude to human beings in the universe. But this
defence of religion falls at the first hurdle. Both superstition and
religious belief rely on the notion that subjective convictions, in
the absence of evidence, are an adequate guide to how things
work in the world. But there is no logical connection between
conviction and truth: a person can be convinced that something is
the case – and be wrong. The philosopher A. J. Ayer commented:

> It may very well happen that even when people's beliefs are false they
> are as fully convinced of their truth as they are of the truth of what
> they know . . . from the fact that someone is convinced that
> something is true, however firm his convictions may be, it never
> follows logically that it is true.[3]

In reality, superstition and religion overlap massively, although, 'as we advance nearer the enlightened ages', the most highly developed religions have been forced to abandon, or at least play down, some of their more absurd superstitions. It is also significant that many supposedly religious experiences, leading to an enforcement of old superstitions and the creation of new ones, are associated with drug taking and what today are recognised as psychiatric conditions (see below).

The problem is that once religion has abandoned its irrational beliefs there is nothing left, since anything of value can be preserved in a purely secular environment. Many Chinese sages, some Greek philosophers and all modern rationalists discuss ethics, death and human nature without recourse to superstitious categories. But religion cannot escape the taint of its superstitious roots, the wealth of fantasy and unreasonable conjecture that has typified its essence over the centuries. It is time to grow up.

The Aztecs believed that without tearing out the hearts of human sacrificial victims on a high altar on a daily basis they could not be sure that the sun would rise tomorrow. The Nuer tribe in Africa, described by the anthropologist Sir Edward Evans-Pritchard, believed that disasters caused by sexual intercourse could only be averted by cutting off the ear of a dog. Roman Catholics believe that by talking in Latin or their vernacular to biscuit and wine they will be magically transformed into the flesh and blood of a dead Semite to facilitate a cannibalistic ritual. In one important sense these beliefs are very similar, involving a mysterious cause–effect relationship that people have employed – or still do – though without understanding it. Most people in the developed world would dismiss the first two beliefs but may hedge about the third, thus making a cultural rather than a rational distinction.

The word *superstition* derives from the Latin *superstitio* – the term used by Tacitus to denote the alien beliefs and practices of the early Christians. This in turn comes from the preposition *super* 'over' and the verb *stare* 'to stand, endure, remain'. Superstitious beliefs survive from one generation to the next, unlike passing fashionable fancies, urban myths and the like. It is clear that superstition, like religion, sprang from human helplessness in the face of nature. Ritual and taboo were invented to shield people from the hostile forces all around, and magic became the key to an understanding, albeit bogus, of natural processes. In this primitive context religion, an associated irrationalism, was created in the image of human fears and imaginings, to propitiate supernatural agencies that operated everywhere. Human inventiveness was never more active than in filling the world with supernatural creatures, spirits of the fields and woods, gods and goddesses, and the mysterious realms in which they dwelt – and in devising weird rituals to cope with all this, enlisting the aid of benevolent entities and striving continuously to keep the dark forces at bay.

Ornithomancy (studying the actions of birds, such as their flight, to predict the course of human affairs),[4] *haruspicy* (examining the entrails of animals),[5] *incubation* (sleeping in a holy place to receive a nocturnal visitation from a divinity),[6] *hydromancy* (divination by water), *astrology* (relying on the heavens to predict events on earth),[7] *necromancy* (divination by means of the spirits of the dead),[8] *sacrifice* (of animals or human beings, including oneself, to propitiate jealous gods), *prayer* (in the absurd belief that a god who is busy creating stars will be ignorant of, or have the slightest interest in, the petty desires of bits of hydrocarbon crawling about on a minor planet in a typical galaxy among billions) and so on – all have been or are enlisted in the fanciful notion that behaviour of an utterly irrational sort is the best way to win a spouse, improve one's love life, cure terminal disease and usher in a new tranquil age without social disturbance or international conflict. Such practices, allied to all the paraphernalia of magic and persistent folk superstition, indicate the extent to which irrational beliefs have shaped human attitudes and perceptions over the centuries.

There have been times when opponents of scientific progress have tried to turn the tables by using 'superstition' as a pejorative term. At the end of the nineteenth century the Christian W. H. Mallock attacked the contemporary laws on marriage and divorce, Fabian socialism and the agnosticism of T. H. Huxley, this last depicted as 'a superstition more abject, more meaningless, and more ridiculous, than that of any African savage, grovelling and mumbling before his fetish'.[9] Many writers have tried to distinguish between religion and superstition, insisting that the former is worthy whereas the latter is disreputable. The anthropologist Bronisław Malinowski even asked whether primitive man had a religion, or was he 'merely obsessed by savage superstitions, surrounded by the darkness of heathendom?'[10] The writer and editor Douglas Hill talked of superstition as an 'illegitimate branch of religious history', as if trying to preserve the propriety of the latter against the false beliefs of competing creeds.[11] And Robert Graves, writing in the *Larousse Encyclopedia of Mythology*, noted that 'mythology is the study of . . . legends . . . so foreign to a student's experience that he cannot believe them to be true'. So whether or not we can believe in fantastic tales is a matter of familiarity rather than reason. If we are bred in a cultural atmosphere of absurdity then we will believe it to be true. But this is highly problematic for the religious believer of whatever sort – namely, that the biblical narratives are closely paralleled by myths from Persia, Babylonia, Egypt, Greece and other ancient cultures.

One heroic but shortsighted way out of the conundrum is to make the whole thing a semantic matter. Thus the celebrated folklore expert and translator Alexander Krappe proposed that it would be best 'to define as *superstition* any belief or practice that is not recommended or enjoined by any of the great organised religions such as Christianity, Judaism, Islam and Buddhism'.[12] So, as we might expect, as soon as an irrational creed gets a grip on society it is quick to label its superstitions as something else. Once a religion has commandeered the education system, much of the media and the vast majority of the political leadership, then anything it represents is by definition praiseworthy, righteous and to be protected against the efforts of mischievous rationalists and other malcontents. But here the beliefs of the predominant religion have nothing to do with reason or evidence. The explorer Sir Richard Burton observed sardonically that the very same missionaries who objected to the natives' use of magic teeth, bones and wizard's mats recommended in their stead relics, medals and consecrated palm leaves.[13]

If religious superstition is so patently absurd then why – apart from the state control of the opinion-forming institutions – do people believe it? The psychologists have answers according to their school of thought. For example, Freudians believe that religion is an illusion and that superstition is generated by the unconscious. William James, in *The Varieties of Religious Experience* (1902), identified a 'full sunlit consciousness' part of the personality to distinguish it from a more mysterious component, 'the reservoir of everything that passes unrecorded or unobserved'. He judged that it was this latter realm from which sprang all our 'intuitions, hypotheses, fancies, superstitions, persuasions, convictions, and in general all our non-rational operations' – with the clear implication that we do not derive a superstition (or religious belief) through ratiocination, as we might a cautious scientific opinion.

Moreover, evidence from the more mysterious element of the mind is notoriously unreliable. Sigmund Freud related how a patient described a supposedly prophetic dream about meeting the family doctor, and then when she went to town she met him where she thought she would. But on examination it transpired that she had no recollection of the dream before actually meeting the doctor. Freud concluded that it was probably during the course of the meeting that the woman acquired the conviction of having had the dream.[14] Much supposed evidence justifying belief in extrasensory or supernatural events is of this quality, unlikely to survive rigorous analysis. Where Freud and other tough-minded psychologists have been predictably hostile to superstition and religion, assuming their falsity, the psychoanalyst Carl Gustav Jung was altogether more sympathetic, going so far in a television interview to proclaim that he did not *believe* that God existed, he *knew* – when in fact he knew nothing of the sort.

The behaviourist B. F. Skinner once wrote a systematic exposition, carrying the unlikely title of '"Superstition" in the Pigeon', to demonstrate that false beliefs could be held by animals as well as human beings. A pigeon was placed in a cage in which food appeared when the bird behaved in a particular way, the particular behaviour to be 'reinforced' not being selected by the experimenters but being left to chance. The pigeon happened to turn its head anticlockwise at a particular crucial moment; the reinforcement strengthened the response and it came to be performed more frequently than other responses. In due course a kind of ritual turning came to be established. Skinner noted that the bird behaved 'as if there was a causal relation between its behaviour and the presentation of food' – demonstrating the familiar point that much superstition (and religion) hinges on a mistaken view of causal relations.[15] He suggested that the principle operating with the experimental pigeon applies also in the formulations of human superstition, and further developed the idea in his book *Science and Human Behavior*.[16] This demonstrates the more general point that irrational beliefs are amenable to scientific enquiry: there is nothing sacrosanct about supernatural commitments.

In a similar fashion the anthropologist John Whiting conducted a field study among a New Guinea tribe with the object in part of examining the social transmission of supernatural beliefs – beliefs in ghosts, sorcery and great monsters called *marsalai*. His conclusion, in short, was that a habit of observing dangers is created, which extends in a non-rational way to non-existent dangers – and which thus provides the essence of superstition and religious belief. It is part of the philosophy of the atheist that, as in Bertrand Russell, 'it is undesirable to believe a proposition when there is no ground whatever for supposing it true'.[17] In this context Russell also identified 'superstitious ethics'; that is, ethics grounded in supposed divine revelation or taboo, moral sanctions that do not accord with reason.[18]

The minor and major religions, from parochial sects to the vast state-sponsored creeds, are replete with superstition. I would go further – *anything that is not consistent with scientific secularism may be regarded as superstition*, and I fully applaud the pejorative judgement that such a statement embodies. It is not difficult to find evidence of religious nonsense and the harm that it causes, and here a few examples will suffice. Some superstitions are harmless, others less so.

One writer in Bangladesh, Syed Kamran Mirza, notes that in markets, bookshops and libraries there are thousands of Islamic *kitabs* (books) that shamelessly promote 'ignorance and cock-and-bull stories'.[19] He cites *Behester Kunji* (The Key to Paradise), *Beheshti Zewar* (The Treasure of Paradise), *Maqsudul Momeneen* (The Destiny of the Believers), *Kassa-suul-Ambia* (The Story of the Prophets) and the *Neyamul Qur'an* (a particular version of the Koran). The publishers of these texts, some of them running to forty editions, can scarcely keep up with the heavy demand. Mirza emphasises that these works serve as primary text books, used by priests to instruct highly gullible Muslims, and he quotes verbatim the material that they contain.

Some texts deal with the business of creation, where Allah seemed to rely on the 'light of Mohammed'. At first Allah divided the light into four parts, using one part to create the supreme throne, one to create his pen and one to create the denizen of souls (al-Lawh al-Mahfouz). The fourth part was itself divided into four parts – the first to create the angels bearing the throne, while the second was made into his throne (a bit of confusion here – Allah seems to have created his throne twice) and the third part was used to create all the rest of the congregation of angels. Then he divided the remaining fourth part into yet more parts – the first used to create the radiance of the eyes of the believers, the second to create the light for the souls, the third to create the light of Kalema (a holy text) and the fourth part used to create all the rest of the materials on earth.

The priorities are clear: let's get the throne, angels and souls sorted out first, and then we can bother about the material world. But the pen, seemingly an anomalous item, is clearly significant. This gets complicated and I advise the reader to study the source. But the gist is that the pen, seemingly acting autonomously, spent 400 years writing a sacred text but failed to complete it. Allah was annoyed, causing the pen to shake with terror, which in turn caused its front part to crack – which is why there is always a crack down the nib of fountain pens.

If the matter of the pen was a trivial matter, the creation of the throne certainly was not. It was raised on 18,000 pillars, with the distance from one pillar to the next requiring a journey of 700 years. We are not told how fast we would need to travel but this is a pretty big throne. And the myth doesn't stop there. The four gigantic angels that carry the throne (why do they bother?) were created in the form of a human being, a tiger, a vulture and a cow. We are not surprised to learn that the legs of the angels are so long that they reach the bottom of the seven heavens situated over the pillars, and that with one step they can travel a distance of 7,000 years (sic – are these light-years?).

After making the denizens of souls, Allah instructed the pen to begin with the first man (Adam) and to tell the stories of the 24,000 prophets. The pen dutifully began the task, stating such obvious details as those obedient to Allah going to Paradise and the rest going to Hell, but then Allah seemingly had a change of mind and instructed the pen to cease its labours and to write something else instead – namely, that if there were some sinners in the ranks of the believers Allah might, as a matter of celestial whim, forgive many of them. It mattered less that people were 'thieves and bandits' than that they were amongst the Muslim faithful.[20]

The light of Mohammed was also used by Allah to create a peacock which was placed on top of a Sajaratul Yaakin tree. From this position the peacock prayed to Allah for 70,000 years using rosary beads, after which Allah constructed a 'mirror of shame' and stationed it in front of the peacock. The bird was so overjoyed at witnessing its extraordinary beauty that it prostrated itself five times before Allah – which is why faithful Muslims are expected to pray five times a day. And so on and so forth . . . Harmless myths or foolish fabrications, conveyed as truths to be believed on pain of eternal damnation, that enslave people from childhood onwards in gullible ignorance of the world?

In early 2008 in Luton a Muslim faith-healer, Mr Wahib, was reportedly taking large sums of money from clients to provide cures for whatever problems they might be experiencing – including sexual impotence, infertility, baldness, depression, financial problems, immigration difficulties and 'domestic problems regarding husband and wife'. Unfortunately – a solution I would not recommend – he was beaten and stabbed to death by two clients.[21] The previous June trading standards officials in Sandwell, in the West Midlands, warned members of the Asian communities to beware of unscrupulous faith healers after receiving complaints from consumers who had spent large sums of money. One family was told by a faith healer that a family member was possessed by black magic that would kill her and her daughters. The solution he advised – for which he was duly paid £16,000 – was that he would go up a mountain to pray for the family.[22]

Another case, one of many, was that of a 22-year-old mother who died after giving birth to twins because her religion would not allow her to have a blood transfusion. She was a Jehovah's Witness who worshipped at the Kingdom Hill halls in Shropshire. A member of the congregation said: 'The basis of the faith is that we follow commands from the scriptures and it is a scriptural command to abstain from blood.'[23] An absurdity of an entirely different order concerned the Dalai Lama, who was faced with Chinese plans to control his reincarnation procedure. In November 2007 the exiled Tibetan Buddhist leader, a Nobel Peace laureate, proposed to hold a referendum among his fourteen million followers to determine whether or not he should be reincarnated. If the vote was against, it would end a religious tradition that dated back to the fourteenth century, when the first Dalai Lama, a young shepherd, was appointed. If the vote was in favour, the Dalai Lama declared that he would 'appoint a reincarnation' while he was still alive: 'According to my regular medical check-up it [the preparation for death] seems another few decades [away] . . . so no hurry.'[24]

The risible nature of the beliefs underlying such attitudes is plain, and we find similar nonsense in all the superstitious cults and religions of the world. Most of these creeds, not all, populate the universe with imaginary creatures performing remarkable tasks in supernatural realms – and, when it suits them, on earth. We have seen that Allah set about creating angels, often mentioned in the Koran, and we are not surprised to find that these are star players in the other Abrahamic religions. Archangels are reckoned to be particularly important. Everyone has heard of the archangel Gabriel, active in both Islam and Christianity, who allegedly brought the Koran – conveniently written by Allah in Arabic – to a bunch of ignorant desert tribes, and who informed Mary that she was pregnant [did she not know?]. The archangel Michael was charged in Islam with various tasks; Israfil is always preparing to sound the last trumpet at the end of time; Israil found copious employment as the angel of death; and Iblis, or Satan, was responsible in both Islam and Christianity for tempting Adam and Eve in the Garden of Eden (Iblis was tossed out of Heaven for his sins). But then it starts to get complicated. There are hierarchies of angels which may be taken as reflecting the structures of societies on earth. In Islam, ordinary angels are superior to human beings in general but inferior to the prophets, who include Jesus Christ. These angels are said to be 'close' to Allah but cannot, unlike faithful Muslims, truly 'know' him. (I haven't the slightest idea what this is supposed to mean.)

In Judaism, from the time of the Second Temple (c.515 BC–70 AD), angels have been busy praising God, their primary task (since he seems to bask in this sort of adulation), and carrying out numerous chores, including protecting the faithful (not very successfully, as history shows). Again, as in Islam and Christianity, some of the Judaic angels were found to be wicked, full of pride and lust, and were banished from Heaven. Angels are scarcely mentioned in the Pentateuch but are busy in the Old Testament books of Ezekiel, Daniel and Zechariah. They can fly, predict the future (just as in the ancient pagan cults) and speak Hebrew – which is convenient (just as Muslim angels are, fortunately, fluent in Arabic). And again four archangels are paramount: Gabriel, Michael, Raphael and Uriel. There is also reference to the significance of light, as in Islamic mythology. Thus the Judaic angels are reckoned to be emanations of divine light (able to speak Hebrew?), and the medieval Jewish philosopher Maimonides (1135–1204) equated them with Aristotle's incorporeal intelligences. Today Judaism tends to view angels as an outdated concept, to be discarded or interpreted 'symbolically'. It's a familiar ploy. When religion is driven onto the defensive by advances in modern science-based knowledge, it invariably opts for a symbolic, metaphorical or allegorical interpretation of central beliefs. Put simply – yes, it's a load of nonsense but what are we to do?

The fate of Lucifer, a wicked angel, is described in Isaiah 14: 12–15, where we learn that his ambition to ascend into Heaven ('I will ascend above the heights of the clouds; I will be like the most High') is brought to nothing as he is cast down to Hell, to the sides of the pit. For a while he battled with his angels in Heaven, but after his defeat his name became the name of the devil. Hence the Christian religion is full of the fall of angels, rebels who were thrown down into the Hell at the centre of the earth (no doubt in all this exactly where the damned would be tortured for all eternity). It was the devil, Lucifer – who served a useful function in giving his name to a brand of matches – who assumed the guise of a serpent to tempt Eve. Jesus allegedly came to earth to sort it all out.

In his 109th letter St Augustine tells us, in accord with some Judaic beliefs, that both angels and devils have slender and agile bodies, but Christianity made some fundamental changes to the tradition it had inherited. In the eighth century Pope Gregory II proclaimed that there were nine choirs (hierarchies or orders) – instead of the Judaic ten – that defined the angelic congregation: seraphim, cherubim, thrones, dominions, virtues, powers, archangels and finally the group that gave its name to the eight other hierarchies. The two cherubim of the Jews, each with two heads, resembled respectively an ox and an eagle with six wings. The French writer Voltaire (1694–1778) observed that such cherubim were painted in the image of a flying head, with little wings below the ears, while other angels are painted in the image of youth, with wings on their backs.[25] St Thomas Aquinas reckoned in *Summa Theologiae* (1265–74) that the thrones were as close to God as the cherubim and seraphim, because it is on them that God is seated. You can't get much closer than that, but there seems to be some confusion between the angelic thrones and the actual pillar-supported thrones favoured in Muslim superstition. The medieval philosopher and theologian John Duns Scotus (c.1265–1308) claimed to have counted a thousand million angels.[26]

These myriad supernatural creatures have to live somewhere, and we immediately think of Heaven and Hell; but allegedly they also populate the terrestrial realm. This has been clear to believers in the Islamic and Judeo-Christian creeds for centuries but there have been particular periods when good angels and bad have been particularly prolific. Demons (fallen angels) were alarmingly ubiquitous in medieval Christianity, when believers worried about inhaling them, sitting on them accidentally in churches and finding them lurking lasciviously under beds. The diligent researchers Colleen McDannell and Bernhard Lang have noted an 'angel fad' that gripped America in the 1990s, and the accompanying proliferation of Hollywood movies and best-selling

accounts of life 'on the other side'.[27] There are a few films that
purport to depict life in Heaven, which demonstrate above all that
the supernatural realms, the inventions of human imagination, are
shaped by the fashion of the time.

The history of Heaven as a concept shows just how much it is
a concoction of human fancy and need. Many religious writers,
distressed at losing loved ones, declare that spouses and other
family members will be reunited in the afterlife – a bit problematic
for bigamists, divorcees, polygamous Muslims and Mormons, and
spouses who don't much like each other. But don't worry if you
are dying of cancer or Alzheimer's disease: your healthy body and
your youth will be restored in Heaven. And it doesn't stop with
human beings. The Catholic author Luise Rinser (1911–2002)
said: 'I will see again my dog and all the dogs of my life, for they
are part of my life, which means they will be saved together with
myself, for they are immortal.'[28] Having to carry a poop scoop
through the celestial streets of Paradise is not my idea of eternal
bliss, but perhaps dogs – like humans – arrive in Heaven minus
their intestinal systems. I myself am acquainted with a woman
who talks, perhaps wistfully, of 'cat heaven', but she is unhappy to
be pressed on the matter. Fervent believers too often seem
reluctant to describe their images of Heaven, perhaps because they
themselves are not entirely convinced of its reality. It is significant
that one Christian burial service includes the words 'in the sure
and certain hope' of eternal life. Yes, there is no doubt about the
hope, but this is scarcely a ringing affirmation.

Muslims, usually less hesitant about the reality of Paradise, have
no doubt that if Allah so chooses they will lead a life of eternal
debauchery, reclining on couches by gushing fountains, and enjoy-
ing the favours of dark-eyed women with big breasts: 'As for the
righteous, they shall surely triumph. Theirs shall be gardens and
vineyards, and high-bosomed maidens for companions: a truly
overflowing cup.'[29] This theme is repeated frequently throughout
the Koran – 'gardens beneath whose shades the rivers flow', 'raised
couches, and goblets ready placed', 'gardens and fountains',
'couches ranged in rows', 'damsels with large dark eyes', 'fruits in
abundance', 'houris . . . ever virgins', 'houris with large dark eyes',
'couches with linings of brocade', 'damsels with retiring glances,

whom no man nor djinn hath touched before them', 'the beauteous ones, with large dark eyeballs', 'soft green cushions and beautiful carpets', 'gardens of delight' and so on. Be assured, it really is better for the average man to spend eternity in Paradise than in the other place (see below). Women too are catered for in the afterlife, but without the lavish promises of hedonistic bliss.

By contrast some commentators have preferred an ascetic vision, suggesting that all the messy sensuality of the body will be abandoned in Heaven as the immortal soul floats free to worship God every day of the celestial week. Philo of Alexandria (20 BC–50 AD), building on earlier Greek attitudes, reckoned that death restores the soul to its original, pre-birth state, the life of the body having been nothing more than an unfortunate episode. In addition the soul, being immaterial, is asexual – neither male nor female. No winsome women here. This sort of view was adopted by later Christian theologians, keen to perfect a gross sexual psychopathology (see Chapter 5). Jesus himself seems to have focused on an afterlife in which the immortal soul would relate to God, rather than to a spouse or other loved ones. In fact both the dead and the living were expected to focus on God and religious notables.[30] Jesus had no interest in the dead meeting their spouses again in Heaven, in part because he saw even the earthly family as an impediment to spiritual growth. Part of his mission was to disrupt the family, setting 'a man at variance against his father, and the daughter against her mother, and the daughter-in-law against her mother-in-law';[31] and even urging a man to hate his father, mother, wife and children in order to be a proper disciple.[32] This attitude helped to bolster the gross misogyny and anti-sexualism that came to dominate the Christian church over the centuries.

It is significant that in modern times some Christian theologians, battered by secularist science, have been forced to admit the purely mythical character of an afterlife in Heaven or Hell. Among them the theologian Karl Barth (1886–1968) and the Jesuit Karl Rahner (1904–84) decided that life begins at birth and ends at death: there are no big-breasted virgins or eternal hymns of praise to look forward to. Barth commented that there could be 'no question of the continuation into an indefinite future of a somewhat altered life . . . no further extension in time of acts and experiences following one upon another'; and in the same vein Rahner said that life could not be understood as a simple change of horses on a continuing journey. In a 1980 interview he explained that 'with death it's all over. Life is past, and it won't come again. It won't be given one for a second time.' He wanted to escape from the continuous struggle of life, from the endless repetition of the same events and experiences. It was time to rest.[33]

Today science has won, to the extent that belief in Heaven is increasingly seen, even by Christians, as an absurdity. But for many people the new vision is a bleak one, with hopes for immortality residing only in the surviving memories of loved ones, and in one's work and enduring causal impact, however slight, on the world. McDannall and Lang comment: 'Scientific, philosophical, and theological skepticism has nullified the modern Heaven and replaced it with teachings that are minimalist, meager, and dry.'[34] And atheists are often too robust to offer much encouragement. We are unlikely to take heart when Bertrand Russell, in one of his best-known essays, comments:

> Brief and powerless is Man's life; on him and all his race the slow, sure doom falls pitiless and dark . . . omnipotent matter rolls on its relentless way . . . for Man, condemned today to lose his dearest, tomorrow himself to pass through the gates of darkness, it remains only to cherish . . . the lofty thoughts that ennoble his little day . . . despite the trampling march of unconscious power.[35]

But perhaps we *should* take heart at the thought that individuals cannot assume that, even as believers, they will finish up blissfully praising a vain and conceited deity: they may not make the grade. And there are other possibilities, much more terrible than a boring eternity, that a robust atheism equips us to avoid. The pious Muslim and Christian have to admit that they may end up in Hell and, believe me, you don't want that. It is time to consort with demons.

Demons, as noted, are usually depicted as fallen angels, thrown out of Heaven by an angry god, but this depiction hardly seems sufficient to account for their sheer numbers. According to ancient

Talmudic computation there were exactly 7,405,926 demons in existence[36] – which raises many questions, not least whether they reproduce and have life spans. Pennethorne Hughes refers to statisticians who computed the infernal population as no fewer than 1,758,064,176 demons,[37] though Jean Wier (c.1515–88), physician to the Duke of Cleves, reckoned that there were only 7,409,127 demons led by 79 princes. According to sums done in the Middle Ages there are nine orders of angels, each order having 6,666 legions and each legion 6,666 angels, which makes a grand total of 399,920,004 – but Satan drew one third with him when he was kicked out of Heaven, which suggests 133,306,668 fallen angels (demons). However, some learned doctors of the church decided that those angels that fell only amounted to the number of one order (that is, 44,435,566 demons). Whichever number you choose, it seems that there are lots of demons in the world. The researcher H. C. Lea (1825–1909) commented on the magnitude of the numbers involved:

> Now all these numbers seem sufficiently large; but when we consider that every man has a good angel deputed for his guardian and an evil one to exercise him it will be seen that there are not enough to go round, even if we restrict this to Christians. The heathen presumably, being inevitably destined to perdition, do not require the services of either kind.[38]

Alfonso de Spina, writing in the fifteenth century, suggested that there were ten varieties of demons: *fates* (said to have been seen by some clerics), *poltergeists* (typically domestic mischief makers), *incubi* and *succubi* (demons who lust after human beings, causing awakening nuns 'to find themselves polluted as if they had slept with men'), *marching hosts* (who appear as noisy crowds of men), *familiar demons* (who eat and drink with men), *nightmare demons* (who bring terror to sleeping men and women), *demons formed from semen and its smell during copulation* (these demons collect nocturnal emissions to 'make therefrom a new spirit'), *deceptive demons* (who confuse men and women by appearing as human beings), *clean demons* ('really most foul', who assail only holy men), and *demons* (*xorguinae* or *bruxae*) who deceive old women into

thinking they are witches.[39] Other demonologists drew up hierarchies of devils for various purposes; for example, indicating
which particular demons were responsible for inducing people to
commit each of the seven deadly sins. In 1589 Peter Binsfield
provided such a list: Lucifer (pride), Mammon (avarice), Asmodeus
(lechery), Satan (anger), Beelzebub (gluttony), Leviathan (envy)
and Belphegor (sloth).[40] Exorcisms were useful in inducing people
to declaim the names of the demons that were possessing them.
Thus when, in 1647, the Louviers nuns were bewitched, Sister
Mary of the Holy Sacrament said that she was possessed by Putifar
and Sister Mary of the Holy Ghost by Dagon.

   The sheer ubiquity of demons encourages us to enquire of their
nature. Are there ailing demons, like David Hume's god in his
dotage, or do they exist in an unchanging state throughout
eternity? Anyone who has seen the feature film *Night of the Demon*
(1957) knows that they can be monstrous, but they are not always
like that. Some of the medieval apologists talked about 'clouds' of
demons, as if they are akin to flocks of migrating birds. Another
talked of them appearing like a swarm of bees. It is fair to say that
they are generally malevolent, consorting with wicked human
beings to bring mischief, or trying to subvert the larger celestial
schemes of a benevolent deity who is seemingly not powerful
enough to extirpate them once and for all. It seems also that they
were not always depicted as fallen angels but, perhaps to facilitate
such proliferation, were depicted also as a personification of blind
forces of nature, capricious spirits but with limited power, and so
could be controlled by any competent magician. But, however
viewed, the demons were everywhere – 'The Demon, everywhere the Demon – *Ubique Daemon.*'

   In the fourth century AD members of the Messalian cult,
thinking themselves to be full of demons, were constantly
blowing their noses and spitting in frantic efforts to rid themselves
of the unwelcome guests. Sometimes the demons appeared to
saints in unmistakable form, complete with horns, tail and cloven
hoofs. At other times they were more subtle. At the end of the
thirteenth century the Blessed Reichhelm of Schongan perceived
them as raindrops or as the dust shown in a sunbeam. And again
there is continuity between the acknowledged superstitions of

'primitive' tribes and the supposedly sacrosanct doctrines of Christianity, Islam and other mainstream religious creeds. Many demonic examples are cited by the anthropologist J. G. Frazer in *The Golden Bough*, a multi-volume epic completed in 1915.[41] The inhabitants of Siaoo, an East Indian island, believed that sylvan spirits dwelt in forests and in solitary trees, and that at full moon the spirits left their abode and roamed about full of mischievous design. Among the people of Nias it was thought that when a tree died its liberated spirit became a demon that could kill a coconut palm merely by alighting on its branches and could kill all the children in a house by landing on one of the supporting posts. In ancient China, fits and convulsions were said to be caused by a demon attempting to draw the soul out of the body. A peasant would not carry food from one place to another without first putting an iron nail on it to stop a demon entering the food and so making the eater ill. Sick men would carry talismans to ward off demons eager to exploit a person's weakened state, and a piece of iron had to be put on sores to stop demons being attracted to that part of the body. On west Africa's Slave Coast, around the Bight of Benin, once a demon had been lured out of an ailing child, talismans were quickly attached to the child's body to prevent re-entry. This is also simple stuff compared with the complex demonic world that emerged in Judeo-Christianity.

The role of Satan and his demons in early Judaism was a limited one, expanded to some extent by Persian doctrines. The prophet Zoroaster was one important source of the doctrine of two great powers, the good and the evil, locked in eternal conflict in a divided universe. The battle would end only with the coming of the Judgement, at which time the forces of light, personified in the great god Ahura Mazda, would triumph, in overcoming Angra Mainyu, the source of all evil in the universe. (This has a nice similarity to the doctrine of modern born-again Christians with their absurd depiction of the 'Rapture', when all true believers will float naked up to Heaven, minus their hearing aids, pacemakers, metal hips and contact lenses.) Angra Mainyu, like Ahura Mazda, commanded vast military hierarchies, but his malevolent forces comprised legions of horrible demons. This doctrine came to

influence Judaism, Christianity and Islam, and invariably won
publicity at times of military expansion (much in the way that
President Bush's fundamentalist Christianity was widely advertised
when in March 2003 he launched his illegal aggression against Iraq).
In 976 BC Jerusalem was conquered by King Nebuchadnezzar and
many Hebrews were deported to Babylonia. Sixty years later,
Cyrus the Great of Persia conquered Babylonia and imported
Zoroastrianism — which impressed Hebrew scholars of the time,
seemingly answering many troublesome theological questions.

In early Judaism two forces — *yetzer ha-tov* (the inclination
towards good) and *yetzer ha-ra* (the inclination towards evil) —
were opposed in a great struggle for supremacy, a division similar
to that between the Egyptian Horus and Set, and the Persian
duality of great divinities. In Judaism the forces were less
personalised, representing instead tendencies in humankind itself.
Belief in Satan and his demons is universal in the history of various
religions. By the time of Abraham (c.2000 BC) the prevailing
polytheism — destined to upset Mohammed — swarmed with
spirits. Spells, incantations, magical texts, exorcisms and various
forms of demonic possession are frequent in archaeological
discoveries from Sumeria and Babylonia. Similarly, abundant
evidence from the civilisations of Egypt, Assyria, Chaldea, Greece
and Rome show them to be rich in alleged demonic phenomena.
The ancient Bible lands swarmed with demons. Thus the writer
George W. Gilmore remarked that 'the entire religious
provenance out of which the Hebrew religion sprang is full of
demonism'.[42] And this was in turn linked to the simple celestial
duality that seemingly gave people a handle on supernatural affairs.
Today it seems obvious that the simple good/bad format belongs
to the infancy of man, whether characterising the attitudes of
primitive tribes or the naïve posturing of Bush and his ilk.

Some writers have argued that in efforts to escape this crude
duality, elements in early Judaism were struggling to grow beyond
the fearful thoughts of ignorant men — but the attempted liberation never represented mainstream Judaism. In Judeo-Christian
orthodoxy the word of God, as revealed in both the Old and New
Testaments, is supposed to attest the reality of evil supernatural
forces as manifested by Satan and his demons.[43] It is suggested that

Satan was a most glorious creature of God, who subsequently sinned before being cast into the pit of darkness.[44] And scripture is cited to indicate why Satanic malevolence is directed so relentlessly against man and the earth. Satan (Lucifer) was created by God to have dominion over the earth: he was entirely sinless before he rebelled – as one might against a celestial tyrant! – and brought chaos to the earth. God, presumably taken by surprise, was now faced with the problem of evil and sin in a hitherto pure universe, and so he chose the earth as the arena in which to stage the great drama of human redemption, culminating in the conquest of evil, its banishment from a sin-scarred universe, and its rigid isolation for all eternity, together with its perpetrators, in the lake of fire, Gehenna or eternal Hell.[45]

Today there are plenty of people – not least, tens of millions of Americans – who believe this sort of nonsense to be literal truth, and it is amply represented in current literature. For example, the fundamental Christian E. G. White describes with relish what will prove to be the final conflict between God and Satan: 'Fearful sights . . . will soon be revealed in the Heavens, in token of the power of miracle-working demons. The spirits of devils will go forth to the kings of the earth . . . to fasten them in deception, and urge them to unite with Satan in his last struggle against the government of Heaven.'[46] But don't worry, it will all come right in the end. 'God's people' will be delivered but it will be tough on the rest. The climax, we learn, will begin with a rainbow that spans the heavens and surrounds the virtuous people in prayer. The mocking cries of the evil-doers die away and they long to be shielded from God's overpowering brightness, and so on and so forth. Mountain chains disappear into the water, inhabited islands disappear, and there is 'the shriek of a hurricane like the voice of demons on a mission of destruction'. Seaports come in for particular attention because they 'have become like Sodom for wickedness': what can God do but inundate them, in tsunami fashion, by a sea 'lashed into fury'. (Even today it is not difficult to find reported pronouncements that every tsunami is a response of a loving God to the wickedness of human beings.) The graves are opened and 'many of them that sleep in the dust of the earth . . . awake, some to everlasting life, and some to shame and everlasting contempt'.[47] It is not surprising that the evil-doers, showing 'horror and despair', are put out by all this: it is not the sort of thing to give the average person a good day. It is clear that we can expect mass slaughter: 'The work of destruction begins among those who have professed to be the spiritual guardians of the people. The false watchmen are the first to fall. There are none to pity or to spare. Men, women, maidens, and little children perish together.'[48] But the whole turgid tale, the great drama of God's victory over Satan and his demons, ends happily: 'One pulse of harmony and gladness beats through the vast creation . . . From the minutest atom to the greatest world, all things, animate and inanimate, in their unshadowed beauty and perfect joy, declare that God is love.'[49] So that's alright then.

Such material sits happily enough in a long tradition, however bizarre and risible. The Christian writer Merrill Unger suggests that 'the New Testament presents overwhelming evidence for the existence of demons'.[50] Jesus gave his disciples the authority to expel demons and on occasions did the work himself. The reality of demons is allegedly attested to by many biblical texts, such as James 2: 19 and Revelation 9: 20 – with other texts describing their nature,[51] their activity,[52] their conflict with the believer,[53] their abode[54] and their eternal doom.[55] In the fifth century St Augustine of Hippo described, in his book *The City of God*, the legions of demons active on the earth; but suggested that it was not the Devil who created evil but God, in order to separate the *elect* from the *damned*. (No, I don't understand this either, but it does accord with Old Testament texts that declare that God created evil.[56]) The fathers of the early church depicted the gods of the pagan world as demons, and those who worshipped them as serving the purposes of Satan – a doctrine that yielded all the horrors of witch hunts (see below). The early Christian writer Tertullian said: 'All the operations of the demons tend to the ruination of man . . . Demons so blind the souls of men that they themselves come to be worshipped, and that sacrifices are offered to their statues.' The early fathers took seriously the efficacy of magic, seeing it as demon-worship and a grave religious transgression. The stage was set for the 'demonisation' of human beings that was to take place, centuries later, throughout western Europe.

In the centuries before the Middle Ages pious and ignorant people had no doubt that demons were all-pervasive and could appear to human beings – beliefs that helped to shape a cultural climate in which persecution could intensify.

The isolation of the desert gave demons many chances to plague the Christian devotees who had decided, following Christ's teachings, to forsake all and follow him. St Macarius the Younger was roused one night by a demon knocking at the door of his ascetic cell and summoning him to where the other monks were assembled – a sort of wake-up call! Macarius bade him begone (or words to that effect) and then went to the assembly, at the same time praying to be shown the truth. He then saw a host of little demons moving among the brethren, distracting their minds from their devotions 'with impure and idle thoughts' (Macarius does not say how he perceived such thoughts in others). Afterwards the monks confessed to the evil imaginings suggested to them by the imps. Sometimes, when the monks were about to take communion, the minuscule demons would play a trick by substituting coal for the host, which then flew back to the altar – all very confusing. On another occasion a demon in the form of a beautiful woman approached Apelles, the blacksmith of a monastery, as though to give him a job, but fortunately he recognised her as a demon – as you would – and smote her in the face with a red-hot iron held in his naked hand. Not surprisingly, the demon howled and fled, its fate unknown. After this remarkable encounter the blacksmith found he could handle hot iron with impunity. The worthy saints Helenus, Apollonius and Hor were privileged to have both demonic and angelic visitors; St Copres, visited by demons only, was less fortunate.

Most demons, we learn, having tempted people into sin, were eager to stop men repenting so that 'they may have comrades in perdition' – and so people needed to be constantly on their guard. A monk named Marinus, known to Pope Gregory VII, scarcely went a day without seeing demons. When the Devil in the shape of an angel induced him to maintain absolute silence he could only be made to talk when the abbot flogged him into speech. Leo IX told of an aunt, a nun who happened to live in a monastery, who was obliged to evict a demon from her cell by making the sign of the cross. And so the bizarre chronology of Christianity ran on . . . demons in the night, demons in the day, demons as animals, demons as raindrops and specks of dust, demons as beautiful women and handsome men, demons as monstrous visions that terrified people into piety, tales and fantasies and dreams, gruesome hallucinations that convinced pious believers that their immortal souls were in danger.

When demons were not creating turmoil and mischief on earth they were performing a host of messy chores in Hell. These consisted mainly of impaling sinners, pushing them into boiling pits, keeping the home fires burning and generally ensuring that a bad time was had by all. There are many depictions of the underworld in ancient accounts, helping superstitious people to glimpse their likely fate beyond the grave. But it was mainly Christianity and Islam – giving vent to a psychopathological sadism – that invented all the horrors of celestial torture that the human mind could imagine. Thus the *Revelation of Peter*, dating to the second century, relates how Christ led his twelve disciples to contemplate the joys of Heaven and to relish the punishment of various categories of sinner in Hell. In the same vein the *Vision of St Paul*, supposedly based on the New Testament book of Corinthians and amplified by other early texts, helped to create a horrific image of Hell for the medieval mind.[57] It is enough to give an extract from the *Vision*, in a typical medieval redaction, to indicate the religious psychopathology at the very heart of Christian Europe:

> Before the gates of Hell were fiery trees, where damned souls hung by their feet, hands, tongues, hair, ears and arms. Paul next saw a multi-coloured furnace with seven separate flames, and sinners pushed within it. Around the furnace were seven torments: snow, ice, fire, blood, serpents, thunderbolts, stench . . . We should fear the dolorous realms of Hell, where there is a fiery wheel with a thousand spokes. It is struck a thousand times a day by a Tartarean angel, and at each turn a thousand souls are tortured. Then Paul beheld a foul river in which swam many infernal creatures, devouring sinners as wolves devour sheep . . . the sinful are immersed in the water according to their deserts . . . For thus saith the Lord: 'Bind them in bundles to burn

them [Matthew 13: 30].' Paul saw some souls immersed to the knees, others to the navel, lips or eyebrows, all in perpetual torment . . . men and women chewing their tongues . . . black girls covered with pitch and sulphur. Round their necks were dragons and fire and serpents. Four demons with fiery horns beat them . . . an old man, weeping and groaning as he was beset by four demons . . . gnawed by snakes and reptiles . . . And Paul asked Michael the number of torments. There are 144,000 . . . Therefore let us follow the Lord, that we may dwell with Him for ever.[58]

Such material, typical of much Christian literature of the time, indicates how numerous pious proselytisers worked to intimidate simple people into trembling obedience. In the Christian world much of this nonsense has ebbed with time, but in Islam it is still taught in an effort to terrorise the child and the adult into blind acceptance of seventh-century doctrine – as if all the intellectual developments spanning centuries had never happened. Any reading of the Koran and its associated texts indicates that the same sickness that once characterised mainstream Christianity is equally manifest today in horrific accounts that a billion people are taught to regard as beyond all question. Mohammed and the many other reciters and scribes of the Koran knew the fate that awaits all sinners:

> Strong fetters, and a flaming fire, and food that choketh, and a sore torment . . . . a crushing fire, God's kindled fire [that] shall mount above the hearts of the damned . . . hell-fire . . . we will brand [them] on the nostrils . . . in the fire shall [they] burn . . . boiling water and running sores, made to drink at a fountain fiercely boiling . . . tormented at the fire . . . dragged into the fire on their faces . . . pour on [their heads] the tormenting boiling water . . . we would surely put out their eyes . . . the fire shall scorch their faces . . . their foreheads, their sides, and their backs shall be branded.[59]

And if anyone should imagine that all this burning should destroy the flesh and end the torment, Allah has an answer. God, 'the compassionate, the merciful', constantly renews the flesh so that the pain will continue for all eternity.[60]

Much of the demonic realm, of which the torments of Hell are only a part, was fabricated by ignorant people who knew no better, and much of it by less ignorant clerics and rulers who, sometimes knowing better, saw widespread superstition as a useful tool of social control – just as cynical pagan priests spoke through the mouths of idols to intimidate gullible people into obedience. And there is yet another important consideration. We have already hinted at the *psychology* of religious belief, explored in a substantial literature,[61] indicating how religious faith can be generated through human fear in a threatening environment. Here it is worth considering another dimension, the role of *psychiatric disease* in causing or shaping religious belief. This further helps to explain how fervent commitment to superstition can be generated in disordered minds that confuse nonsense with truth, and how such confusion can aid the persecution of vulnerable people in theocratic societies.

There are many ways in which demons were alleged to afflict people – and many of these superstitions have survived into the modern world. Notable among these is the demonic habit of possessing or taking over a human being. Anyone who has seen the feature film *The Exorcist* (1973) knows that this is not always a pretty affair. Belief in the reality of demonic possession has existed in all cultures and nicely illustrates the obvious links between mental disease and religious conviction. The theologians, ever busy with such topics, made a distinction between *possession* and *obsession*: in the latter, the demon was thought to besiege or 'sit without' the body of the victim, where in the former the demon actually entered the body of the afflicted person. In the mid-seventeenth century Bishop Montagu contrasted the power of Satan 'to move and actuate' (obsession) and 'to possess and rally inhabit' (possession). It was sometimes thought that a virtuous person was immune to possession – so the early saints suffered only obsession. Another view was that, since all people were infected with original sin, none was wholly virtuous and so all were vulnerable to demonic wiles.

There are numerous descriptions of obsessions and possessions in the theological literature. For example in the fourth-century *Catechisms* of St Cyril of Jerusalem we are told how the Devil tyrannically uses another's body, another's instruments, as his own property; he throws down him who stands upright; he perverts the tongue and distorts the lips. Foam comes instead of words; the man is filled with darkness; his eye is open, yet his soul sees not through it; and the miserable man quivers convulsively before his death.

Henry More noted in *Antidote against Atheism* (1653) that the various symptoms and signs were proof that 'the devil got into the body of a man . . . making use of the organs of the body at his own pleasure, for the performance of such pranks and feats as are far above the capacity, strength, or agility of the party thus bewitched or possessed'. Sometimes there was learned discussion, as in Robert Burton's *Anatomy of Melancholy* (1621), as to whether the Devil acted directly on the mind, or indirectly by means of the body which affected the mind. It was noted that some victims stank, inducing theologians to the latter view. In the fourth century St Hilary of Poitiers reckoned that he could tell by the smell which demons were present in his locality.

In 1830 a certain Dr Bardili in Germany came across a case which he considered to be one of possession.[62] And in the twenty-first century such cases continue to be reported throughout the world. Christian orthodoxy remains certain, despite all the volumes of psychiatry science, that demons exist and can possess the bodies and minds of human beings. Thus the Roman Catholic neurologist Jean Lhermitte, writing in the 1960s, stated that demonic possession and obsession 'are still extremely frequent . . . scarcely a month passes without some example being brought to my own notice . . . whatever skeptics, unbelievers and the ill-informed may think, demonopathic manifestations are not extinct, we still observe the phenomena which startled and alarmed our forefathers'.[63] But today it is rational to interpret such conditions, and other aspects of religious belief, in terms of psychiatric disorder, amenable in many cases to the therapeutic procedures available to medical science.[64]

Research has shown that one pathological use of religion is 'sacrificing the intellect', where the critical faculty is suspended and people are 'duped' into following blindly after undeserving persons.[65] This is particularly the case with religious sects (see later), such as David Koresh's manipulation of a large number of people in the Branch Davidian sect in Waco, Texas (which ultimately led to many fatalities); but the phenomenon is also discernible in mainstream religion where normally adult individuals are determined to abandon any mature analysis in favour of a childlike acceptance of nonsensical doctrines. This blind following and uncritical evaluation of the evidence – often proclaimed as 'faith' – has also been found to be an aspect of the cognitive style of some people with schizophrenia. Various studies have shown that deluded people make observations based on a less critical evaluation of the evidence than is normal for people without delusions.[66]

The psychologist Ronald Siddle notes that there are various other similarities between the cognitive style of some religious individuals and that of people suffering from schizophrenia. For example, he emphasises the irrational adherence to forms of 'magical thinking' – for example, telepathy and extra-sensory perception (ESP) – where the causal concepts of the person's normal culture are abandoned, and he comments:

> If the doctrines of Christianity . . . were examined according to modern day scientific knowledge . . . there would be insufficient acceptable evidence for these established Christian beliefs . . . This involves suspension of disbelief, and the person, and many other perfectly normal and sensible religious people, retain this magical thinking in spite of their own scientific knowledge.[67]

Moreover, magical thinking has been shown to be associated with a 'cluster of personality traits' that are linked to schizophrenia.[68]

It has been found also that religious experiences – and for our purposes this includes the experience of demon possession by both the victim and the witnesses – are linked to psychotic experiences. (One study remarks that a defining attribute of these is the defiance of logic.) Siddle notes that religious experiences 'can be ecstatic, in which the body is active with excitement, trances, glossalalia (the "gift of tongues") and being moved by the spirit'[69] – all highly suggestive of what conventional theologians have regarded as demonic possession. In one study a number of the experiences described verged upon being, or were even overtly, psychotic.[70]

The researcher W. P. Wilson described three main types of religious delusion: *persecutory*, often involving the Devil; *grandiose*, including the Messiah complex; and *belittlement*, including such things as unpardonable sins.[71] Siddle adds hallucinations to this categorisation: 'since auditory hallucinations are common symptoms of schizophrenia, [they] would be a major category in the classification of religious delusions in schizophrenia'.[72] It is well known that auditory hallucinations are a common feature of demon possession: in both historical and modern accounts the victims claim to have heard horrible voices, to have heard the Devil speaking to them or through their own mouths, to have had conversations with demons and so on.

It is interesting that possession by demons has been the religious delusion most studied in psychiatric research. The descriptions of demon possession in the Bible (Luke 4: 35; Luke 8: 27) are clearly akin to accounts of epileptic seizure and mental illness; and possession syndrome itself has a number of recognised symptoms – including the acting out of a different personality.[73] Here the new personality identifies itself as a demon and talks in the first person, referring to the victim in the third person. The 'demon' evinces knowledge allegedly unknown to the victim, and typically shows an aversion to religion and a complete change of moral character. Demons that possess human beings in the West are typically depicted as grotesque men and women, but in other cultures – for example, Chinese folklore – they may be turtles, foxes and the like.

It is known also that religious delusions are typically associated with lower educational attainment, with self-harming activities (responding to biblical texts urging people to pluck out an offending eye etc.)[74] and with dangerous acts allegedly prompted by the Devil or other demons. In 1991 researchers showed that more than half of twenty-seven dangerous psychiatric inmates in an American penal institution, some of them with schizophrenia, appeared to have religious delusions. In twelve of the cases the inmates said that

God or the Devil made them do things, and seventeen believed that God or spirits communicated directly with them.[75]

Hence it seems clear that a wide range of religious experiences are associated with mental illness – for example, schizophrenia – and that delusional states can induce a fervent belief in religious phenomena, including possession by demons. All this is conducive to the generation of persecutory cultures in which vulnerable people, often mentally ill, are abused for alleged links to the Devil and other evil spirits. It is not only the prevailing superstitious beliefs rooted in scriptural texts that contribute, but also the mental states of both accusers and victims. The accusers are likely to have their own psychiatric problems, being constantly worried by the malevolence of mysterious forces that threaten disease and death. And the victims themselves may contribute to the prevailing paranoia and sense of dread, believing in their own guilt and their vulnerability to all sorts of demonic influence. Such a culture is ripe for witch burning.

The medieval Christian church was not the first superstitious organisation to celebrate the execution of alleged witches, but it refined the procedures to an unprecedented degree and surrounded them with theological justification and pious homilies. As we have seen, the practices of Judeo-Christianity and Islam were irredeemably rooted in the superstitions of earlier cultures – and remain so. In the Code of Hammurabi, dating to the eighteenth century BC, there is reference to men being charged with witchcraft; and according to an Egyptian papyrus of the nineteenth dynasty (1292–1190 BC) 'two harem conspirators were condemned to death because they made magical writings to lead astray and work mischief, and made certain gods of wax and certain medicines to weaken the limbs of men'. However, it was early Judaism that supplied much of the scriptural authority, built on by later theologians, for what would become a horrific period in Christian Europe. The most famous injunction in this respect is Exodus 22: 18 ('Thou shalt not suffer a witch to live') but, as Rossell Hope Robbins and others have pointed out,[76] the Hebrew word *haskagh* (sometimes *chasaph*), which occurs twelve times in the Old Testament, more usually means 'prisoner' and has nothing to do with the Christian concept of a witch. Hence a possible mistranslation helped to send thousands of women in medieval Europe to agonising deaths. As one example, after the execution of Goody Knapp at Fairfield, Kent, in 1653, a neighbour was reported as saying: 'It was long before she could believe this poor woman was a witch, or that there were any witches, till the word of God convinced her, which saith: "Thou shalt not suffer a witch to live."' Robbins cites a dozen passages from the Old Testament to indicate how 'erroneous translation and tendentious interpretation fostered the growth of obscurantism'.[77]

Such an attempt to exonerate sacred texts from complicity in the later horrors of the witch trials, and so to redeem Judeo-Christianity, is understandable but not altogether convincing. If mistranslation occurred then it served the medieval climate only because of what Christianity was at that time. The early church fathers saw nothing inconsistent between the biblical condemnation of witchcraft and the Christian tradition as they saw it. A host of superstitious beliefs, many of them derived from ancient paganism, were feeding into early Christianity and helped to shape pious attitudes to witchcraft. And centuries of horrific persecution were sustained in large part by papal and other authoritative pronouncements indicating ways to recognise witches, how to torture them to obtain confessions, and the appropriate methods of execution – the whole sadistic and superstitious framework of the holy inquisitors.

The Talmud states that in the first century BC a certain Rabbi Simeon ben Shetah caught eighty witches performing their rituals in Ashkelon; he hanged them all in one day. In ancient Roman law the Twelve Tablets condemn maleficent magic; and Tacitus recorded that magicians were expelled from Italy: 'Among them was Lucius Pituanius, who was hurled from the Tarpenian Rock, and Publius Marcius, who was stripped and lashed to death outside the Esquiline Gate.' In the third-century *Sententiae* Iulius Paulus declared that those who gave potions to induce love, 'though they act without malice, yet commit an act of evil example'. Lowly offenders were banished to the mines, the more honourable ones to an island, with confiscation of their property.

In England royal decrees against magical practices were issued as early as the eighth century; in 901, during the reign of Edward the Elder, laws were passed punishing diviners with banishment; in 940 King Athelstan made witchcraft a capital offence; and in 959 Edgar issued an edict against enchantments, necromancies and divination. Hérard, the ninth-century Archbishop of Tours, went to great length to condemn witchcraft and related practices, and one of the laws of Charlemagne decreed the death penalty for 'agents of the Devil who arouse tempests'. A twelfth-century law of the Forum Turolii in Spain stated that a woman should be burnt if she bewitched 'men or beasts or other things'. Similarly, Nicholas Remy declared in his *Daemonolatreiae Libri Tres* (1595) that clemency should never be granted to witches: 'It is like sparing mad dogs, that everyone knows are incurable.' And Martin Delrio stated in the *Disquisitionum Magicarum Libri Sex* (1599) that witches should be executed even if they had committed no malevolent act ('killed no one . . . [done] no harm to crops and beasts'), simply because they were possessed by the Devil. In 306 AD the church addressed the notion that human beings could form a pact with the Devil; in 314 the Council of Ancyra forbade witchcraft as a branch of pharmacy, demanding several years' penance for anyone found guilty of it. St Basil of Caesarea urged an atonement of thirty years – in contrast to an ancient Anglo-Saxon law that exacted three years' penance if the malevolent witch's magic failed, and seven if it succeeded and the victim died. By the time of Canute, however, the penalty for witchcraft was banishment or death.

On 5 December 1484 Pope Innocent VIII issued the famous anti-witchcraft bull, *Summis desiderantes affectibus* ('Desiring with supreme ardour'), which helped to sustain the terrible work of the inquisitors. It was written in response to the request of the Dominican inquisitor Heinrich Kramer for explicit authority to prosecute witchcraft in Germany. In this case the local ecclesiastical authorities had declined to assist Kramer's pious endeavours but the Pope proved more amenable. The bull, issued with all papal authority, recognised the existence of witches and gave full approval for any measures to tackle the problem. It affirmed Kramer's view that there had been an outbreak of witchcraft and heresy in the

Rhine valley, and urged the local authorities to cooperate with the hardworking inquisitors on pain of excommunication.[78]

Kramer did what he could but combating witchcraft was a mighty task, and in due course he retired to write *Malleus Maleficarum* (The Hammer of Witches, 1487) with James Sprenger, another Dominican monk. They included *Summis desiderantes affectibus* as a preface to the work to signal papal approval, so providing an authoritative handbook for the persecution of witches throughout Europe. The book covered the powers and practices of witches, their relationship with the Devil, their detection, the setting up and conduct of the inquisitorial courts, and the use of torture as a means of punishment and eliciting the truth.

Apart from the repulsive sadism that runs through much of this work, it is easy to see the gross misogyny that has characterised the Catholic Church through all its history. For example, the two worthy Dominicans explain in detail 'Why Superstition is chiefly found in Women' That this is so 'is indeed a fact that it were idle to contradict . . . it is good, for the admonition of women, to speak of this matter' – and they cite biblical and later pious authorities to justify the charge.[79] Did not Ecclesiastes say that a wicked woman was 'more bitter than death', and what his soul had sought through life was rarely found among men and never among women?[80] And what of St John Chrysostom's considered judgement on the matter: 'What else is woman but a foe to friendship, an inescapable punishment, a necessary evil . . .'? And so Kramer and Sprenger run on:

> All wickedness is but little to the wickedness of a woman . . . She is more carnal than a man, as is clear from her many carnal abominations . . . [She is necessarily defective] because she was formed from a bent rib . . . an imperfect animal, she always deceives . . . a wicked woman is by her nature quicker to waver in her faith, and consequently quicker to abjure the faith, which is the root of witchcraft.[81]

Moreover, since women have defective intelligence and 'inordinate affections and passions' they are more likely to abjure the faith than are men, again making them prone to witchcraft:

'They search for, brood over, and inflict various vengeances either
by witchcraft, or by some other means. Wherefore it is no wonder
that so great a number of witches exist in this sex.'[82]

The papal support for the campaign against witches was one of
the factors that made 'witch finding' a respectable profession.
New bodies of male professionals evolved, touring Europe to
indulge their sadistic fantasies and to pick up some easy money. At
first the persecution of witches had relied upon the vindictive
testimony of neighbours, but with the advent of the witch finders
the matter was put on a more systematic basis. Matthew Hopkins,
pre-eminent among the breed, adopted the title 'witchfinder
general' and used James I's work *Daemonologie* as a textbook.[83]
Hopkins, the son of a vicar in Great Wenham, Suffolk, charged a
community twenty shillings a visit, whether or not he found
witches there – he usually did – and expected to be provided with
board and lodging and some travelling expenses. In addition he
was given an extra twenty shillings for every witch he discovered
– which no doubt induced him to work hard and produce results.
In one highly successful fourteen-month period, from 1645 to
1646, Hopkins managed, by dint of various tortures applauded by
local clerics, to send to the gallows more women than did all the
other witch finders in England.

It was not only the witch finders who found the execution of
witches a profitable enterprise. In one account, dated 11 September
1646, the fee for the imprisonment of the alleged witch Cathin
Joyeuse in Nancy, France, lists fourteen items, including those
listed in Table 1. In the same vein an account for the burning of
two Aberdeen witches, Janet Wishart and Isabel Crocker, in
February 1596 runs as shown in Table 2.[84]

At the same time, despite the general approval by the church,
there was some fervent contemporary opposition to the activities
of Hopkins and the other witch finders. For example, in
September 1645 a parliamentary news magazine, the *Moderate
Intelligencer*, expressed doubts about Hopkins's methods, and the
following year at least one churchman, resenting his excursions
into Huntingdonshire, preached against him. Hopkins quickly
replied to the Houghton town council to ask if they had many
witch-lovers ('sticklers for such cattle') and threatened to bring his

methods to the town. One clergyman, the ailing eighty-year-old
Rev. John Lowes of Brandeston, Suffolk, denounced Hopkins
and was arrested as a warlock for his pains. Hopkins had the man
tortured for a few days 'til he was weary of life and scarce sensible
of what he said or did'. The man confessed. By now, however,
Hopkins's reputation was on the wane and in 1647 he died of
tuberculosis.

Table 1

Item	Francs	Gros
For wine (including wine for the guards)	13	0
Additional for other expenses . . . from the announcement of the sentence to torture to the time of that torture	3	6
For the woman who shaved her	1	0
For the torturer	20	0
For the man who had to go . . . to fetch the said torturer	4	4

Table 2

Item	Shillings	Pence
For 20 loads of peat to burn them	40	0
For a boll [6 bushels of coal]	24	0
For 4 tar barrels	26	8
For fir and iron barrels	16	8
For a stake and dressing of it	16	0
For four fathoms of rope [hangman's rope]	4	0
For carrying the peat, coals and barrels to the hill	8	4
To one justice for their execution	13	4

We have seen that in addition to papal authorisation for the
burning of witches there was also royal authorisation. Hence G. B.
Harrison emphasises in the introduction to *Daemonologie* what the
'Royal author' writes in his preface, that the book was written to
show that the 'assaultes of Sathan are most certainly practized, &
that the instruments thereof, merits most severly to be punished'.[85]
Here James describes the practice of 'diuelish artes' and indicates
'what exact trial and seuere punishment they merite'. Well,
someone has to do it. So the King describes what the witches get
up to and cites in approval the fate of one suspect, a maidservant
called Geillis Duncane. With the help of others, her master
subjected her to 'the torture of the Pilliwinckes vpon her fingers,
which is a greeuous torture, and binding or wrinching her head
with a corde of roape, which is a most cruell torment also'. Even
this treatment did not induce the girl to confess, but when the
'enemies marke' was found in her throat she confessed that 'all her
dooings was doone by the wicked allurement and inticements of
the Diuell, and that she did them by witchcraft'.[86]

Duncane was then imprisoned and forced to give other names,
whereupon other women were tortured – with full Christian
approval – as was the custom. In one verbatim report of a woman
accused of witchcraft at Prossneck, Germany, we learn what befell
her on the first day of torture:

> The hangman bound her hands . . . threw alcohol over her head and
> set fire to it so as to burn her hair to the roots. He placed strips of
> sulphur under her arms and around her back and set fire to them . . .
> [He] pulled her up to the ceiling [leaving her hanging] while the
> torturer went to breakfast . . . He poured alcohol over her back and
> set fire to it . . . [He] placed a very rough plank full of sharp points
> against her body [and] jerked her up to the ceiling. Then he squeezed
> her thumbs and big toes in the vice . . . [then] the calves and legs . . .
> then he whipped her . . . [then the vice again] . . . then they whipped
> her again in a frightful manner . . . The next day they started all over
> again, but without pushing things quite so far.[87]

This procedure followed the advice in the papally approved
Malleus Maleficarum: if the accused refused to talk, the answer was

simple – 'other forms of torture must be placed before him'. But even this did not always work. In 1630 Barbara Schwartz was tortured eight times in Bamberg without confessing. In England the punishment for 'taciturnity' was *pressing to death*. Thus in 1654 an accused man in Maidstone refused to talk, whereupon he was stripped and 'upon his body must be laid so much iron and stone as he can bear no more'; Giles Cory at the Salem witch trials was killed in this way. It was not until 1722 that this method of 'inducement' was abolished in England. Here the last execution for witchcraft took place in 1685, and the last known trial was in 1717.

A principal factor in the decline of witchcraft was the increasing secularisation of society, but the victories of enlightened thought were never complete. The human propensity towards the marvellous has never been totally satisfied with 'Einsteinian religiosity' or the zoological enthusiasms of Richard Dawkins, but has characteristically opted much of the time and throughout the world for supernaturalism, magical ways of thinking – for nonsense. In England the Witchcraft Act 1604 was repealed in 1736 and replaced by a provision which permitted no more than minor penalties for fraudulent occultism. The removal of the legal machinery for prosecution had as a consequence the ending of courts charting the exact chronology and distribution of subsequent witch accusations and suspicions. But the superstitions persisted – as shown, not least, by all the battles that the evolutionary scientists would be forced to wage in the nineteenth century and beyond.

Many writers have argued that the Industrial Revolution finally killed the social influence of witchcraft: Max Gluckman declared that 'in our own country accusations of witchcraft were ruled illegal when the industrial revolution began to develop'.[88] In such a view, witchcraft beliefs are seen to typify small communities; the growth of large-scale societies, where relationships are 'impersonal and segmental', precludes the need for such superstitions. And associated with this idea is the notion that a developing technology makes magic superfluous. Belief in witchcraft persists – as do beliefs in telepathy, ESP, alternative therapies, ghosts, gods, poltergeists, souls, spirits, precognition and all the rest of the superstitious paraphernalia – throughout the world, but its incidence is less than in medieval Europe. But modern societies are far from immune. France is said to have more witches, today differently defined than in the Middle Ages, than other European countries; and the Basque provinces are said to be particularly rich in such people – there the *sorguin* still exists in her coven, and there is evidence of the continuation of *sabats* (ritual encounters) and other practices.

The persistent human need for witches as scapegoats or suppliers of beneficent magic has always led to their association with areas of deprivation. Perhaps, in this connection, it is significant that the Basque provinces are more deprived than Paris; and so there are Basque rather than Parisian 'wise women'. In 1954 the writer Gerald Gardner, himself a coven member, admitted to witch cults in Britain:

> I have been told by witches in England: 'Write and tell people we are not perverts. We are decent people, we only want to be left alone, but there are certain secrets that you mustn't give away.' . . . I am permitted to tell much . . . I write only of what takes place in the North, South, East and West of England today in covens which I know.[89]

Today such practices are regarded as mere eccentricities, of little social consequence in the developed world. In March 2008 fresh archaeological research was reported that shows the incidence of seventeenth-century rituals involving witchcraft in the Cornish countryside. Work in thirty-five pits at a site in a valley near Truro revealed swan pelts, dead magpies, unhatched eggs, quartz pebbles, human hair, fingernails and part of an iron cauldron. Jacqui Woods, leading the excavation, commented: 'A lot of the paganism of the Celts was wiped out by the Romans, but not in Cornwall . . . It really makes me wonder whether . . . [witchcraft] is still going on.'[90] In one recent estimate there were still about 10,000 witches in Britain, with young women showing unprecedented interest in witchcraft. According to a report in *Youthwork*, a monthly magazine published by Christian Communications Partnership, about a hundred teenage girls a month were wanting to join covens to learn about casting spells. This was seen as a means to female empowerment, as a route to passing exams, finding boyfriends and becoming wealthy.[91]

At the same time a campaign was being waged to achieve a pardon for Helen Duncan, an English witch who was accused of leaking military secrets during a séance in Portsmouth during the Second World War. Winston Churchill denounced her conviction as 'tomfoolery', and later repealed 200-year-old witchcraft legislation.[92] Such antics indicate how witchcraft is regarded in modern Britain. Today, though theologians are less keen to talk about witchcraft than in the days of the *Malleus*, the business of exorcising demons continues to thrive. On 26 January 1999 the Chilean cardinal Jorge Medina Estévez, prefect of the Congregation for Divine Worship and the Discipline of the Sacraments, presented at the Holy Office in the Vatican a new rite of exorcism, which contained 'no radical changes' to the traditional rites: 'The language is more sombre and fewer adjectives are used; however, the expression of faith in the power of God to expel the Devil is the same in both cases.'[93] Well, I suppose it is necessary to give the impression of modernisation, albeit half-hearted, from time to time. The Vatican still maintains exorcism colleges, instructing clerics on how to combat demon possession, and the Anglican Church supports exorcism practices used to expel ghosts and other unwelcome spirits from buildings and the human body. Elsewhere belief in witchcraft and exorcism still remains a dangerous force. The further following examples, culled from the mainstream press, could easily be extended:

- On 25 November 1994 Mona Rai, a Muslim holy woman who lectured on the Koran in mosques, schools and private homes, was convicted of manslaughter for beating 22-year-old Farida Patel to death in a 'bizarre and barbaric' exorcism. The Muslim priestess led a two-day beating of the young woman in an attempt to drive evil spirits from her body. The prosecuting counsel, Julian Bevan QC, told the jury: 'This case will introduce you to the ways and customs and beliefs of people whose world, no doubt to most of you, is entirely alien. Who amongst us has experience of evil spirits in the body and of driving them away by beating the individual?'[94] Rai hit Patel with a vacuum cleaner tube until it broke, beat her with a walking stick and jumped on her body, breaking nine ribs.

- In Madrid in 2001 'possessed individuals' were found performing satanic rites in blood-soaked nocturnal rituals involving the killing of eagles and goats. Those involved managed to escape over a roof, leaving the police to examine bloody walls on which was written 'Satan will conquer'. In September 2002 the Kentucky prison service suspended satanic rituals in jail pending an enquiry into whether they were legal: 'We are researching it to see what we are required to allow under the law.'[95]
- In 1998 in Pakistan, an old woman, Maradam Mai, diagnosed as a paranoid schizophrenic, was tortured and burnt to death as a witch. After villagers alleged that she was seen mutilating the Koran, a group of men dragged her to the village square, cut her fingers off, gouged her eyes out, poured petrol over her and then lit it. When the police arrived a crowd of about seventy gloating men were surrounding the corpse: 'She burnt the Koran, so we burnt her,' they said. The head of the community, Ishfaq, said the woman died because the villagers 'love Islam'. Then it emerged that she had probably not burnt the Koran but only paper charms given to her by a local holy man. The alleged burning of the sacred text was only 'an excuse for the lynching', said a local teacher. 'It was a witch hunt, like in Europe centuries ago.'[96]
- In November 2007 detectives began a murder enquiry in Wainuiomata, near Wellington, the capital of New Zealand, after a mother died and a fourteen-year-old girl, her cousin, had her eyeballs scratched during a Maori exorcism ceremony. The 22-year-old mother, Janet Moses, also had her eyes scratched before she was drowned in an attempt to lift a curse or *makutu*, in which a spirit takes over the body of a person. Three other teenagers also underwent exorcism but were unharmed.[97]
- In November 2000 Derek Taylor, who had been involved in witchcraft since 1975, was found washed up dead on a beach at Rustington, West Sussex, after a bizarre ceremony involving a sword and a symbol marked out in the sand. His

wife commented that he thought he was the corn king and
would have to be sacrificed: 'He said he had killed himself in
former lives . . . and . . . said he would have to kill himself
again. He said he would have to return the children to the
stars.'[98] (The following year Jane Swift, the acting governor
of Massachusetts, approved a bill that exonerated the last of
the Salem witches hanged in 1692 and 1693. Twenty-four
men and women were variously hanged, crushed to death or
died in prison during the witch-hunt, which became a
symbol of the perils of religious superstition.)[99]

- In 2004 Amar Jatar, an Indian villager, desperate to rekindle
his wife's love for him turned to a tantric, a traditional witch
doctor who calls on supernatural powers to heal those in
need.[100] Jatar had tried tenderness and beatings, but nothing
had worked. At first the tantric offered an amulet but that too
was useless, and so he advised the husband to lift the curse on
his marriage by killing his four-year-old son. Jatar carried out
the tantric's instructions, strangling his son as he played in the
back yard and throwing his body down a well.[101]

- In February 2008 Human Rights Watch and other activist
groups were campaigning to halt the execution in Saudi Arabia
of Fawza Falih, an illiterate woman accused of witchcraft. She
had been arrested by the religious police in 2005, beaten and
forced to sign a confession that she could not read. Among her
various accusers was a man who claimed she had made him
impotent through sorcery – a common charge against
thousands of alleged witches in medieval Christendom. Falih
had exhausted all her chances of escaping the death sentence by
beheading, and she could only be saved if King Abdullah
intervened.[102] In the event a global campaign proved sufficient
to prevent the execution.

- On 24 October 2007 a judge in Michigan ruled that 31-year-
old Jennifer Kukla, found guilty of first-degree murder,
would spend the rest of her life in prison. She had testified
that the Devil had told her to kill her two daughters and the
family pets.[103]

- In October 2007 Muslim leaders in Nigeria were claiming
that a tribe led by a woman was using black magic to keep

men off the throne, since every man who had become king in the northern kingdom of Kumbwada had died under mysterious circumstances. Aminuddeen Abubajar, a prominent cleric in Kano, the north's main city, said: 'The fact that any man who assumes the throne dies in a week strongly suggests the use of black magic which Islam absolutely condemns.'[104]

- In November 2007 Bradford Crown Court was told that a devout Christian, a Nigerian keen to quote the Bible, had sealed his sons' lips with safety pins and clothes pegs to save them from the Devil. In addition the boys had been beaten with poles, a long stick and an electric cable. One boy was locked in a cupboard, the other forced to spend a night blindfolded and tied to a chair, with a safety pin through his tongue and bottom lip. The father filmed some of the cruelties using a camcorder so that a copy could be sent back to Nigeria. The family attended a Pentecostal church and the children were being brought up to be obedient and 'to put their morality in order'.[105]

It is plain that many of these bizarre superstitions, often leading to torture and murder, are intimately connected with mainstream religions such as Christianity and Islam. Faith, involving the suspension of common sense and critical analysis, inevitably keeps people locked in obscure and nonsensical beliefs, which are at best harmless diversions and at worst wholly destructive of domestic and social harmony. Consider, for example, the Muslim belief in jinn, the supernatural creatures for which there is no evidence but which obedient followers of the prophet are expected to accept as part of the fabric of reality.

Orthodox Muslims remain fearful of jinn, allegedly fashioned by Allah out of smokeless fire along with the angels made out of light. Jinn, we learn, come in various shapes and with various abilities: some fly, some crawl, some are invisible, some drink blood, and some take on the form of human beings but with their feet turned backwards. Muslim clerics have described jinn as bestial, giant, hideous, hairy, ursine and so on; and some holy men, having fallen into trances, have afterwards claimed that bare rooms had become filled with jinn seeking favours or release from amulet charms. Women, we are not surprised to find in misogynistic Islam, are more susceptible than men to the influence of jinn – and illiterate rural women are particularly prone to witnessing the presence of jinn (just as in Catholicism ignorant rural women are most likely to have visions of the Virgin Mary). Some superstitious, or opportunistic, Muslim women have exploited jinn presence to earn a living as fortune tellers, answering such troubled questions as 'Will my husband take a second wife?'. Shrines, often carrying no more than a prayer flag, are said to attract jinn.

In August 2006 Muslims in the central Ugandan town of Kikandwa were terrified by reports that jinn were haunting and raping women in the district, so when an unkempt and deranged young woman stumbled out of the forest she was denounced as a jinn in disguise. The villagers beat her almost to death and then the local police shot her dead. In her last moments she called out for her children. It emerged later that, searching for her lost husband, she had spent days without food and water. This in turn produced a secular backlash, and editorials in Ugandan newspapers called on the government formally to deny the existence of jinn – but they were forced to contend with the superstitious weight of traditional Islam.

A few Islamic scholars have denied the existence of jinn, but the modern consensus is that good Muslims should believe in them. But there is learned debate about the purpose and character of jinn. Are they moral or immoral? How exactly are human beings supposed to relate to them? Are jinn physical or purely spiritual creatures? Some Islamic jurists consider that marriage between jinn and humans is lawful, and there is a provision for the inheritance of jinn property. If a Muslim woman consents to having sex during menstruation – against Koranic prohibition[106] – then a jinn child may be the result. Alleged yeti sightings in Pakistan's Chitral district were believed by local superstitious Muslims to be of jinn, ones fortunately vulnerable to date or plum stones fired from a sling. Mohammed allegedly preached to bands of jinn and converted some of them to Islam. Some scholars have taught that jinn may be saintly or demonic. These latter are dubbed *shaytan*, demons that are 'firewood for hell' along with human sinners; and the common malevolence of such jinn can have a political significance.

Thus Muslim factions in Somalia and Afghanistan have accused their enemies of being backed not only by the CIA but by jinn, who are also said to whisper into the ears of suicide bombers. Mubarak Ali Gilani, a Pakistani cleric associated with the resistance group Jamaat al-Fuqra, has warned America that jinn will guide jihadists' missiles. Ahmed Shah Massoud, the commander of Afghanistan's Northern Alliance, eventually killed by al-Qaeda terrorists on 9 September 2001, was said by his followers to have enlisted the support of Muslim jinn – and in consequence Osama bin Laden was declaring war on the jinn also.[107]

Just as superstition is irretrievably enmeshed with religious belief, so cults have obvious kinship with mainstream religions. In its early years Christianity was a cult, in fervent competition with many other cults, such as Mithraism. The eternal logics of cults and religions are the same: all depend upon a suspension of the critical faculty, blind faith, the unquestioning obedience of followers, mind control or 'brain washing' and the vesting of authority in some inspired leader, godhead or dogmatic creed. What distinguishes a cult from a religion is the scale of its success as a proselytising group. A cult that remains small and powerless is always a cult. A cult that wins millions to the cause and captures the commanding heights of sociopolitical power becomes a religion. But all cults and religions maintain their DNA kinship – all rely on superstition and irrational polemics, an inevitable posture in defence against the corrosive power of science and reason.

Cults are more numerous than religions, simply because they are smaller and parochial. A cult can form around a few dozen people with a singular preoccupation; and there cannot be more than one state religion in any country. And their modest size allows for immense variation in character and style. The proliferation of cults shows that they are often little more than schismatic offshoots, highly derivative of mainstream religious movements. Hence there are cults with obvious and undisguised links to Christianity, Islam, Buddhism, Shinto and so on.

In Japan, for example, there are 183,000 officially recognised religious organisations, many of which are cults, in our terms. One of these, the Shinto-based Kigen-kai, in the town of Komoro, recently received publicity when 63-year-old Motoko Okuno was punished by cult members after her daughter jokingly suggested to the 'Great Deity's' granddaughter that a condom could be used as a protective amulet. She was beaten up, her face chalked as ritual humiliation, and she was forced to endure cult members riding on her back and grabbing her hair as 'reins'.[108] As she lay motionless on the floor the women cult members sprinkled her body with Kigen-sui, a 'magical' water and supposed elixir of life, but Okuno was dead. The subsequent police enquiry admitted that there were many unanswered questions. How had entire families been sucked into the belief system? Why were so many women members involved in the beating? Had there, as the townspeople of Komoro claimed, been other deaths due to cult activity?[109]

In September 2006, farmers on Dartmoor found dozens of their sheep mutilated and laid out in bizarre patterns. Some had their eyes gouged out, and their tongues and sexual organs removed; most had been strangled or had their necks broken. Early in January the previous year seven dead sheep had been found laid out in the pattern of a seven-pointed star, and since that time the killings increased – possibly, some said, the work of Satanists.[110] Sometimes, following deaths and police enquiries, people admit to Satanic practices. In January 2002 in Germany a young married couple, having admitted to diabolical practices including drinking the blood of their victim, were told that they would spend the rest of their lives in a secure psychiatric unit.[111]

In some accounts little attempt is made to distinguish cults from religions. For example, the researchers George Chryssides and Margaret Wilkins have considered a wide range of 'new religious movements' that, in another context, may be regarded as cults.[112] One of these is Scientology, founded by L. Ron Hubbard (1911–86) and currently gaining notoriety for its celebrity support.[113] As befits a cult or 'new religion', Scientology has its full measure of original jargon and absurd claims. 'Dianetics', we learn, is what the soul is doing to the body and provides a route to how we can become healthy. People are essentially souls or 'thetans' trapped in matter. Events sometimes 'drop out of time' into a reactive mind which stores 'engrams', memories of unpleasant or painful events, which need to be 'audited' out of the system if a person is to become healthy. The thetan may have inhabited different bodies in past lives and so the engrams may have arisen centuries ago. Take out of this the familiar Freudian notion of suppressed traumas, and some well-intentioned social programmes, and we are left with nonsense. For example, an Australian woman accused of killing her father and mother in 2007 and diagnosed as psychotic was denied psychiatric treatment on account of her parents' Scientology convictions.[114]

Other cults that have gained dramatic notoriety are David Koresh's Branch Davidians, slaughtered at 'Ranch Apocalypse' in 1993 by the FBI in Waco; the Kingdom of Hell, involved in the killing of film star Sharon Tate and her friends by Charles Manson, self-proclaimed 'God and Devil', in 1969;[115] the Gospels Polygamists, sharing many of the social beliefs of the Mormons; the People's Temple, involved in the suicides or murder of 914 people in Jonestown, Guyana, in 1978; the Temple of Love in Miami, where cult followers were induced to beat a man to death; and the America-based Movement for the Restoration of the Ten Commandments, which proclaimed of the French, for example: 'Your laziness will not permit you to endure the chastisement that will be inflicted upon you until you are destroyed in lamentations.'[116]

To such examples can be added the Unification Church (the 'Moonies'), led by the Rev. Sun Myung Moon; the John Frum 'cargo cult' on the Vanuatu archipelago in the Pacific; the Order of the Solar Temple, implicated in cult killings and mass suicides in Switzerland, Canada and France in the 1990s; the Old Believers in Siberia, with a leader who believes he is Jesus Christ;[117] the Children of God, who drove a cult member to kill a woman and then commit suicide; the American Rapturists, a growing sector of Christianity, who predicted the end of the world for 4 October 2005; the Exclusive Brethren, responsible for countless family break-ups; Jehovah's Witnesses, many of whom have died rather than have blood transfusions;[118] and so on.

★

It is obvious that the human propensity towards the marvellous has stimulated immense creative efforts throughout history. This has yielded a vast cultural heritage, of which all the paraphernalia of cults and religions are but one part. It is significant for our purposes that these are rooted not only in ignorance and superstition, but in mental aberration and disease. St Paul and Mohammed are thought by some analysts to have suffered epileptic seizures, and it is easy to speculate on the paranoia and delusional megalomania of many cult leaders. Researchers have shown that cult members typically have a psychiatric history before joining,[119] and that though membership may satisfy various psychological goals – for example, by providing a useful 'escape route' from the pressures of life – this in turn can lead to immersion in other-worldly fantasy and irrational attachment to a cult leader or dogmatic creed. In extreme cases the upshot can be a surrender to psychological infantilism and intellectual impotence, which in turn can lead to psychological abuse, suicide, torture, murder, war making and genocide. In all this, cults and religions are one – nonsensical and dangerous. It is time to grow up.

3

What do you mean?

'When *I* use a word,' Humpty Dumpty said . . . 'it means just what
I want it to mean, neither more nor less.'
'The question is,' said Alice, 'whether you can make words mean
so many different things.'

Lewis Carroll, *Through the Looking Glass, and
What Alice Found There* (1871)

In the New Testament St John declared: 'In the beginning was the
Word, and the Word was with God, and the Word was God.'[1] As
befits theology we are immediately plunged into confusion. Was
the Word 'God' (or its Greek or Hebrew equivalent), or was the
Word 'with' God – and what does that mean? Whichever
alternative we opt for, it does not matter. Neither of them makes
any sense. How were there *any* words before the evolution of
language – or, liberally put, the evolution of animal sounds used for
communication? And if God invented language 'in the beginning',
what use was it until the creation of animate species? Or did God
talk to itself? Or perhaps it created its own celestial library,
including the Arabic Koran, for purposes we can only imagine.
Were there spiritual membership cards? And did it give away
redundant copies, or recite befuddled bits and pieces, as it allegedly
did to an illiterate Arab? Being charitable, we can acknowledge
that John's comments did emphasise the crucial importance of
language – an importance that, as obtained in all ignorance in
primitive societies, assumed a deeply spiritual significance.

In many primitive societies, such as the early Hebrew tribes, it
was believed that magic might be wrought on a person through
the use of his name, just as hair, nails or any other bodily part
might be used for the same purpose.[2] North American Indians,
and members of many other tribes from the Atlantic to the Pacific,

regarded someone's name not as a mere label but as an important part of their personality, like their eyes or teeth, and reckoned that as much harm could be done to them by the malicious handling of their name as by a physical wound to their body. Some Eskimos assumed fresh names when they were old, assuming that they might thereby be reborn with all the vigour of youth. The Tolampu of Sulawesi, in Indonesia, were terrified that if you wrote a man's name down you could carry off his soul with it, and one writer noted that Australian aborigines kept their names secret so that they would not fall into the hands of sorcerers.[3] Some of the tribes of central Australia opted for two names for every person – one a common name available to everyone, the other a 'real' name that was kept secret to protect it from bad magic. Here again we encounter the misogyny that infects all religion and superstition: to reveal one's real name to a woman of the tribe would be particularly reckless. In some tribes women were not allowed to speak the names of relatives, lest evil befall them – a superstition which, in some tribes, has led to the evolution of an almost distinct language, 'women's speech', designed to protect people from malign female influence. Men were also often prohibited from speaking names in order to avoid malign supernatural influences. In the same way the ancient Egyptians each received two names – a 'good' or 'little' name that was made public, and a 'true' or 'great' name that was carefully concealed.

The natives of Nias believed that a person might be harmed if demons heard a name said out loud, and so the names of infants, who were particularly vulnerable to demonic forces, were never spoken; and in allegedly haunted places, where the demons thrived, men refrained from calling to each other by name for the same reason. And we find similar superstitions surrounding names among the Chilota and the Mapuche of Chile and Argentina, the Ojibwa in North America, the native tribes of British Columbia, the Papuans of New Guinea, the Melanesians of the Bismarck Archipelago, and many South African tribes. When warriors of the Nandi, a Kenyan tribe, were away on a foray, no-one at home was allowed to pronounce their names so that malign supernatural forces would not be able to use the information. Instead the absent men were referred to as birds, so a child who carelessly mentioned the name of an absent warrior would be rebuked by its mother: 'Don't talk of the birds who are in the heavens.'[4] In the same vein the Bangala of the upper Congo refrained when fishing from speaking each other's names, so that the malicious spirits of the river could not exploit the information to prevent any catches.

In these and many other ways the magical power of names – and, by extension, the power of words in general – was assumed in countless primitive societies. The origins of language were not understood, and so the very existence of words was regarded with wonder and superstitious dread. Hence the names of relations were tabooed, as were those of kings and other sacred persons, and people were not allowed to speak the names of the dead. And even the gods had problems with words, often determined to hide their true names from ambitious sorcerers and from other divinities who would usurp their power. J. G. Frazer relates the story of how the subtle Isis managed to worm the secret name from Ra, the great god of the sun, and so to acquire fresh powers.[5] If the gods had problems with names, what hope was there for simple folk in primitive societies? As always, and as with the major religions of the world, people were seen as at the mercy of incomprehensible supernatural forces, with words being one of the many phenomena open to abuse by spirits, demons and gods.

The superstitions surrounding names in particular and words in general – like all superstitions, including the essence of the world religions – derive from human ignorance in the face of reality. It is only in modern times that rational theories have emerged to explain the origin of the great language families and how language itself may have originated. As with biological species, there are 'genetic' links between various languages. For example, researchers in the nineteenth century provided proof of the connections between Indo-European languages, and identified the rules that governed linguistic change. This work, deriving from what has been called comparative grammar, has facilitated the emergence of scientific linguistics, structuralism and other disciplines.[6] Today the very structure of language has been explored with reference to its underlying logic and its significance for such topics as syntax and semantics and broader questions of psychology and philosophy.

For our purposes it is enough to note that simple and complex belief systems, invariably conveyed and preserved through language, whether oral or written, are subject to evolution over time. There are ample reasons in this context why meanings can be obscure and confused, and why interpretations can proliferate in any one society and over time. Here it is significant that religious apologists often seize interpretation as a silver bullet, a magic wand, a linguistic device to save this or that supernatural claim. Thus when a doctrine is exposed as absurd they frequently adopt the ploy of saying 'it all depends on how you interpret it', 'what this really means is . . .', 'you shouldn't take the words out of context'. Perhaps, they hope, the words – often from a sacred text – can be recast to make them intelligible to a modern mind. But, far from providing an escape route, interpretation is the theologian's Achilles heel. If sacred texts are so amenable to reinterpretation in the light of new scholarly discoveries or shifting cultural trends, then what price the word of the gods? Any divine message becomes subject to human intercession, human editing, human caprice – which in turn serves to advertise the obvious fact that sacred texts are creations of the human mind, the products of particular cultures facing particular existential problems.

Of course many theologians recognise this problem – which is why they heroically assert that the Bible or the Koran or whatever is *unchanging*, composed of infallible words of God that cannot be tampered with by fallible mortals. Alas, this strategy solves no problems. It totally ignores the internal contradictions of the texts, and also the fortuitous and random circumstances of their genesis. It was human beings who decided what would constitute the sacred texts, and any modern ignorance of the relevant circumstances in early primitive tribes goes no way to establishing the divine character of the surviving words. In short, relatively ignorant men with vested moral and political interests chose, discarded, hacked and cobbled together this or that sentence, this or that paragraph, this or that chapter, to constitute the so-called canonical works. The gods had nothing to do with it. This was a flawed and capricious human enterprise, and no talk of people being inspired to juggle the texts can save the case. No modern student found to be plagiarising off the internet would get away with such undisciplined and arbitrary behaviour.

The matter of interpretation is relevant to many human activities. We all appreciate particular interpretations of pieces of music and theatrical performances; language translators are concerned to provide reliable interpretations of oral and written material; scientists need to interpret their data according to consensually agreed protocols; and, at the most basic level, we all need to interpret sensory information as accurately as possible to avoid delusion, hallucination and wrongful assumptions. This last one has represented particular problems for religious believers, for massive edifices of theological dogma have been erected on hallucinatory visions that rational interpretation would see as no more than interesting psychological experiences that say nothing about the real world.[7] And textual translations have brought further difficulties. If different translators disagree about how a text should be rendered, who are we to settle the matter? The theologian A. C. Bouquet (1884–1976) has pointed out that religious enthusiasts can make assumptions about texts without ever having read them; and the quality of texts can be wrongly judged as 'it is often assumed that the translators have found it easy to arrive at the true meaning, which is far from being the case, since *some of the texts are capable of very diverse renderings*, and must not in any case be modernized, if they are to be judged fairly' (emphasis added).[8] This, he suggests, is especially true of the Gathas, the Upanishads and the proverbial sayings of Confucius. In fact Bouquet is unconsciously making a broader point, which is bound to be unwelcome to believers. We can never be sure that a translation is accurate, and even the original is inevitably prone to error since perhaps the scribe was having a bad day or he was not listening carefully when the god was dictating.[9] (The issue of the reliability of sacred texts is considered in more detail below.) And what of supposedly sacred texts – such as Joseph Smith's *Book of Mormon*, allegedly translated from golden plates mysteriously donated to Smith by the angel Moroni, and Mary Baker Eddy's *Science and Health with Key to the Scriptures* – which both appear in

English and claim to be faithful interpretations of English translations of the Bible? The plot thickens.

It does not help that the sacred character of the texts implies that mere human beings should not deign to tamper with them – so the Koran, for example, should not be held in dirty hands, placed beneath other books or used as diversionary reading in the lavatory; and the task of translation is particularly fraught. What non-Arabic speaker can presume to say what Allah wrote? Early literature was not uniquely associated with religion, but sacred texts were an essential part of any developed belief system. In Tibet the only word for 'literature' was synonymous with 'religious literature'; in Western courts people swear on sacred books; synagogues protect their priceless Judaic writings; and the Catholic inquisitors were keen that torture instruments should carry inscriptions from the Bible. With religious words being so important in all societies, it is not surprising that much of human creativity has focused on the creation of verbal materials that supposedly bring believers closer to their gods. The sheer wealth of sacred literature considered by Bouquet and others is a testament not only to human inventiveness but also to the human indifference to philosophical consistency. It seems that whatever you believe or want to believe regarding supernatural or ethical matters, there is a sacred text to underwrite it.[10]

The central purpose of the sacred texts is to give meaning to supernatural belief systems. Of course, not all the texts deal with otherworldly phenomena – some, as with Confucius and some Buddhist schools, are more interested in ethical protocols, rules for life – but most are bothered by the gods and what people can expect after death. The texts sometimes contain poetry, parables, historical chronologies, analyses of battles and so on, but the underlying theme generally concerns the fate that powerful divinities will inflict on wayward or virtuous human beings once their disembodied souls escape the flesh. And in this context the most common theme in the major religious texts is God – its nature and intentions in the vast scheme of things. The Bible suggests that man was made in God's image, from which we are not intended to believe that an ageing deity – it has been around for a long time – suffers from a thickening waistline or erectile dysfunction. The Koran suggests that God will torture many men and more women for all eternity, while at the same time managing to be compassionate and merciful. Happily the atheist does not have to make sense of such unpleasant nonsense. For the believer the unanswerable question remains – what is God? Or, put in linguistic terms, what does 'God' mean?

The entity denoted by 'God' is often portrayed in terms of a sum of attributes. So God is changeless, loving, wrathful, transcendent etc. The fact that many incompatible qualities are often assigned to the same entity causes confusion, obvious paradoxes to be resolved or ignored, contradictions that may impress the pious observer or irritate the unbeliever. It is sometimes suggested – by people who would never embrace absurdity in any other context – that God's manifest contradictions are a sign of its greatness. This is a useful ploy, analogous to how the Christian mysteries show the glory of the faith. Here the underlying logic is age old. If something is manifestly incomprehensible but at the same time has to be believed, say that human ignorance is merely contrasted with the greatness of the deity. This of course is the logic of the primitive mind – to bow down before the inexplicable force, be it sun, rain or god, that shapes human destiny.

The term 'God' has variously denoted beings, persons, souls, forces, essences, powers, grounds, spirits, absolutes, presences, infinities and so on and so forth. (In the same way 'religion' has come to mean many different things, so, if inclined, you opt for the one that best suits your own psychology.) The term has proved to be promiscuous in its range of applications. The God of today is not the God of yesterday or the God of tomorrow, thus making the divine entity just as vulnerable to evolutionary pressures as any biological system in the observable world. The word 'God' remains useful, even when the semantic framework shifts, acquiring new layers of significance or connotation, like rust or barnacles. It is of course obvious that 'God' exists – you have sensory corroboration of the symbol – but the existence of God is an entirely different matter. In this context the religious contortions are truly remarkable.

The modern philosopher Alister Hardy (1896–1985) went so far as to consider the biology of God, by which he meant that Man's 'experience of what may be called God' has 'some biological connections'. What Hardy is implying here is that human emotional behaviour, 'both sexual and religious', is explicable in biological terms – to modern science, nothing surprising here.[11] (Of course the book is mistitled: it should have been *The Biology of Religious Belief*, but perhaps the marketing department wanted a more catch-penny label.) The French Jesuit Pierre Teilhard de Chardin (1881–1955) liked to regard evolutionary biology as an upward development towards God, suggesting that evolution 'proceeds towards spirit' and that God is both the power 'within' evolution and the goal 'ahead of creation' to which evolution aspires. So Darwinism is enlisted to interpret the meaning of 'God', revealing Teilhard de Chardin's failure to grasp that evolution needs no spiritual infusion to make it work.

The countless primitive meanings of 'God' (or 'gods') derived essentially from terror and superstition. In simple animism, malign supernatural forces were everywhere – in rivers and trees, storms and malformed babies, crops and natural disaster – inducing fear and attempts at propitiation. Even stones could be interpreted in anthropomorphic terms. Thus in *The Attis of Caius Valerius Catullus* (translated by Grant Allen in 1892) we encounter simple folk who worshipped 'very large stones, saying that they were once men'; likewise the Iroquois Indians reckoned that stones were, in some mysterious sense, living human beings. In 1880 the American Report of the Bureau of Ethnology noted tales from native folklore that describes the metamorphoses of men into stones. So God models can be born in absurdity as well as in terror.

Some ideas about God go far beyond the fantasies of ignorant tribes: there are relatively sophisticated absurdities as well. From Indian philosophy we learn that God is full of good qualities but is also 'acosmic, qualityless, indescribable'. Moreover, 'the cosmic Brahman is regarded as the cause of production, maintenance and destruction of the universe' and 'all things arise from Him, live in Him and are absorbed by Him'.[12] This sort of thing is par for the religious course. Once we are told that God has many good qualities, we are invited to believe that he is 'qualityless'. I feel no obligation to make sense of any of this, only to stress that such meaningless jargon typically permeates the pious mind. By contrast, the Sankhya creed, originating in the eleventh century, began as a theistic creed but evolved through monism to atheism. Here it was found that the God hypothesis was redundant at best, contradictory at worst: the paradox of a free god creating a world of pain and misery was seen as inescapable – but perhaps God is subject to the law of karma, in which case it is not free. In addition, the Sankhya believers introduced a subtle argument that hinted at the modern conservation laws of physics. A physical world could not spring from a non-physical entity, as God is supposed to be: if God is 'pure knowledge, this material world cannot spring from Him'.[13]

In the more familiar mythologies of the West the many God models are unashamedly anthropomorphic. Zeus is supreme in physical strength, a manifest virtue; Odin is the supreme war maker (with war depicted as 'the oldest law') – these and other deities sped down to help their favourites, much in the way that Christian saints appeared during battles in the Americas, according to testimonies by the Spanish conquistadors. Similarly the Celtic god Lugh, protected by a golden helmet and breastplate, fought on battlefields and restored dead warriors to life by dipping them in a magic well. God as magician, a miracle worker – a model that has enjoyed much popularity over the centuries. And the gods, manifestly 'made in man's image', have frequently shown jealousy, greed and lust. Hence W. Raymond Drake, espousing the 'gods as spacemen' notion, asks: 'Who could lock up their daughters against the lust of the gods?' 'God' is often represented as a symbol, but we should remember that gods have often been *sex* symbols, eager to copulate with human women and so to sire mythical figures such as Hercules, Mithras and, indeed, Jesus Christ. (Now I hear you ask: 'Jesus, mythical?' See below.)

There is also the problem of whether God is one or more. Primitive polytheism was once widespread and in some sense still is (in Chapter 1 we noticed that the design argument conducts us to many intelligences framing the world), since mainstream Islam and Christianity both insist that we believe in angels, demons, jinn and the like – demi-gods all – and even the Catholic saints have a quasi-divine status, able to hear prayers and work miracles. I have always wondered at the multitasking abilities of God, but of course it has always delegated magic powers to spread the workload. Perhaps there is a divine designer of trees, a divine designer of the rabies virus, and a divine designer of big cats that eat the testicles of living mammals. So perhaps God is one and a delegator, but that still leaves the problem of the Trinity.

Here I am reminded of the answer to the young boy asking a teacher to explain the Trinity: 'Three in one, one in three . . . it's obvious. Any doubts, see the maths master.' Of course the Trinity is a leftover from the divine trinities of paganism in which father, mother and child were revered with superstitious awe, as in Egyptian and Hellenistic belief systems. Christianity, as befitted a comprehensive misogyny, was forced to jettison the woman in favour of something more acceptable (and more incomprehensible). On the doctrine of the Trinity the Catholic theologian Hans Küng has been forced to remark: 'Even in Catholic churches it is frequently possible to hear either a scarcely intelligible explanation of traditional teaching or a deafening silence.'[14] And he cites the case of the Bavarian priest who announced to his congregation that the Trinity was so great a mystery, of which he understood nothing, that unfortunately on that day there would be no sermon. In fact the main contribution of the Christian Trinity – traceable to the third century and introduced by Pope John XXII for the whole church in 1334 – was to bring further confusion to a belief system already layered in mystery and obfuscation.

Christian art struggled to cope with the concept of the Trinity in various ways: triangles and even three-faced deities (*trikephalos*) appeared in paintings as artists tried to depict the sacredness of an idea which none of them understood. In the eighteenth century Benedict XIV warned against the frequent depiction of the Trinitarian concept as three men with one figure. Speculation about the nature of a triune god did nothing to dispel the air of confusion that has persisted throughout church history. We see the difficulty in Küng (and others): 'It is essentially a question of the *right coordination of God, Jesus* (Son, Word, Christ) *and Spirit* that brings out both the real distinction and the undivided unity.'[15] So paradox is celebrated, mystery is a virtue, and language is used to obscure rather than to illuminate.

The words are familiar enough in Christian orthodoxy. The Christian deity is depicted as 'the union of God the Father, God the Son, and God the Holy Ghost – a threefold diversity within the never-doubted unity of the divine life'.[16] In such a fashion we are urged to equate one and three as a mark of pious insight, and so what can we say of a creed that so blatantly celebrates such an affront to common sense? The problem is often admitted by religious thinkers who typically don't have a clue what it all means. The Christian A. R. Peacocke, for one, notes that the Trinity 'can easily be reduced to what appears to be arithmetical nonsense'. But he should take heart. Mere nonsense has never been allowed to inhibit the proclaiming of the doctrine. The trick is simply to rely on the old formula of declaiming the incomprehensibility of God: the affirmation of the Trinity 'remains the over-arching keystone of the Christian insight and its very difficulty serves to remind us that a complete harmonization of all our understanding of God lies beyond human language and imaginings and beyond life itself'.[17] This is a familiar ploy. Religious apologists use language where they can, and where they cannot they proclaim the mystery and wonder of their abject failure.

If God becomes synonymous with the 'laws of nature', as he did for the seventeenth-century philosopher Benedict de Spinoza, or with the 'ground of our being', as he did for John Robinson, Bishop of Woolwich during the 1960s, he can no longer do for people what they wish of him. He can no longer comfort in times of adversity, justify an afterlife, wreak vengeance on one's enemies, reward believers for their piety, and in general under-write a person's take on reality. Sir Leslie Stephen wrote in *An Agnostic's Apology*: 'The word God is used by the metaphysician and the savage. It may mean anything from "Pure Being" down to the most degraded fetish.' But it is only when science got going that God became 'Pure Being'. The fetish is essentially an empirical concept, understandable in empirical terms, but 'Pure Being' is a typical piece of theological nonsense, graphically exposing the religious dilemma. If God is not part of the world then it is a meaningless irrelevance; if God *is* part of the world then scientists are likely to investigate it as they would any other empirical entity. The philosopher A. J. Ayer pointed out that any investigation of the word 'God' quickly exposes its vacuity: 'The mere existence of the noun [God] is enough to foster the illusion that there is a real, or at any rate a possible, entity corresponding to it. It is only when we enquire what God's attributes are that we discover that "God" . . . is not a genuine name.'[18]

Let's assume, to simplify matters, that there is one god and that it has certain attributes. What might these be? The 'standard proofs' for God's existence are intended to be independent arguments for establishing that a deity exists. But if valid (I think they are all demonstrably false) then they individually establish various particular attributes of God. So it may be a creator, a designer, a moral source and so on. But even all this is insufficient for the true believer — it is essential also that the one true God, needing yet more remarkable talents, be omnipotent, omniscient, omnipresent, perfect, indivisible, immanent, transcendent, immutable and all the rest of the mysterious and baffling synonyms. In addition, God needs to be a person. Only as a person can God fulfil the task required of it, the 'it' being conveniently transmuted into a 'he' (never a 'she', except in feminist satire). Only when God has emotions, knowledge, intelligence etc. can he satisfy the people who are desperate to believe in him.

It is important in this context not to neglect the quota of celestial emotion, the capacity of the deity to experience pleasure, distress and other feelings. It is obvious that the God of the Old Testament is capricious, wrathful and brutal; and that the Allah of the Koran relishes the torture of helpless people in Hell. All this requires a highly emotional divine disposition. An introductory booklet to Catholicism, in answer to the question 'Why did God make me?', offers the illuminating answer 'Because He liked the idea of me'. Did God create paedophiles and mass murderers because he 'liked the idea' of them? Similarly the Catholic catechism defines 'sin' as 'something that displeases God'. God, so depicted, is an oddly vulnerable fellow, likely to be distressed if we commit adultery or eat meat on Fridays. Is someone with such fragile sensitivities really fit to be the CEO of the universe?

It is alleged that God is interested in the fate of human beings, and that he provides various routes for their salvation as a rebirth to eternal bliss. This means, in traditional theology, that if they do as he commands he will protect them from demonic influences in this life and refrain from torturing them in the next. Thus the demonologist Merrill Unger comments that 'when men [and women] violate the moral laws of God, they subject themselves to the satanic yoke that binds them in opposition to God and brings them under the sway of occult powers in the hidden realm of evil supernaturalism'.[19] In such an alarming situation there is obviously a great need for salvation – from demons, death and eternal torture. It all stems from the natural human fear of extinction.

It is significant that, for example, Golden Age mythologies describe a time when there was no death, and a later period of degeneration, when mortality was introduced to the human race through mischance or sin. In Greek mythology death originated – like the cosmos of the theologians – at a particular time. Night gave birth to Doom (Moros), to Fatal Violence (Cer) and to Death (Thanatos) – then Sleep and the retinue of Dreams were born. In Vedic mythology the abstract Absolute (Mahabharata), without beginning or end, was identified with both Time and Death, which absorb all things and bring them to nothingness. In Egyptian mythology the monstrous figure of Zurvan-Chronos, assigned the attributes of Time, has been linked with Iranian deism, which posits a dual concept: namely, *zrvan-akarans* ('infinite time') and *zrvan-dareghochvadhata* ('time of long dominion'), this latter being finite time, the source of decay and death in the world. An ancient Pahlavi text declares: 'For Zurvan there is no remedy. From death there is no escape.'

All this pessimism conducts us to another role of God – that of saviour. Reality is a pretty bleak affair and so it is necessary that the deity act as a protective father, a sort of celestial comfort blanket. If religion cannot be flavoured to serve as a reliable prop for fragile human beings in a frightening world, then it loses much of its purpose. But even this obvious role could not be guaranteed. In the Greece of Homer men survived their deaths, yet in the *Iliad* Hecuba could still say to Andromache: 'Death cannot be what life

is, child. The cup of Death is empty, and Life hath always hope.'
And in the same vein a dead wife in Egyptian mythology addresses
her husband and implies that death is always the victor: 'Death, his
name is "Come"; every one to whom he calleth comes to him . . .
The great and the small alike rest with him . . . All men fear and
make petition before him.' But it is all a waste of time, since Death
'turns not his face towards them . . . He hearkens not, even though
any manner of bribe be given to him.' This is all a somewhat
gloomy picture, from which Christianity, Islam and other religions
promise escape. God as a multitasking saviour – another of his
roles. But there are many hazards on the way, not least because it
suits the theologians to keep people terrified and insecure.

The Christian *good news* is not stated without ambiguity. We are
told, for instance, that at the time of the Second Coming, we will
see 'the abomination of desolation' (Matthew 24: 15), which
will weigh heavily on pregnant and lactating women; and we are
urged to fear the god who is able to destroy both the body and the
soul in hell (Matthew 10: 28). Here there is not much comfort or
solace. Instead, we are encouraged to fear, to tremble and to feel
insecure. The Abrahamic religions promise salvation – on the
terms specified by a brutal celestial tyrant – but they do not want
to make it all sound too easy. In this harsh spirit Mohammed
speaks enthusiastically about the Day of Doom 'when the Terror
descends' – that is, when the saved are divided from the damned
and the unbeliever is cast into the flames: 'Lay hold of him and
bind him. Burn him in the fire of Hell, then fasten him with a
chain seventy cubits long. For he did not believe in God, the Most
Great, and nor did he care to feed the destitute. Today he shall be
friendless here; only filth shall be his food, the filth that which
only sinners eat.'[20]

Hence the doctrine of the saviour God is ambivalent. God
cannot save everyone, otherwise what's the point of it all? He has
to be a judge – and not one who is appointed or elected. He's just
there, and accountability and democracy have nothing to do with
it. He rejoices in his role as tyrant, and mere human beings are
impotent in the face of almighty power. Bertrand Russell talks
scathingly of a being of infinite power 'who chooses that children
should die of meningitis, and older people of cancer . . . We shall

have to reckon Nero a saint in comparison with the author of that Plan.'[21] Fortunately there is no reason to believe in any such celestial dictator: 'We are, therefore, spared the necessity for that attitude of impotent hatred which every brave and humane man would otherwise be called upon to adopt towards the Almighty Tyrant.'[22]

The doom of souls, divine vengeance against sinners, is the stock in trade of such religions as Christianity and Islam. Thus we find the vengeful old deity graphically depicted in eighteenth-century hymns – for example, in the *Divine Songs for Children* by Isaac Watts (1674–1748). At Sunday school it was fashionable to tell infants the story of the forty-two children who mocked old Elisha, and who were thereby killed by bears at the behest of the merciful god ('God quickly stopt their wicked breath | And sent two raging bears | That tore them limb from limb to death | With blood, and groans, and tears'). In this context children from one year old should be taught to 'fear the rod and to cry softly; from that age make him do as he is bid, if you whip him ten times to effect it . . . Break his will now, and his soul shall live, and he will probably bless you for all eternity.'[23]

We now have some grasp of what 'God' means, of what God is intended to be. It's not a very savoury package, comprising in the main a set of all-too-human attributes and activities which in any civilised society would get a person thrown into jail. God emerges as a vindictive and capricious egotist, likely to hold a grudge and to punish mercilessly any people he does not like. He is alleged to have demanded and sanctioned human sacrifices,[24] killed the first-born babies and children of Egyptian families, sanctioned slavery and the selling of one's daughter, and urged death for a wide range of human acts – heresy, violation of the Sabbath, cursing one's parents, adultery, blasphemy and unchastity (this latter reserved for women). The Israelites, 'only following [divine] orders', killed men, women and children through conquest on many occasions. Consider for example Joshua 6: 21, which tells how the holy warriors 'utterly destroyed all in the city, both man and woman, young and old, and ox, and sheep, and ass, with the edge of the sword'. In Numbers 31 we find Moses urging his officers to kill 'every male among the little ones, and kill every woman that hath known man', at the time telling the men to keep all the young girls alive 'for yourselves'. This is the work of the law-giver deity, the source of all morality, the divine standard to which mere mortals are supposed to aspire.

We have seen that all this causes problems for pious believers, many of whom are quite decent people. What are they to make of a Judaic god who urges piles of foreskins from slaughtered men to be built, a Christian god who urges all who will not be ruled by him to be killed, and an Islamic god who sanctions the rape of slave girls and the merciless extermination of infidels? Today it is generally far too heroic in civilised societies for believers to take the gods at their (holy) word, and so various strategies are adopted. It is easy to ignore what the sacred texts say, to pretend that they say something entirely different, to look to 'new' or 'modern' interpretations, and to recast God as a largely non-human phenomenon. This last ploy puts the deity beyond the reach of probing rationalists but entirely defeats the object. As noted, the character of God has to have some human elements, if it is to work.

Some modern theologians have liked the idea of God somehow being 'at the root of our existence', 'the sustaining presence', 'the ground of our being' and such like. We all know that the 'ground' model is most closely associated with the once Bishop of Woolwich, Dr John Robinson, formerly fellow and dean of Clare College, Cambridge. In March 1963 he published an article, 'Our Image of God Must Go', in *The Observer* – and provoked a heated nationwide debate. Within a few days of the article appearing, SCM Press published the associated book, *Honest to God*; and for the first time in many years the anti-intellectual English found themselves discussing the profoundest religious and metaphysical topics, though they managed to recover from it before too long.[25] Within months, hundreds of thousands of copies of the book, a conveniently small paperback, had been sold, with translations hastily arranged for editions in German, French, Swedish, Dutch, Danish, Japanese, Italian and other languages. The bishop was soon widely perceived to be a radical, if not an atheist. In fact *Honest to God* was clearly an atheist tract, though a dishonest one, since it struggled to dress up imaginary religious concepts in secular language – sometimes on the level of the theologian who states that 'everyone believes in God, but some people don't know it'.

In Chapter 3 of the book we are invited to consider 'The Ground of Our Being', a largely meaningless phrase otherwise known as 'A Depth at the Centre of Life'. Such phrases have a ring to them, but to suggest the ring of truth is an altogether different matter. The influential theologian Paul Tillich (1886–1965) also preferred 'depth' to 'height', the better to convey the nature of God and ultimate truth – which perhaps suggests that important people should be called 'Your Depth' or 'Your Lowness' instead of 'Your Highness'. Robinson quickly leads us to a definition of 'the infinite and inexhaustible depth and ground of all being'. This, we are told, is our *ultimate concern, what we take seriously without reservation.* So if we value anything, if anything is ultimately important to us, then we are believers. A neat trick! Atheists are defined out of existence: most people, we can assume, value something. We may as well define religious believers as all those who believe that food and drink and oxygen will sustain their lives: not many exceptions to that, though perhaps we should wonder about Christian Scientists, who have eccentric medical theories of their own.

Tillich, quoted approvingly by Robinson, is prepared to go further. God, we learn, has acquired too many layers of confusing associations. Now there's a surprise. For example, we are inclined to think of God as a being 'out there'; so, declares Tillich, 'you must forget everything traditional that you have learned about God, perhaps even the word itself'.[26] With such a sleight of hand God goes, and so does 'God' – and all this from the respected theologian Robinson (until he became known as the 'atheist bishop'). In this view theological statements are not to be regarded as describing the 'highest Being' but the depths of our emotional natures. But then Robinson loses his nerve and we are back in familiar territory. The *ground of our being* is 'the love of God in Christ Jesus our Lord'. So much for forgetting 'even the word itself'.

The atheist bishop did not stop there. In 1965 he published *The New Reformation?*, which failed to explode in the national consciousness like the earlier text, but which clearly deserves equal attention.[27] If anyone still doubted that Robinson was an atheist he was happy to confirm it here, but not many people noticed. The titles of the first two chapters – 'Troubling of the Waters' and 'Starting from the Other End' – suggest an element of dissidence, hints of further attacks on orthodoxy, but it is Appendix I, 'Can a Truly Contemporary Person *Not* Be an Atheist?', that is genuinely devastating from the pen of an Anglican bishop. Here Robinson offers three summary statements and considers each in turn:

> God is intellectually superfluous.
>
> God is emotionally dispensable.
>
> God is morally intolerable.[28]

The conclusions, unlike much of the material in *Honest to God*, are clear and direct. Any attempt to bring in God to fill the gaps in our science or to deal with life's many difficult questions is 'intellectual laziness or practical superstition'. In support Robinson quotes *Letters and Papers from Prison*, by the theologian Dietrich Bonhoeffer (1906–1945):

> Man has learned to cope with all questions of importance without recourse to God as a working hypothesis . . . It has become increasingly true of religious questions also . . . Everyone gets along without 'God', and just as well as before . . . What we call 'God' is being edged out of human life.

In *The Secular Meaning of the Gospel* Paul van Buren, another religious thinker, makes the same point with his graphic example of the mythical garden with a gardener who can never be detected. The Believer says: 'But there is a gardener, invisible, intangible, insensible to electric shocks [an electrified fence has been set up to detect him], a gardener who has no scent and makes no sound [bloodhounds detect nothing], a gardener who comes secretly to look after the garden which he loves.' The Sceptic despairs: 'Just how does what you call an invisible, intangible, eternally elusive gardener differ from an imaginary gardener or no gardener at all?' Robinson concludes this section by urging believers to feel the 'full force' of the atheist's attack.

Then Robinson declares that it is impossible to save the traditional Christian father-figure from death using artificial respiration. Jesus makes an occasional appearance from time to time, but in a desultory way that adds nothing to the destructive analysis. Even prayer is demolished. Does it help to pray that the plane will 'make it and leave the ground'? – 'I think not . . . This is where the Christian *ought* to be a practical atheist – and trust the pilot.'[29] And finally God *is* morally intolerable. Robinson quotes a nineteen-year-old girl interviewed in the *Daily Mirror* who used to believe in God but now finds it impossible: 'I don't see how there can be a benevolent God. There are too many tragedies – personal and in the world . . . RELIGION IS DISGUSTING.'[30] So does the salaried Anglican bishop attempt a riposte? Quite the contrary: 'Religion is disgusting. God does not solve the problem of suffering: he only marginalises it. To push off evil on to God simply makes him into a Devil – and in any case represents a cowardly evasion.'[31]

Robinson then considers what is to be done *post mortem dei.* This is a tricky one for the bishop and we do not need to dwell on his lapse back into opaque prose, but his dramatic conclusion leaps from the page – *the obituary read by the atheist is valid, even if sometimes shrill.*[32] So, says the churchman, God is dead and that's that. We are forced to consider Appendix II, 'Spiritual Education in a World without Religion' in which God, having being roundly dismissed a few pages earlier, pops up again like a vampire at nightfall.

The task, as always, was to make sense out of traditional religious language which had passed its sell-by date, in the hope that enough verbal contortions would allow a vast body of jargon to survive in the modern age. The problem was well recognised. For example, the philosopher Peter Donovan, in a book exploring religious language, felt compelled to include an early chapter entitled 'Avoiding Empty Talk'.[33] Here it is deemed necessary to propose tests or observations 'not so much with putting meaning into the completely meaningless or explaining the utterly nonsensical' –

who'd have thought of any such thing? – but as substantiating 'what are otherwise at best pretenders to, or candidates for, informativeness'.[34] In short, the task of the sympathetic linguistic philosopher is to show that seemingly vacuous (religious) statements can mean something. Why bother?

It is reasonable to suggest that religious language, highly ambitious, is in fact nonsense. It fits neatly into the syntax of language, creating the illusion of meaning, but in fact conveys no information about the world. It is a closed symbolic system, defining this or that meaningless word in terms of this or that other meaningless word, phrase or book. The self-contained nature of the jargon conveys the impression that important matters are being covered, if only they could be understood – so the symbols carry the connotation of expertise, like the language of physics and chemistry.

This situation is well illustrated by a quotation used by C. K. Ogden and I. A. Richards in their classic *The Meaning of Meaning*:

> Suppose someone were to assert: *The gostak distims the doshes.* You do not know what this means; nor do I. But if we assume that it is English, we know that *the doshes are distimmed by the gostak.* We know too that *one distimmer of doshes is a gostak.* If, moreover, the *doshes* are *galloons*, we know that *some galloons are distimmed by the gostak.* And so we may go on, and so we often do go on.[35]

Here the argument suggests that if the rules of syntax are followed, totally meaningless symbols can be manipulated to create the impression that something intelligible is being conveyed. If the structure of the propositions and the appearance of the symbols suggest that some of the words are verbs, others plurals, others subclasses etc., then the vacuous manipulation can go on endlessly. This is exactly what happens in theological language when efforts are made to describe God in terms of transcendence, divinity in terms of perfection, deity in terms of immanence and so on. A gostak may distim a dosh. An immanent deity may be the ground of our being. It's all the same really.

This, then, is what the religious apologist is reduced to – having to say that God is a humanlike super-creature of the universe (living where exactly?), or struggling to breathe some semantic significance into vacuous symbols. Not a job I'd relish. Today it is easy to see how believers have arrived at this predicament. One particular problem is that they have been forced to rely on texts the genesis of which is shrouded in confusion, mystery and all the hazards of human fallibility.

All the major religions, and many of the minor ones, have adherents who like to believe that their sacred texts arrived on earth in a pristine form, complete and bearing the imprint of a divine hand. In this context human beings simply received the tablets or the recitation, and then prostrated themselves before the wonder of it all. There is no suggestion in this view of things that ordinary people were involved in writing the texts, editing them, discarding items they did not like, and generally shaping what would eventually emerge as an approved body of work on which all the alleged certainties of religious belief could rest. Who were mere human beings to tamper with the word of the Almighty? In fact at every stage the sacred texts were tailored to particular purposes by people with various axes to grind. There was no divine authorship, no celestial voice dictating from on high, no angels delivering messages. No god spoke to Moses on a mountain, the archangel Gabriel did not communicate with Mary and Mohammed, no magic tablets in a strange language were delivered to L. Ron Hubbard. Instead a variety of human beings, with great ambitions and perhaps mental disease, generated a wealth of confused and highly influential texts, and shaped them over the months, years and centuries to come. It seems that most of the faithful, content to rely on authority, did not notice the process that was under way.

It is alleged that sometimes God presented physical scrolls to likely recipients, with the aim of supplanting earlier writings. Ezekiel was instructed by the deity to eat the roll he was carrying, and then also to eat a new roll that God was offering ('fill thy bowels with this roll that I give thee'),[36] perhaps a magical way of acquiring fresh wisdom, just as a savage would aim to acquire new strength by devouring the testicles of a fallen warrior. Anyway it saved all that messy business of reading, understanding and remembering. Once Ezekiel had eaten the new roll ('it was in my mouth as honey for sweetness') he was able to speak to the house of Israel. But, fortunately, not all the scrolls were eaten. Many of the Jewish exiles from Jerusalem brought scrolls to Babylon, which they studied and edited.[37] The scribes felt free to edit as they saw fit, to add new texts and to adapt the material to the new circumstances. There was no suggestion in any of this that the scrolls contained unique divine knowledge that should be preserved intact. Later generations added further to the corpus of written material, thus enshrining its essentially human character.

In one of the older extant accounts Moses, allegedly inspired by God, passed on the divine instructions orally; but later reformers preferred the idea that he had 'put all the commands of *Jahweh* into writing' and read the results to the people.[38] God judged this to be insufficient, so, as related in Exodus, he instructed Moses to climb Mount Sinai to receive 'tables of stone, and a law, and commandments [the Ten Commandments] which I have written; that thou mayest teach them'.[39] The religious writer and ex-nun Karen Armstrong points out that the next book of the Bible, Deuteronomy, is 'an entirely new scripture', following the familiar reform custom of attributing fresh ideas to figures of the past: 'In other words, this was what Moses would say to Josiah if he were delivering a "second law" today.'[40] Put simply, human beings with new ideas were happy to inject their thoughts into the sacred texts and to assume that unquestioning followers would regard the new material as the Word of God. In addition the scribes 'actually changed the wording of earlier law codes, sagas and liturgical texts to make them endorse their proposals . . . [They introduced] radical change . . . adding fresh material.'[41] So much for divine authorship.

Any interpretation of the Bible requires extensive judgements on what is intended to be literal truth and what allegorical insight – and these shift over the generations. What was regarded as factual material yesterday is seen as figurative or metaphorical today, and what is accepted as true today will probably be discarded tomorrow. Again this endless process vitiates any pretence that the Bible and other sacred texts are the unchanging message of this or that deity. The task of detailed exegesis, as performed by such scholars as Armstrong and others, offers a perennial quest to uncover meaning, to determine how one text relates to another, to emphasise the shifting character of material that the faithful laity sees as immutability and inspired. But there is little in all this of how any deity communicates with human beings. We can learn about St Benedict's *lectio divina* ('sacred study') and Martin Luther's *sola scriptura* ('scripture alone') but such historical detail offers few philosophical insights. Such material is an inevitable diversion from the central difficulty in establishing that there is a god behind it all. The atheist is happy to note that exegesis serves to emphasise the essentially human character of all religious texts. This is not something that the religious believer wants to hear.

Armstrong emphasises that if we want to understand someone, we must assume that 'he or she is speaking the truth'.[42] But she should have added 'as they see it'. We cannot assume that even an honest person never lapses into conveying falsehoods. Armstrong's *allegoria*, an 'attempt to find truth in texts that seem barbarous and opaque and then [to] "translate" them into a more congenial idiom',[43] is a recipe for infinite gullibility and confusion. With such an approach it could never be concluded that people were simply mistaken or, as happens all the time in theology, uttering meaningless sounds. The writer N. L. Wilson is quoted in support. A critic who is approaching alien material should adopt the 'principle of charity', seeking an interpretation that 'will maximise truth among the sentences of the corpus'.[44] The same point applies – abandon the rules of rational analysis, abandon proper scrutiny. What does 'maximising truth' mean? Propositions are either true – making due allowance for mathematical concepts of probability – or they are not. Imagine a scientist struggling to 'maximise the truth' of hypotheses based on inaccurate data. It is hard to avoid the conclusion that the 'principle of charity' is an excuse for sloppy thinking.

It is acknowledged that in the modern world the Bible 'is in danger of becoming a dead or irrelevant letter . . . derided – often unfairly – by secular fundamentalists . . . a toxic arsenal that fuels hatred and sterile polemic'.[45] But here the implication is that in earlier times the Bible was *not* a source of conflict and empty disputation. In fact all the sacred texts have traditionally diverted people from social reform and the accumulation of knowledge about the world. In its early days the church frequently became involved in 'sterile polemic'. Later, when it gained social and political power, the Inquisition 'fuelled hatred' and social turmoil. It is useful to remember that, as Armstrong has demonstrated, the history of the church does not exhibit one fixed, divinely inspired corpus of textual material but an untidy conglomeration of vacuous theorising, empty pontificating and rank absurdity.

Once the Christian church had won secular power in Rome under the brutal imperium of Constantine, it seemed that many of the old theological disputes had been settled. The church had repelled, mainly by suppression, any existing cultish or pagan challenges, and it was content to bask in its new social status. But no sooner had the church escaped from centuries of persecution than it was shattered by a fresh wave of internal dissent, namely, the Arian controversy. This was the first of many theological crises that the ecclesiastical authorities, now secure under state protection, were forced to face. It revealed the proneness of religious creeds to schism and disarray: in the absence of any consensually agreed protocols for seeking objective truth, dissidents can always make inroads into the fabric of orthodoxy.

Arius (c.250–336) was born in Libya, trained in Antioch and became a presbyter in Alexandria. So what was the controversy that rocked the early church? He claimed that in the doctrine of the Trinity the Son was not co-equal or co-eternal with the Father, but only the first and highest of all finite beings, created by God as an act of celestial free will. This was serious stuff – to the point that Arius was excommunicated in 321 by a synod of bishops, but this did not settle the matter and the controversy continued to rage. Then the special Council of Nicaea was called in 325 to settle the issue once and for all. Here it was decided that the divine essence had an absolute unity, and that the three persons of the Trinity were equal. Arius died in Constantinople, but the dispute continued until it was finally suppressed by the end of the fourth century.

There were many pitfalls on the way to a solution. On one occasion the cleric Eusebius of Caesarea read out an influential creed at Nicaea, which he hoped all would accept, but some thought it insufficient to rule out all Arian possibilities. There was then much debate about *homoousios* ('the same substance') which led to some small alterations. Finally an express repudiation of the Arians was included to define a creed that began with the words:

> We believe in one God the Father all-sovereign, maker of all things both visible and invisible. And in one Lord Jesus Christ the Son of God, begotten from the Father as only begotten God from God, that is from the very being of the Father, light from light, very God from very God, sharing one being with the Father . . .[46]

This, please note, is a *clarification*.

It wasn't over. The issue was raised again at the Council of Antioch in 341 – then, as today, there were 'conservatives' and 'moderates'. The latter succeeded in winning acceptance for yet another redrafting of the creed to expunge any residual hints of Arianism;[47] in 343 a contingent of Western bishops expressed opposition to any further tinkering; in 344–5 yet another synod met to deal with the case of Bishop Stephen, who had proposed a fresh version of the 341 creed . . . and so it went on until 381, when the final victory of the Nicene interpretation was achieved at the Council of Constantinople. Still, dissidents were keen to dispute church consensus on various topics – so we encountered Apollinarianism, Nestorianism, Eutychianism, Pelagianism and others.[48] Throughout its history the Christian church has been rent by division, dispute and controversy – in the early days over matters of 'sterile polemic', and in modern times over such doctrines as contraception, the role of women, homosexual priests, just war and papal infallibility. Much of the early discord related to 'substance metaphysics' – were God and Christ made of the same stuff? But the absurdity of such disputation gradually penetrated the clerical mind, and other contentious issues took the floor. As always, there were ample texts within the tradition to support any position.

The matter of God was never settled, as noted. Was it a real person or an abstract and eternal essence? And the matter of Christ proved to be equally problematic. Forgetting such imponderables as whether or not God and Jesus were made out of the same spiritual substance, what can be said about the nature of Christ himself? Most people outside the United States seem to have arrived at the view that Jesus was a good man and a moral teacher, but not necessarily the Son of God. Can even this much be said? How, in fact, are the gospels to be interpreted?

The first points to emphasise are that the existing gospels are incompatible with each other in important respects, making contradictory statements about Jesus and other matters; that individual gospels are self-contradictory, carrying incompatible statements within their own texts; and that there is a substantial apocrypha from the Old Testament and a similar apocrypha from the New Testament. This latter constitutes a wide range of documents from the early Christian centuries – gospels, acts, epistles and apocalypses – that are often attributed to New Testament characters but which are not widely accepted as canonical. This underlines a key point made earlier. There is no complete Christian document that suddenly appeared in an unambiguous form. The current material in the New Testament, like the Jewish texts of the Old, was edited, added to, shaped, expanded and reduced according to the whims and prejudices of the early clerics. Doubtless many disputes raged about what should be included and what left out, as a broadly agreed canon eventually emerged over the centuries. Much of the apocryphal material derived from sources that were regarded as heretical, but who was to say? The 'successful' texts were generally the upshot of clerical struggles for power and influence, rather than any analytical studies designed to establish veridical sources. Had a different group of clerics won the day, perhaps we would have an entirely different Jesus today. As just one example, the apocryphal Gospel of Thomas, while conveying much that is familiar about Jesus, carries many elements that cannot be found in the canonical texts. True to the misogynistic flavour of Christianity, Jesus here declares that 'women are not worthy of life' but he will help them to become men so that they 'will enter into the kingdom of heaven'.[49]

As it is, we do not need to be too impressed. The 'gentle Jesus, meek and mild' is obviously a fabrication. Such a creature would not have dared to overturn the money changers' tables. But does an alternative consistent character emerge from the canonical gospels? It is difficult to find one. In the Beatitudes Jesus declared: 'Blessed are the peacemakers,' but elsewhere he points out that he did not come 'to send peace on earth: I came not to send peace, but a sword'; [50] and urged his followers, if they had no sword, to sell their garments to buy one.[51] He urged people to 'resist not evil, but to turn the other cheek', implying forgiveness, but elsewhere declared that anyone who spoke against the Holy Ghost would never be forgiven, 'neither in this world nor in the world to come'.[52] In addition, he urged people to hate their mothers and fathers, and wives and children, so that they could follow him.[53] He had come to earth, after all, to spread domestic discord.[54] And, like Mohammed after him, Jesus had no scientific grasp of reality, damning the fig tree for not bearing fruit out of season[55] and urging people to eat food with dirty hands – when the Pharisees asked him why he ate bread with 'unwashen hands', he replied: 'There is nothing from without a man, that entering into him can defile him.'[56]

The picture of Jesus that emerges from the gospels is of a charismatic but ignorant man, inconsistent in his moral teachings and likely to be violent and intolerant when he encountered hostility or resistance. Like many preachers of the day and since, he was prepared to denounce opponents as a 'generation of vipers' and consign them to 'the damnation of hell'.[57]

Perhaps this allows too much. It assumes what most of the world does, that there was such a person as Jesus and that he lived about two millennia ago. He figures in the New Testament and the Koran, and that means that there are an awful lot of people who believe in his historicity. They debate his nature and purpose, but assume that such a man walked upon the earth (and sometimes the water). But are they right? Is it possible that Jesus was an invention, useful for the creeds of the day but lacking the substance of other historical figures?

The argument that Christ was a mythical figure gains considerable weight from the similarities between the gospels and other contemporary legends. The miraculous birth is paralleled in the traditions associated with Buddha, Krishna, Mithras and many other figures, just as the resurrection is a variant on the theme of the dying and rising god that can be found in many mythological tales. The notion that Jesus was a healer is pre-dated by the Greek god Asclepius, who could work magic to cure the sick and raise the dead. The researcher J. M. Robertson (1856–1933), author of *Christianity and Mythology* (1900) and *Pagan Christs* (1903), at first accepted the historical existence of Jesus but later came to believe that the whole of the gospel tradition was so steeped in super-naturalism that none of it was reliable.[58]

In its early days Christianity was a cult much like most of the others that were thriving at the same time. The researcher H. W. Wood mentions such contemporary cults as the Ebionites, Nazarenes, Naassenes, Ophites, Peratae, Elkesaites and Maneans. Some of these groups practised ritual human sacrifice and cannibalism, as Christianity still does in the modern age.[59] It is likely that the turmoil following the fall of Jerusalem in 70 AD led some of the cults to unite in the face of increased Roman persecution, and to merge some of the myths that had dramatic appeal. Robertson suggested that the Crucifixion and other key elements of Christianity were myths retained because they graphically conveyed the idea of a messiah who sacrificed himself for the sake of his followers. It has been suggested also that the cross is not necessarily the method of crucifixion used to execute Jesus, that in fact he was nailed through his arms to a T-shaped structure commonly used by the Romans for executing criminals.[60] (Muslims, required to believe every word of the Koran, declare that the Romans did not crucify Jesus but someone who looked like him.)[61] Thus Robertson argued in *Pagan Christs* that (a) the gospel story of the last supper, the agony, the betrayal, the crucifixion and the resurrection were demonstrably not originally a narrative, but a mystery-drama 'which had been transcribed with a minimum of modification', and (b) the mystery-drama was 'an evolution from a Palestinian rite of human sacrifice in which the annual victim was "Jesus, the Son of the Father"'. These two propositions were explored in detail by H. G. Wood (1879–1963), who in 1938 noted the use of the 'Christ-myth assumptions in any Marxist anti-God campaign' and aimed to provide a book that 'may serve as a kind of spiritual air raid precaution – a preservative against poison gas'.[62] Wood criticises the Christ-myth school but is still driven to ask whether 'the Christian faith needs a historic Christ'.[63]

Just think of it. After nearly two millennia committed Christians are still wondering whether Jesus actually existed, and whether, if he did not, it would be possible for Christianity to rub along without him. Perhaps, as Wood suggests, to show that Jesus is merely a symbol provides 'a great service to faith' since the term 'symbol' is the watchword of the whole Christian movement. Perhaps the gospels are merely allegories like Bunyan's *Pilgrim's Progress*, with 'the story of the Virgin-birth [enshrining] the way in which truth comes to birth in the pure soul'.[64] Here Wood suggests that 'the miracles in Mark are as purely and as deliberately symbolical as the miracles in John' and that 'the whole tradition concerning Jesus has its value, not as a record of actual facts, but as a symbol of spiritual truths'.[65]

On 25 December 2007 – Christmas Day, of all days – a Channel 4 television programme, *The Hidden Story of Jesus*, emphasised the unreliability of the traditional account of Christ's birth, life and death, and indicated the similarities between Christianity and other early religions. Here we were reminded that Mithras presided over ritual meals involving bread and wine; that the Egyptian god Osiris was baptised in the Nile, died and was resurrected, and was sacrificed as a saviour god; that the Hindu god Krishna, like Jesus, had been attended by angels and shepherds; that Buddha had been tempted by the Devil, walked on water and fed a multitude; and that, according to Muslims, Jesus will return at the end of time – and later occupy a tomb already prepared for him next to that of Mohammed in Medina. Krishna had an immaculate conception and his birth was attended by angels; wise men travelled to see Buddha soon after his birth, and he espoused the Buddhist equivalent to 'turn the other cheek': 'If anyone should give you a blow with his hand, with a stick or a knife, you should abandon any desires and utter no evil words.'

The programme also included testimony from Fida Hassnain, the former director of archives, archaeology and museums for Kashmir, who claimed that a wealth of Indian and Tibetan documents proved not only that Jesus visited India but that he died there. Here the accounts – conveyed in many languages

(Persian, Urdu, Kashmiri, Chinese, Sanskrit, Tibetan and Arabic) – sometimes overlap the traditional story. Jesus was born of a virgin and was the son of God, but he married and had a child.

Hence there is ambiguity about Christ's birth, confusion in his teachings, uncertainty about where he died, grave doubts about his very existence as a historical figure. There were some sixty historians active during the first century in the Roman world, and they provide no corroboration of the Jesus story. Where he is mentioned – for example, in Josephus, Tacitus, Suetonius and Pliny the Younger – the material is brief and inconclusive. The gospels were not eyewitness accounts, but were written some forty to eighty years after the death of Jesus. It is highly question-able that any of the sayings attributed to Jesus were ever spoken by a historical figure, but were added later to embellish a very thin tradition. The researcher R. Joseph Hoffman, quoted by Ibn Warraq, concludes:

> It is difficult even to speak of an 'historical' Jesus, given the proportions and immediacy of the myth-making process that characterises the earliest days of the Jesus cult. Whether or not there was a historical founder (and such is not needed . . . for the success of a cult . . .), scholars now count it a certainty that the Gospels are compilations of 'traditions' cherished by the early Christians rather than historical annals.[66]

So what can be said about the principal character, God apart, of the Christian faith? How can a consistent moral message be gleaned from the contradictory texts? Was Jesus born of a virgin, like a host of mythological gods in the ancient world? Did he walk on the water, like Buddha? Was he resurrected, like Osiris? Was he a saviour god, like Mithras? Did he even die in the Middle East? Was he even crucified? Did he even exist? Is all this mythology and uncertain history sufficient to support the vast superstructure of Christian pretension and practice?

This is all mind-numbing stuff. It reflects what has already been indicated in the present chapter – that, by the twentieth century, the most progressive thinkers in Christianity were being driven to examine its most basic categories of belief. God was in trouble –

and, if anyone bothered to look at Robertson, Hassneain and their ilk, so was Jesus. The Catholic Church chose not to notice any of this and, by dint of characteristic obscurantism, was still propagating a superstitious faith that had not yet emerged from the Middle Ages. Outside the suffocating confines of Rome, much of Christian thought was in crisis.[67] Long-held superstitions were being abandoned, much of the teaching was being secularised in one way or another, with many salaried clerics continuing to mouth the old magic formulae without believing a word of them.

Today the greater part of Christianity, as represented by Rome, has not yet fully adjusted to the seventeenth-century teachings of Galileo and is struggling desperately with nineteenth-century Darwinism, but another great world religion is experiencing even greater problems. In the early twenty-first century, Islam has not yet escaped the jinn and the demons in the desert sands of seventh-century Arabia.

The whole of Islam – all the dogmatic scholars, centuries-long schisms, minor and major sects, conservatives, moderates, peace makers, terrorists etc. – rests on the assumed authority of the Koran, the alleged communication of God's message by the archangel Gabriel to an illiterate and ignorant desert dweller. The Koran is about 80,000 words long and comprises 114 chapters (surahs) containing between 6,200 and 6,240 verses. The text itself, a copy of the pure Arabic version in heaven, celebrates its own special nature by saying that it is a transcript of the eternal book (Surah 43: 3) and a well-guarded tablet (Surah 85: 22).

As the allegedly perfect revelation from God, the Koran is often used as a magical charm on the occasions of birth, death and marriage. It must never be obscured by other books or papers, must never be recited when anyone is drinking or smoking, and can serve as a talisman against disease and disaster. Muhammad ibn Muhammad al-Nafzawi, in his erotic classic *The Perfumed Garden*, celebrated the Koran's aphrodisiacal power: 'It is said that reading the Koran also predisposes [the person] for copulation.'

Mohammed (c.570–632) allegedly heard the lengthy Koranic message over a period of years, and informed various scribes and friends as to what it contained. An authorised version of the Koran did not emerge until long after the Prophet's death, with its accuracy supposedly guaranteed by the third caliph, Uthman (see below). Some Muslim scholars (for example Patricia Crone) have found no reliable evidence for the existence of any Koran before the last decade of the seventh century.

The Koran itself, when it eventually emerged as a canonical document, was in fact regarded as insufficient by Muslim believers, and so they supplemented it with the Hadith, the alleged sayings of the prophet and his companions. (This was a useful adjunct for Mohammed since he could claim fresh revelations: for example, that he had been inspired to take yet more wives.) The writer and activist Tariq Ali dubs this a 'wonderful game of Arabian whispers that began in the peninsula and moved to Damascus [and] could not be restricted to four or even five slim volumes'.[68] Hundreds of scholars and scribes, many of them 'intellectually ill equipped for the purpose',[69] were employed in the crucial task of formulating the new tradition defined by the Hadith. This inevitably led to angry disputes about authenticity. Who could say that any particular Hadith was accurate? The scholars disagreed with one another, and so the tradition became confused and unreliable. Today the arguments continue, with nominally highly educated scholars (almost always men) occupied in endless disputation about what should really constitute a part of true Islam: 'The war of traditions still goes on, raising the basic question whether any of them are authentic.'[70] And many of the ambiguities that surround the Hadith also characterise the Koran, potentially a much more serious problem.[71]

There are uncertainties about the proper order of the surahs, with some suggestion that the early surahs had short verses, and the later ones long verses – which has encouraged their categorisation into three Meccan periods and one Medinan, though this approach alone has not solved the dating problem.[72] There is also a suggestion that some of the Koranic material might have originated from non-Arabic sources, since foreign accounts of the mission of Mohammed are different from what the Muslim tradition says. 'On the other hand, there seems little reason to doubt that the Qur'an is *substantially* a document of seventh-century Arabia, although it may have taken some time to assume

its definitive literary form [emphasis added].'[73] Moreover, there
are some elements in the traditional texts that indicate attempts 'to
fit Mohammed into the Near Eastern image of a holy man, and
the Arabian pattern of a noble descent';[74] in addition, the early
writings reflect particular doctrinal controversies, suggesting that
the early tradition was shaped in part by invention and polemic.
All this is bad enough, indicating that the Koran, the Hadith and
the surrounding literary materials are untidy compilations
produced by people with vested interests at different times and in
different places. This is far from a divinely inspired doctrine: it is
a typically confused accretion of contributions from, by today's
standards, ignorant tribesmen who knew little history and no
science.[75] But there is worse. The Koran can be shown to be a
completely unreliable document, totally unable to support the
gullible weight of a billion-plus believers.

It is significant that despite the textual claim that God had made
an Arabic Koran (Surah 12: 2), philologists have argued that it
contains many foreign words: for example, Professor Arthur
Jeffrey found about 275 words in the Koran from Aramaic,
Hebrew, Syriac, Ethiopic, Persian and Greek.[76] It is suggested that
the word 'Koran' itself was taken from the Syriac language.[77]
Other difficulties arise from the chaotic state of the written
materials on Mohammed's death. Many of his followers tried to
gather together what would be a consistent body of sacred texts,
but attempts to produce an authoritative codex in fact produced a
number of competing codices from such scholars as Ibn Mas'ud,
Ubai bin Kab, Ali', Abu Bakr, al-Ash'ari, al-Aswad and others;
and, with the spread of Islam, so-called metropolitan codices
emerged in Mecca, Medina, Damascus, Kufa and Basra.[78] Uthman
tried to bring order to this chaos but the problems remained.

There were still various technical reasons why different interpretations of the Koranic materials were possible. One problem
was that consonantal texts were 'unpointed'; that is, they lacked
the dots used in modern Arabic to distinguish between different
symbols. In addition, since Arabic originally contained no signs for
short vowels, decisions had to be taken at a later date about what
vowels to use – and this in turn allowed different readings of what
were supposed to be unchanging and unambiguous divine texts.

Many different scholastic centres developed with their own ways of pointing and vowelising the texts – which only added to the confusion.[79] The linguist Charles Adams commented:

> It must be emphasised that far from there being a single text passed down inviolate from the time of Uthman's commission, literally thousands of variant readings of particular verses [of the Koran] were known . . . These variants affected even the Uthmanic codex, making it difficult to know what its true original form may have been.'[80]

It was not until the tenth century that the great Koranic scholar Ibn Mujahid (d. 935) managed to standardise the consonants and limit the vowel variations. Even then Muslim scholars were divided about what canonical texts should be accepted; and today, as emphasised by Ibn Warraq, the survival of several variants presents problems for Muslims wanting to believe in the unchanging and unambiguous word of God. One strategy has been to conceal various extant codices in order to create the impression that the variants no longer exist. In addition, it is possible to identify stylistic weaknesses in the Arabic Koran, verses missing, verses added, and serious contradictions from one verse to another.[81]

Warraq emphasises the much-rehearsed moral weaknesses of God, an allegedly omnipotent, omniscient and benevolent creature that reveals itself as 'a petulant tyrant, unable to control his recalcitrant subjects . . . proud [and] jealous . . . all moral deficiencies'. If God is self-sufficient and all-powerful, why does he need the help of humans; and, above all, 'why does He pick an obscure Arabian merchant in some cultural backwater to be His last messenger on earth?' Why should this allegedly supreme moral being demand praise and worship from the creatures he has allegedly created?[82] Finally Warraq argues that the historical material in the Koran is inaccurate, that Islam is a religion of fear, that the moral precepts – amputation, crucifixion, the immurement of women, flogging etc. – are barbaric. Much of this is not a matter of interpretation but the literal word of the Koran that has survived from one historical codex to another.[83]

Hence the Koran, the foundation of Islam, emerges as a brutal document of uncertain origins and questionable authority. As with the compilations that came to form the Old and New Testaments of the Judeo-Christian tradition, it has nothing to do with a deity but bears the indelible imprint of the wild fantasies, bigotry and fallibility of ignorant minds in primitive tribes. It is obvious that the problems of interpreting the confused and inconsistent texts have continued to plague believers, struggling to determine authenticity, over the centuries. For example, the ninth-century imam al-Bukhari (810–70), recognised as one of the most authoritative compilers of Hadith, is said to have travelled for sixteen years in search of authentic narrations, but selected only 7,500 of the half-million that he collected – so a single wandering scholar determined the most reliable Hadith. Just imagine a process that would have inevitably involved fatigue, hostile receptions, texts in many different media, questionable sources, different languages – all assessed by the subjective judgement of a single human being in an ancient period long before scientific dating, modern philological methods and computer-based textual analysis. It is difficult to avoid the conclusion that the Hadith, as represented in Bukhari's selection, is no more than a mishmash of items selected for purely personal reasons. Does a principal Hadith compilation really rest on such an arbitrary process? Or perhaps he relied on inspiration, on the magical forces that were ubiquitous in ancient times.

The researcher Yoginder Sikand emphasises the relevance of human interpretation of the Koran and the Hadith, and has traced the evolution of some of the principal Islamic schools and traditions.[84] Here, as elsewhere, we find religious beliefs and attitudes shaped by prevailing political and socioeconomic forces, suggesting that Islam and other cults, sects and religions are no more than outgrowths from prevailing cultural circumstances. Through all their periods of development, and at all levels, the religious belief systems in their entirety are mediated by human beings with their own agendas, ambitions, prejudices and convictions. The gods have nothing to do with it.

We need only glance at the world to see how true this is of Islam. Muslims are keen to say that their religion defines life for them in every detail, whilst at the same time they deny its manifestly totalitarian character. In particular, for our purposes, orthodox Muslims – not the 'moderate' species that are forced to adapt to infidel states – insist that religion and politics are one: if you are a Muslim then Islam will determine your political position. But just consider, for example, the Middle East. The Hamas Muslims in Palestine disagree with the Fatah Muslims; the Hezbollah Muslims in Lebanon disagree with other Muslims in government; in Saudi Arabia the Wahhabist authorities persecute the Shi'ite minority; in Egypt, Muslims in government suppress the Muslim Brotherhood; and in Iraq the Sunnis and Shi'ites are currently engaged in bloody sectarian cleansing. The one unchanging word of the Holy Koran, allegedly recited by an almighty divinity, seems to have invited a remarkable number of interpretations.

The task of interpretation continues – as if God could not make up his mind in the first place, did not speak clearly enough or did not chose the right people to talk to. So in February 2008 the Turkish prime minister, Recep Tayyip Erdoğan, was reportedly sponsoring a 'bold and original attempt' to rewrite Islamic jurisprudence, the Sharia law based on the Koran.[85] It was suggested that the 'ambitious experiment' would diminish Muslim discrimination against women, banish such barbaric punishments as amputation and stoning, and redefine Islam as a dynamic force in the modern world. A team of Islamic scholars at Ankara University, acting under the auspices of the Diyanet or Directorate of Religious Affairs, was reportedly close to concluding a 'reinterpretation' of parts of the Hadith. A liberal commentator, Mustafa Akyol, said: They have problems with the misogynistic Hadith, the ones against women. They may delete some from the collection, declaring them not authentic . . . Or they may just add footnotes, saying they should be understood from a different historical context.'[86] In the same vein Fadi Hakura, of the London-based International Institute of Strategic Studies, suggested that the project was an attempt to make Turkish Sunni Islam 'fully compatible with contemporary social and moral values . . . a return to the original Islam . . . akin to the Christian reformation, though not the same'.[87] The task involved scrutinising some 162,000 Hadith, and was expected to take years. The aim, according to Avuz Unal, who was heading the Hadith

Project, was 'to present the intentions of the prophet Mohammed to the people of today in a language they can understand'.[88] So what was to be done with Hadith urging believers to kill apostates, repress women, ban fine arts, stone adulterers and all the rest? There was only one answer if Islam was to be rendered 'fully compatible with contemporary social and moral values' – jettison the lot and adopt an adult rationalism suitable for the modern age. Many of the Muslim reformers, evident in Iran, Egypt, Turkey and elsewhere, admit that obscurantism and literalism are impediments to a modern interpretation of Islam, and that a new phase of *ijtihad*, allowing scholars to address contemporary issues according to the *spirit* of the Koran, is essential. Well, it won't work. They may as well discuss modern 'interpretations' of how the sun circles the earth or how the stork brings babies. Salaried imams are unlikely to admit that they have been talking nonsense all their lives, so the only option is reinterpretation of the texts. And where will that get them? To the ultimate demise of irrational belief systems – unless we are headed for a new Dark Age, which is certainly the aim of some Muslim proselytisers.

And while reformist Muslims were busy rewriting the Hadith, the Pope was busy rewriting the Good Friday prayer and adding to the seven deadly sins. If the Muslims could set about improving the word of God, why shouldn't the Catholics have a go as well? The traditional prayer called for the 'salvation' of Israel and asked Almighty God to 'enlighten' the hearts of the Jewish people so that they would acknowledge Jesus Christ as their saviour. This prayer, which appears in the 1962 Roman Missal, was quietly put to one side by the liturgical reforms of the Second Vatican Council – much in the way that Muslims play down inconvenient Koranic codices. Alas, the papal move did not go far enough. The prayer still explicitly aspires for Jews to accept the Christian faith, and there is no acknowledgement of the importance of the Torah as a route for salvation for the Jewish people.[89]

Perhaps the Vatican will have more luck with its expanded list of deadly sins, published in *L'Osservatore Romano* on 9 March 2008. Here the Pope sadly acknowledged the 'decreasing sense of sin' in today's 'secularised world', and doubled the number of sins laid down by Pope Gregory the Great in the sixth century and popularised by Dante in *Inferno*.[90] So now there are fourteen deadly sins, today including drug abuse, genetic manipulation, morally debatable experiments, environmental pollution, social inequalities and social injustice, causing poverty and accumulating excessive wealth.[91] Perhaps the scholastic philosopher William of Ockham (c.1285–c.1349), of 'razor' fame, could look at these since they obviously overlap. Social inequalities are obviously related to poverty and accumulating excessive wealth. No matter. At least the church is acknowledging that its traditional doctrine is in drastic need of a makeover. We have seen what has happened to God and Jesus, so it is unsurprising that prayers and sins need to be dusted up for the modern age.

And so the debate runs on. In March 2008 two former Islamists were reportedly launching a Muslim think tank, the Quilliam Foundation, to challenge 'extremist' ideologies by removing certain 'obstacles' to a modern interpretation.[92] The persecution of the English teacher Gillian Gibbons in Sudan for naming a teddy bear after Mohammed was reported as in accord with 'one of the most violent interpretations of Islam'.[93] In February 2008 Seyed Davoud Salehi, Iran's ambassador to Spain, compared chopping off the hands of thieves to a 'surgeon amputating a limb to prevent the spread of gangrene'.[94] The beating and imprisoning of Muslim girls who have offended 'family honour' is often said to have nothing to do with 'real Islam',[95] as if religion and culture exist in totally separate bubbles. In September 2007 thousands of enraged Hindus took to the streets when the Archaeological Survey of India, an arm of the culture ministry, suggested in court that there was no evidence to support the existence of the divine characters in the *Ramayana*, a revered ancient text.[96] Another, more rational, interpretation of the sacred work was possible.

We have seen that, in the last resort, the persistent need for interpretation of ancient texts totally undermines their credibility. What are supposed to be divinely shaped works are in fact created, edited, synthesised and embellished by human beings. All the texts – shaped as they are by personal idiosyncrasy and cultural pressure – bear the marks of their human origins. They never contain knowledge that goes beyond the knowledge of the times, they never contain science that goes beyond the contemporary state of learning; the gods of the Bible and the Koran clearly knew nothing of the DNA double helix or the fusion of hydrogen atoms at the centre of stars. And it is for these reasons that religion is so vulnerable to scientific criticism. Religious scholars have never managed to evolve universally acceptable protocols for settling disputes regarding the character of spiritual knowledge, the authority of particular schools and the authenticity of specific elements in the sacred works.

If the New Testament says that Jesus was crucified and the Koran says he was not, how do we choose between them? Most frequently, in fact, by where we happen to be born. An Arab born in Mecca will 'know' what the truth is, just as a white American in Alabama will 'know' what the truth is. But to rely on nothing more than the accidents of geography and genetic endowment is a poor way of settling disputes. Religion, by its nature, cannot do any better. By contrast, science, despite being occasionally distracted by charlatans who tell lies and governments eager to hijack its powers, provides consensually agreed methodologies which yield doctrines that are the nearest to an objective truth that human beings are likely to achieve. Scientists running nuclear programmes in Israel and Iran may disagree politically but they are sure to agree on the basic procedures for uranium enrichment.

I well remember my fascination when I first came across D. J. West's *Eleven Lourdes Miracles* (1957).[97] Here was a detailed medical analysis of eleven cures (1937–50) at Lourdes pronounced miraculous by the church. West undertook a detailed examination of the patients' dossiers and enlisted the help of various medical experts to make an independent appraisal of the evidence. He deplored the general absence of laboratory tests and comparative X-ray examinations before and after the cures, and concluded that there was 'absolutely no convincing evidence' for miraculous intervention in the official Lourdes cases.[98] Such scientific enquiries, long after David Hume's sceptical commentaries on the 'concept' of miracles, illustrate a general point: the more religious categories and assumptions are opened up to scientific analysis, the emptier they appear. Few modern psychiatrists, even within the Catholic and Muslim traditions, believe that schizophrenia is an example of demonic possession.

Today archaeological excavation has made it possible to query many specific texts in the Old Testament and other textual compilations, and to offer possible explanations for supposedly divine involvement in human affairs. For example, was ancient Israel more the 'creation of politically correct biblical scholars than a matter of historical certainty?'[99] Likewise many parts of the Old Testament are probably 'imaginative fictions' unsupported by available archaeological evidence.[100] In November 1996 Professor Ian Plimer, head of the School of Earth Sciences at the University of Melbourne, took a creationist to court over claims that he had discovered part of Noah's ark: 'For what the creationists say to be true, you would have to discard all theology, astronomy, physics and biology. Do we really believe as a matter of literal truth that our flat Earth, formed from water, stands on pillars and that the sun rotates around the earth?'[101] In the summer of 1997 a conference in Cambridge heard that Sodom and Gomorrah had perhaps been destroyed by comet debris. Marie-Agnès Courty, a French archaeologist, provided powerful evidence for this hypothesis: samples dating from 2200 BC from three Middle Eastern regions containing meteorite material. Other research suggested that the two cities might have been destroyed by huge underground fires ignited by an earthquake.[102] In 1998 two Israeli archaeologists, striking at the heart of Judaic assumption, presented evidence suggesting that King Solomon was not the builder of the first Jewish temple in Jerusalem, and at the same time science was offering an explanation for the ten plagues of Egypt: they were all down to a family of deadly single-celled creatures known as dinoflagellates.[103] In summary, research had shown that the principal events in the Bible – Adam and Eve, Moses and the burning bush, David and Goliath, Moses and the tablets, Abraham and Isaac, Solomon and the Queen of Sheba, etc. – are no more than colourful myths, invented to embellish historical events of doubtful authenticity. An Israeli doctor, Vladimir Berginer, while accepting the historical reality of Goliath, suggested that his defeat might have been caused by defective eyesight rather than divine intervention. He pointed out that a recognised eye condition, associated with gigantism, can lead to poor peripheral vision: 'Giants of staggering proportions generally suffer from acromegaly.'[104]

In 2002 the biblical scholars Roberto Beretta and Elisabetta Broli published *Gli undici comandamenti* (The Eleven Commandments), showing that many of the cherished Bible stories 'derive from subsequent apocryphal writings or medieval fables and embroidery'.[105] The title of the book is meant to emphasise that whereas Deuteronomy records ten command-ments, Exodus says there were twelve. Modern translations of the Bible, describing events in the Garden of Eden, talk of 'fruit', not an apple, just as they state that Jonah was swallowed by a 'great fish', not a whale. Jesus was not born on 25 December, which in fact was a date chosen by a fourth-century pope because it coincided with the Roman *sol invictus* festival. St Luke, the main source of the Christmas story, says that an angel told the shepherds, 'watching their flocks by night', of Christ's birth but does not say at what time of day the birth took place. St Matthew talks of the wise men entering a house, not a stable, 'where they saw the child with Mary his mother'. Images showing Jesus wearing a loincloth on the cross are mistaken since, according to Matthew, he was stripped and the soldiers 'shared out his clothes by casting lots after they had crucified him'. Beretta comments that Bible 'embellishments' had arisen because of 'people's natural desire to improve on a good story and fill in the gaps'.[106]

Professor Colin Humphreys, a materials scientist at Cambridge University and a Baptist, argues in his book *The Miracles of Exodus*[107] that Mount Sinai, where Moses allegedly received the divine commandments, was located in Saudi Arabia, not Egypt's Sinai Peninsula, throwing yet more doubt on the traditional account.[108] And even Jesus's profession, if he existed at all, is in doubt. Jesus and Joseph have been described as carpenters, when the Greek word *tekton* meant 'something more like architect or master builder'; and Gianfranco Ravasi, a member of the Pontifical Commission for Culture, has said that many of the myths that had grown up around the Bible stories were the result of 'a mixture of popular imagination and devotional fervour'.[109] It has also been suggested that the biblical plagues and the parting of the Red Sea were caused by a huge volcanic eruption on the Greek island of Santorini in the sixteenth century BC,[110] and that Jesus's ministry was fuelled by mind-altering substances such as cannabis.[111] When he walked on the water, Jesus may have been walking on thin ice.[112] And perhaps he was a victim of deep vein thrombosis (DVT), since thrombophilia, in which blood has an increased tendency to clot, was common among natives of Galilee.[113] In recent years, a papyrus found in the Egyptian desert was hailed as an authentic copy of the lost Gospel of Judas, suggesting that Judas Iscariot sacrificed himself for his divine master;[114] research has shown that hundreds of biblical artefacts in museums all over the world could be forgeries;[115] and new translations of the Bible, all giving different emphases in important respects, have been published.

Current research, in such fields as philology, archaeology, medicine and history, is showing what has been manifestly obvious for centuries – that sacred texts have been subject to variations in translation, factual errors, confusions in witness testimonies, manifest contradictions, additions and deletions, censorship, and all the other depredations of fallible human beings with their own agendas, ignorance and prejudices. Whatever the texts tell us, it is nothing to do with the existence and intentions of gods in the world.

4

Less than human

O women! Give alms, as I have seen the majority of the dwellers in Hell-fire were you.

Among the inmates of Paradise the women would form the minority.

Mohammed, Hadith (Bukhari)

In the sixth century AD a synod of bishops in Gaul, striving to chart the development of early Christianity, debated the important question of whether women were really human beings.[1] Opinion was divided and the matter was never fully resolved. Today the question could not be seriously posed, except for rhetorical or other similar purposes,[2] although women continue to suffer throughout the world as if they were less than human. This dismal situation has evolved for various reasons, not least the muscular superiority of male animals and the primitive fears surrounding menstrual blood. Thus the sociologist Edward Westermarck conveys one of the simple attitudes regarding menstruation that has helped to shape religion, in many of its baleful manifestations, throughout history: 'Such regular temporary defilement . . . may easily lead to the notion of a permanent uncleanness of the female sex.'[3] For this reason and many others the great religions have conspired over centuries, sometimes millennia, to afford women a status inferior to that of men – a pattern of discrimination rooted in gross superstition that has sustained blighted lives and the worst excesses of abuse.

However, there are many periods in history that pulled against the prevailing and deeply entrenched misogynies in ancient religions such as Hinduism and Judaism, and what would become the overwhelmingly discriminatory impact of Christianity and Islam. The feminist Rosalind Miles and many others have highlighted the reverence given to Woman, as signalled in the mythologies of the day. More than two millennia ago, Enheduanna, a female priest-poet in Sumeria, wrote 'The Exaltation of Inanna', a passionate hymn, to celebrate an omnipotent female deity who combined all the eroticism and power[4] that later would be so comprehensively denounced by male clerics in all the major religions of the world. In the same vein the archaeologist Sir Arthur Evans, discoverer of the Minoan civilisation, stated that the many goddess figures revealed through excavation all represented 'the same Great Mother . . . whose worship under various names and titles extended over a large part of Asia Minor and the regions beyond'; it was 'a worldwide fact' that 'The Great Goddess, the "Original Mother without a Spouse", was in full control of all the mythologies'.[5]

The celebration of women, often in connection with fertility and female sexuality, was manifest in much of the ancient world. 'Venus figurines' of stone and ivory, perhaps dating to 20,000 years BC and symbolising 'the Great Mother',[6] have been found in Europe and Egypt; the ceremonial burials of bodies coated in red ochre, originating around 10,000 BC and found in the former Czechoslovakia and Iraq, have been associated with goddess worship; shrines to the Mother Goddess, dating to 7000 BC, have been found in Jericho; other manifestations of goddess worship have been found in Turkey (forty shrines, 6000 BC) and Iraq (temple inscriptions to the Queen of Heaven at the ancient Sumerian site of Uruk, 4000 BC); and by 3000 BC Woman was celebrated and worshipped 'everywhere in the known world . . . [with] statues, shrines and written records'.[7]

As early as 1000 BC the Celts observed equality of the sexes, with a possible weighting in favour of women, who often presided over tribal councils.[8] The leading males in the community were elected, while the monarchy observed matrilinear descent. In observing the female line, Celtic society followed much of the rest of the ancient world. Tacitus saw the Celts as blue-eyed giants, and the Greeks called them 'Keltoi' – possibly, according to one authority, the name of the royal family.[9] In the fourth century AD the Roman historian Ammianus Marcellinus wrote that a troop of foreigners would not be able to withstand a single Gaul 'if he called his wife to his assistance, who is usually very strong, and with blue eyes';[10] and in 58 BC Julius Caesar recorded in *The Gallic Wars* that the joint chiefs of staff of the Celtic people were women: 'It was for the matrons to decide when troops should attack and when withdraw.' A treaty drawn up between the Celts and the Carthaginians under Hannibal included the words: 'If the Celtae have complaints against the Carthaginian soldiers, the Carthaginian commander shall judge it. But if the Carthaginians have anything to lay to the charge of the Celtae, it shall be brought before the Celtic women.'[11] According to Herodotus, the Celts worshipped the goddess Tabiti as their supreme deity. For a thousand years they were able to maintain their reverence for women, until conquered by Germanic tribes and later succumbing to Christianity.

Where once the Celtic woman had presided over tribal councils and led troops into battle,[12] she surfaced again in the Dark Ages of Christian Europe

> cringing at her cottage door, a whimpering slave, branded by the church as a thing of evil, sans soul, sans rights, sans humanity. No longer arbiter of her people or priestess of her goddess, she is debarred from the courts of justice, debarred from serving at the altar of the new God, deprived of her right to own property, even deprived of her rights over her own body.[13]

In the shift of power to Christianity, Celtic women were enslaved, exploited in marriage and abused by their liege-lord and priest. Here was the state which Christian women would be forced to endure for centuries to come.

The celebration of womanhood among Celtic and other ancient communities lasted, perhaps intermittently, at least 20,000 years. During the same period, parallel forces hostile to the status of women were evident in early paganism and would feed through and sustain the gross misogyny of Judaism, Christianity and Islam. For example, Aristotle's disparagement of women was adopted as a benchmark by St Thomas Aquinas and other fathers of the church (see below). Pagan cults, even those typically focusing on a goddess, often involved paying obeisance to the phallus, seen as a symbolic image of the penis and celebrating the role of the male in procreation. Thus a wooden phallus was installed in the temple of Isis at Thebes, and Greek women carried a string-controlled phallus during ceremonies involving goddess worship. At such events the senior matrons of the town would honour the phallus with garlands and kisses as a sign that the Great Goddess acknowledged the tribute of phallic service.[14] And gradually the male element began to supplant the female in religious mythology and the associated ceremonies, with phallic worship spreading throughout the world, even in circumstances where the role of women in procreation was plainly acknowledged.

Hence in the centuries immediately before Christ all the mythologies relate the overthrow of the Great Mother Goddess. In one version, the Babylonian Epic of Creation, the solar god Marduk, replete with four eyes and four ears and able to breathe fire, challenged the domination of Tiamat, the ancient Mother of All Things, and hacked her into two pieces like a cosmic clam. It was in death that Tiamat aided the creation of the world. One half of her was raised to become the roof of the sky, the other became the earth above the subterranean waters. From her eyes Marduk created two rivers; from her udder, mountains and foothills; from her saliva, rain and clouds; and from her lethal poisons, fog. Marduk then named each element and set the stars and gods in their places.

It is interesting to note an analogous Tiwi tale from central Africa in which the creator goddess Puvi made the land, sea and islands. The god Iriti killed her with a strike on the head, whereupon her urine made the sea salty and her spirit went into the sky.[15] Other accounts relating the defeat of the Great Goddess occur in Celtic folk myth, in the Greek story of how Apollo took over the goddess's most sacred site at Delphi, in the Kikuyu myth of how ancient ancestors overthrew their women by making them pregnant and vulnerable, and in the tale of how the son of the Aztec earth mother Xochiquetzal killed her daughter the Moon Goddess and supplanted her as ruler of heaven. In Egypt the goddesses Nut, Isis and Osiris were subordinate to the sun god Ra, the divinity of light and the virile force. In Babylon, after the dismemberment of Tiamat, Ishtar was no more than a servile wife to Marduk. When the Greek Zeus won power, the goddesses Gaia, Rhea and Cybele were forced to abdicate; and the Roman Jupiter was supreme in his realm. When the Vedic gods had spouses the female deities had a lesser claim to worship. And the Semites adopted a male god. In all mythologies, reflecting terrestrial events, the triumph of the male became established. But with the spread of Christianity, eager to celebrate the dethronement of Woman, the pagan devotions centred on the phallus were soon confronted by church fathers obsessed with the sins of the flesh. Sex worship, 'never before consciously associated with anything immoral, degenerated into a frankly licentious cult'.[16] One of the main fruits of Christianity was to transform one of the principal joyous instincts of humankind into disreputable sin (see Chapter 5).

Various mythologies had come to provide patriarchal prototypes that the early ascetic Christians found congenial. In particular, the biblical Old Testament, which includes the Judaic Pentateuch (the Torah), presents an image of woman that would help to shape discriminatory attitudes through all the succeeding centuries in the Middle East, Europe and beyond. This is never more explicitly advertised than in the differential monetary values assigned to males and females in particular roles. At all ages, men are worth more than women: for example, 'thy estimation shall be of the male from twenty years old even unto sixty years old . . . fifty shekels of silver . . . And if it be a female then thy estimation shall be thirty shekels' (Leviticus 27: 3–4).

Like most religious writings, the Old Testament was in part a description by men of male-dominated society. There are famous female characters, either sinful or heroic (Eve, Sarah, Deborah, Ruth, Esther, Jezebel, Delilah and others) but for the most part they are subordinate to men, significant only in relation to male ambitions and activities. Phyllis Bird has indicated the rich variety of female images in the Old Testament,[17] but the society portrayed is marked by the invariably male activities of war, cultish practices and the business of government, all presided over by a jealous, capricious and violent male deity. The various books in the Old Testament were compiled over a millennium (from the twelfth to the third century BC) so the images inevitably shift over the period, reflecting changing mores and the contingencies of political development. Bird notes that the consistent themes in Israeli law differ little from those of Syria and Mesopotamia, among which is a 'thorough-going institutionalisation of the double standard',[18] whereby women are to be judged according to one set of criteria and men according to another. It is significant that the laws are framed by men with men in mind. Thus 'thou shalt not covet thy neighbour's wife' (Exodus 20: 17). Not much here about lusting after your neighbour's husband. In a similar vein, 'ye shall not afflict any widow, or fatherless child. If thou afflict them in any wise . . . your wives shall be widows, and your children fatherless' (Exodus 22: 22–4). All the early Judaic laws suggested a society in which males are regarded as the only responsible members. There was no point in addressing laws to women since they were regarded as less than full citizens: they would derive their social status from men and be controlled by them. In this fashion women were dependent upon men and had no authority to act as mature political actors in society. Hence discrimination against women – as reflected in the laws dealing with inheritance, divorce, sexual transgressions, religious vows, cultic observances and ritual purity – was inherent in the socioreligious organisation of Israel.[19]

The interests of the family were identified with the interests of the male head, who had rights and responsibilities with respect to other men and their property. The woman's sexuality, whether generating pleasure or offspring, was regarded as the exclusive property of her husband. Thus 'the man that committeth adultery with another man's wife . . . the adulterer and the adulteress shall surely be put to death' (Leviticus 20: 10) may appear to mete out equal treatment to both miscreants but here the transgression is against the property of the wronged husband. There is no equivalent law condemning to death 'the woman that committeth adultery with another woman's husband'. In fact there was no general prohibition against extramarital sex – this was a

contribution of later Christianity – only the particular denunciation of the damage to a man's authority and honour within his
family. By contrast, a man who seduces an unmarried girl is not
executed but simply ordered to marry her, making a proper
marriage gift to her father to protect his honour.

The discriminatory Judaic attitudes and laws have survived over
the millennia. Every morning many adult male Jews still recite the
heartfelt prayer 'Blessed be God, King of the universe, for not
making me a woman' – an extraordinary sentiment in the twenty-
first century that has justly attracted feminist scorn. This prayer,
above all other Judaic statements, encapsulates the doctrine that
religion regards women as inferior to men and that in consequence men should be grateful for their good fortune.[20] In this
context the role of Jewish women, as socially inferior to men, is
to serve their husbands.

After a detailed survey of how women are regarded in the
Talmud, Rabbi Judith Hauptman, a professor at the Jewish
Theological Seminary in New York, lists some of the traits that
typify them. In addition to a number of positive qualities, 'the
Talmudic stories run the entire gamut of negative evaluations':[21]
women are typically sharp tongued, arrogant, outspoken, cruel,
jealous, vengeful, abusive, superstitious, desirous of luxury and
quick to anger. Hauptman concludes that 'a woman's prime
function in life is to concern herself with man's welfare and
to provide for his physical comfort'.[22] Where the rabbis sought to
improve the lot of women, care was taken not to erode men's
dominant position, with the consequence that women should be
modest in dress and behaviour, confine themselves to the home
and free their husbands to fulfil their religious and ethical duties
elsewhere. Hauptman acknowledges that Judaic doctrine still
reflects an outdated social structure: 'women should no longer be
used as the means with which men achieve their ends'.[23]

The more religious the Judaic school is, the more unpleasant the
doctrine – a feature of all religions. It seems that religious belief
becomes progressively more acceptable to reason and compassion
as it becomes attenuated and diluted by secular and other modern
pressures. The Jewish Haredim, religiously devout, illustrate the

point. Adherents to this brand of Judaism not only restrict the rights of women but view them with contempt. They typically refer to Jewish women active in politics as 'witches, bitches or demons', which largely mirrors the traditional Judaic attitude to women.[24] The Haredim prohibit women from participating in politics at any level and in any other public activities in which they may surpass men. They are not allowed to drive taxis or buses, and are forbidden from driving cars if any males outside their own family are passengers. Women judged to be dressed immodestly are likely to be insulted and assaulted. Such rules and attitudes are not merely the unpleasant excrescences of a minority sect, but rely on support from mainstream Talmudic literature that men – but not women – are expected to study diligently. Hence a statement in *Tractate Shabat* defines a woman, any woman, as 'a sack full of excrement'. The *Talmudic Encyclopedia*, written in modern Hebrew for access by all educated Israeli Jews, indicates that because sexual intercourse is more important for men than for women a wife is punished more by the halacha (religious law) for refusing her husband sexual relations than vice versa.[25] For the same reason a prospective husband is entitled to see his wife-to-be before marrying her, but the prospective wife has no such right.

There is a traditional halachic prohibition on teaching Talmudic literature to women, whereas it is a sacred duty for every Jewish male to 'learn the Torah'. And the religious inferiority of Jewish women is manifest in many other ways. For example, the religious act of hearing the ram's horn being blown on New Year brings a greater reward to a man than to a woman because she is not obliged to do so. The seemingly greater freedom of a woman in this regard signals her diminished status as a spiritual being. The great Jewish authority Maimonides, writing in the twelfth century, pointed out in his *Talmud Torah Laws* that women never intend to learn anything and if they should happen to read the Torah, which they are not obliged to do, they will convert its pronouncements into nonsense because of their weak under-standing.[26] Since the time of Maimonides there has been some progress. Today the Haredim teach the simpler parts of the Torah to girls, while shielding them from rabbinical arguments that are not suitable for the 'weak female mind'. Similarly, girls are allowed some contact with the Pentateuch but the more serious commentaries are reserved for the boys.

One stipulation in the *Kitzur Shulchan Aruch* (Abridged *Shulchan Aruch*), an elementary textbook for Jews, dictates: 'A male should not walk between two females or two dogs or two pigs . . . the males should not allow a woman, dog or pig to walk between them.'[27] All Haredi boys between ten and twelve are expected to observe this rule, just as the Haredim insist that all Jewish women shave their head and cover it with a coif before marrying. Many Jews cut some of their hair as a partial acknowledgement of the Haredim prescription, while secular Jewish women are enraged by such rules. Some of the secular response to the traditional Judaic abuse of women is found in articles in the Israeli Hebrew press. For example, the secularist Kadid Leper, a well-known journalist, wrote an article in *Hai'r* under the heading 'Woman is a sack full of excrement', drawing on the *Tractate Shabat*, protesting at what could be found in the Talmud: 'Beatings, sexual brutality, cruelty, deprivation of rights, use of a woman as merely a sexual object . . . the place of women is in the garbage heap together with cattle and slaves. According to the Jewish religion a man buys himself a slave woman [a wife] for her entire life.'[28]

It is plain that many current Jewish attitudes to women have been shaped by traditional teachings, and that discriminatory practices are rooted in Jewish religious law. The academic Israel Shahak (1933–2001) gave examples of what the applications of such law involve in the case of women. Jewish women are allowed to testify in rabbinical courts in a few limited matters considered 'female affairs', but if the case involves 'a major judicial effort' a woman's testimony is regarded as invalid because 'all women are lazy by nature'.[29] Even in cases not involving a major effort, the testimony of a man and a woman may not be in accord. In such cases the court relies on the principle that 'a testimony of 100 Jewish women is equivalent to the testimony of a single Jewish man'.[30]

A further example offered by Shahak concerns the definition of 'harlot' in Jewish religious law. The Torah, following Maimonides, regards a harlot as any woman who is not born Jewish, or a Jewish woman who has sexual intercourse with a man she is forbidden to marry. This means that the Torah is unambiguously racist, perceiving all women not born as 'daughters of Israel' as harlots, with the corollary that even a woman who converts to Judaism is still considered by Jewish religious law to be a harlot.[31]

Today thousands of Jewish women are living in a state of *aguna* (the Hebrew word for 'chained'), in which the rabbinical courts prohibit them from divorcing their husbands, even in the celebrated case of Sarah, whose husband was a convicted child rapist. Here there is no separation of church and state, and the religious law says that both the husband and wife must agree before a divorce can be allowed by the courts. One woman in Bnei Brak, a conservative suburb of Tel Aviv, was forced to endure this limbo for well over twenty years. Another, Daniela Valeny, wore down the rabbis over a twelve-year period until her divorce was granted, but by then it was too late for her to have more children. Men too are prohibited from divorcing without permission, but unlike women they are allowed by the rabbinical courts to remarry without first securing a divorce. This means that the subsequent children of a 'chained' woman by another partner are regarded in Jewish law as bastards, whereas the children of an undivorced man to a new partner are seen as legitimate, provided that the new partner is not a chained woman.

Another case concerned a man who attacked his wife with an axe. He declared that he would agree to a divorce if his wife compensated him for his £50,000 lost earnings in drug deals. The sympathetic rabbis asked him to provide receipts for his previous earnings. In yet another case Susan Zinkin was 'shackled' in such a fashion for more than forty years, unable to obtain a Jewish divorce even after her marriage had been dissolved: 'I would have liked to have had more children, but they would have been deemed illegitimate . . . In the Jewish faith you're treated as a second class citizen [if illegitimate] . . . No Jewish man wants illegitimate children – and so when people heard I hadn't got a get [a permission granted by the rabbinical courts to divorce], they realised it couldn't go any further. That spoils any relationship.'[32] In many cases the husband sells a get, effectively blackmailing the woman for money. Some women commit suicide under the strain and misery.

In 1998 a panel of rabbis in Haifa, prompted by divorce
proceedings, ruled that wives must be home by midnight. The
man had complained that his wife had been visiting singles bars
and sometimes not arriving home until the morning. The wife
protested that her husband was sleeping with other women,
which the court did not dispute, but the ruling stood. The
previous year, Rabbi Ovadiah Yosef, the spiritual leader of the
then government's ultra-orthodox partner, Shas, warned women
that if they took a shower on the Sabbath they were committing
a crime. Another Jewish sage, Rabbi Kadouri, achieved fame by
flying round Israel's borders and chanting prayers to throw a
protective mystical cloak over the country. He also proclaimed
that women would 'burn in hell' if they wore wigs.[33]

Judaism, in concert with various pagan elements, had prepared
the ground for the coming of Christianity and for the
development of what history would recognise as the Judeo-
Christian tradition. A main feature of the new religion would be
a comprehensive misogyny intent on maintaining the suppression
of women and blighting their lives for the centuries yet to come.
The nineteenth-century philosopher John Stuart Mill commented
that it was the Jewish religion, 'barbarous, and intended for a
barbarous people', plainly steeped in woman-hatred and superstition, that had formed the basis of 'Christian morality'.[34]

The feminist writer Elizabeth Gould Davis (1910–74) noted
how the Christian church itself 'initiated and carried forward the
bitter campaign to debase and enslave the women of Europe'.[35]
There had been a revival of feminism in imperial Rome, and in
Celtic Europe the favourable status of women had been
seemingly secure. As one example, the Celt authority Thomas
Powell (1916–75) commented: 'It is generally assumed that the
right of a wife to hold property or of a daughter to inherit, is a
late development. But a more liberal practice seems to have been
operative in Rome and Celtic legal custom.'[36] All this was set to
change. When the Christians gained secular power, in one
country after another many ancient rights afforded to women –
divorce, abortion, birth control, property ownership, the bearing
of titles and the ownership of estates, the making of wills,
bringing suits at law and much else – were progressively eroded

and have not yet, even under the pressures of secular ascendancy, been fully restored.

It is significant that the leaders of the early church were Jews, accustomed to regarding women as fit only to serve men. It was the Jewish St Paul who said:

Neither was the man created for the woman; but the woman for the man.[37]

Let your women keep silent in the churches: for it is not permitted unto them to speak; but they are commanded to be under obedience, as also saith the law. And if they will learn any thing, let them ask their husbands at home: for it is a shame for women to speak in the church.[38]

Wives, submit yourselves unto your own husbands, as unto the Lord. For the husband is head of the wife, even as Christ is head of the church . . . Therefore, as the church is subject unto Christ, so let the wives be to their own husbands in every thing.[39]

Let the woman learn in silence with all subjection . . . I suffer not a woman to teach, nor to usurp authority over the man, but to be in silence.[40]

In the same spirit, St Peter, one of the apostles of Christ, urged women to be 'in subjection' to their husbands and to indulge in 'chaste conversation coupled with fear'.[41] Again the very humanity of women was in question.[42] Perhaps, like mere animals, they did not have souls. What conceivable rights could such degraded creatures have? All they could do was to submit themselves to priest and husband. In the second century AD St Clement of Alexandria proclaimed: 'Every women should be overwhelmed with shame at the very thought that she is a woman.'[43] He noted that women

throw back their heads and bare their necks indecently . . . and gulp down the liquor as if to bare all they can to their boon companions

. . . Nothing improper is proper for man, who is endowed with
reason; much less for women, to whom it brings shame to reflect of
what nature she is.

And women should be allowed to 'uncover and exhibit' no part
of their person, lest both fall – the men being excited to look, they
by drawing on themselves the eyes of men.[44] Women were seen
as deficient in intellect, as temptresses already steeped in sin,
untrustworthy and liable to lead men astray. Clearly only the
harshest punishments were fit to address their crimes.

It is also significant in this context that Constantine, the first
Christian emperor of Rome, ordered the execution of Fausta, his
own wife, on suspicion of adultery.[45] She was boiled to death in a
cauldron of water brought to a slow boil over a wood fire – a
precedent for the next fourteen centuries throughout Christendom.
Thus the Abbé de Brantome (c.1540–1614) later deplored the
freedom with which 'our Christian lords and princes murder their
wives. To think that the pagans of old, who did not know Christ,
were so gentle and kind to their wives; and that the majority of our
lords should be so cruel to them.'[46] In Christian Rome husbands
were entitled to kill their adulterous wives, but male adulterers
could only be killed if they were slaves.[47]

The persistent double standard was evident through all of
Christendom and constantly reinforced by the fathers of the
church. Gratian, the great canon lawyer of the twelfth century,
wrote: 'Man, but not woman, is made in the image of God. It is
plain from this that women should be subject to their husbands and
should be as slaves.'[48] At the same time St Thomas Aquinas was
drawing on the pagan Aristotle to demonstrate the gross inferiority
of women to men. Aristotle (constantly referred to in adoration as
'the Philosopher') had declared that woman was 'misbegotten', to
be considered only with respect to the body and not the soul. So
Aquinas adopted the Latin phrase *deficiens et occasionatus* to depict
woman, an epithet that is variously translated as 'defective and
misbegotten' or 'unfinished and caused accidentally'. In any event
there was no doubting woman's inferior status in the realm
of creation.

In *Summa Theologiae* Aquinas considered the implications of woman's defective nature. Here the question is raised as to whether woman, an imperfect creature, should not have been part of the original creation:

> It would seem that the woman should not have been made in the first production of things. For the Philosopher says that 'the female is a misbegotten male'. But nothing misbegotten or defective should have been in the first production of things. Therefore woman should not have been made at the first production.

Alas, Aquinas cannot escape the fact that women are necessary for procreation so he is forced to allow them a place in creation, but their inferior nature is plain. Yes, woman is

> defective and misbegotten, for the active force in the male seed tends to the production of a perfect likeness in the masculine sex; while the production of woman comes from a defect in the active force or from some material indisposition, or even from some external influence; such as that of a south wind, which is moist, as the Philosopher observes.[49]

It is unsurprising that Aquinas should regard women as fit only for subjection, albeit benevolently enforced, by men: 'For good order would have been wanting in the human family if some were not governed by others wiser than themselves. So by such a kind of subjection woman is naturally subject to man, because in man the discretion of reason predominates.'[50] But she should not be treated as a slave: the woman 'should neither use authority over man, and so she was not made from his head [but from a rib]; nor was it right for her to be subject to man's contempt as a slave, and so she was not made from his feet'.[51]

Some of the worst excesses of religious misogyny are found in the work of clerics associated with the Inquisition (see also Chapter 2). In the fifteenth-century *Malleus Maleficarum* the Dominican monks Heinrich Kramer and James Sprenger, seeking to justify the sadistic treatment of alleged witches, go to great lengths to demonstrate the evil nature of women.[52] St John Chrysostom is cited to show that a woman is a 'punishment', an 'evil', a 'temptation', a 'calamity', a 'danger', a 'detriment' and the like; Cicero to show that women are avaricious; Seneca to show that they are evil deceivers. Women have 'slippery tongues', are intellectually 'like children', have 'many carnal abominations', are 'defective animals', have 'weak memories', are 'secret and wheedling enemies' of men and so on and so forth.[53] The early authorities of the church knew where they stood with women.

Roman Catholic apologists are keen to point out that canon law allows women to be deputed as readers, servers, cantors, preachers, leaders of prayer services, and ministers of baptism and communion (Canon 230, Sections 2 and 3), signalling that there are ways in which women can teach in church and have authority over men, but such areas of discretion are immensely limited and the central Catholic constraint has not changed in two millennia. Aquinas declared that woman's deficiency was confirmed in her inferior intellectual powers, prohibiting her from being fully an image of God as every man is judged to be. One consequence is the administering of the Eucharist, where the priest is proxy for Christ: 'Since it is not possible in the female sex to signify eminence of degree, it follows that she cannot receive the sacrament of Holy Orders.' So women priests are banned in the Catholic Church and a female pope would be unthinkable.

The absurdities of Gratian, Aquinas and their ilk, by modern standards ignorant men, still have an enormous impact through much of Christendom. In 1879 Pope Leo XIII issued a rescript ordering that the philosophy of Aquinas had to be taught in all Catholic educational institutions as the only correct one. Christianity is still plagued by pagan nonsense and medieval obscurantism.

A combination of Jewish doctrine and early Christianity had reduced women to a pitiable state. The Christian fathers delivered endless invectives denouncing Woman, seen as the chief source of temptation to virtuous men. She was represented as 'the door of hell', the mother of all human ills. Her only recourse was to acknowledge the shame of being a woman and to live in a state of continual penance on account of the curses she had brought upon the world. Her dress, signalling her femininity, constantly reminded her of her shame since it served as a memorial of her fall.

And her physical beauty, a potent instrument of the demon, was a perpetual theme of ecclesiastical denunciations.[54] Of course one solution to the appearance of an alluring female face was the veil, certainly not the prerogative of Muslim women (see below). St Ambrose, like other fathers of the church, demanded that women go veiled in the streets: 'Let the woman cover her head, so as to secure her modesty in public. Her countenance should not be readily offered to the eyes of a young man, and for that reason she should be covered with the marriage veil.'[55] The fourth-century Apostolic Constitutions likewise called for the veiling of women in the street.[56] These regulations stipulated also that women should not wash too often, presumably in the belief that excessive washing signalled vanity and an interest in carnal matters: the woman 'should not wash all too frequently, not in the afternoon, nor every day'. And of course women should avoid improper sports, but 'should be made to practise spinning wool and weaving, and helping with the baking of bread . . . Women should also fetch from the pantry the things we need.'[57]

Chrysostom, clearly disturbed by the female of the species, was forced to admit that women, although disreputable, had a certain allure – 'a necessary evil, a natural temptation, a desirable calamity, a domestic peril, a deadly fascination, and a painted ill'. He also judged that since 'the whole [female] sex is weak and flighty' women might seek salvation through children[58] – not a solution that appealed to Ambrose since women might experience carnal pleasures during conception ('The daughter of Heaven refrains from all fleshly lust') and because children would only bring grief. Perpetual virginity was the only solution (see Chapter 5). And so it ran on in the minds of all the ascetic fathers of the church. Tertullian ranted:

> A veil must be drawn over a beauty so dangerous as to have brought scandal into heaven itself . . . I am speaking of her condition as a woman . . . hot after pleasure and finery. Rather would she wear rags and mourning, weep and show an Eve plunged in penance, trying to expiate by her contrite appearance the disgrace of that first crime and the shame of having brought ruin to humanity . . . You are the devil's gateway; you are she who first violated the forbidden tree and broke

the law of God . . . Because of the death you merited, the Son of God had to die. And yet you think of nothing but covering your tunics with ornaments.[59]

At the beginning of the fourth century the Synod of Elvira stipulated in Canon 81 that women should neither write nor receive letters in their own name – presumably in an effort to maintain male control over any female efforts at communication with the outside world.

In the fifth century the Christians pillaged the great School of Philosophy at Alexandria, which at the time was headed by Hypatia, 'a remarkable woman of great learning and eloquence, the charm of whose rare modesty and beauty, combined with her great intellectual gifts, attracted to her lectures a large number of disciples'.[60] Cyril, the Christian bishop of Alexandria, was incensed that this female mathematician and philosopher should be teaching men, and so resolved to destroy her. In a passionate sermon the bishop denounced Hypatia and urged his congregation to kill her. The mob caught Hypatia in her chariot, whereupon they stripped her, cut her to pieces with oyster shells and burnt her body piece by piece. One of her former pupils, Synesius, later became Bishop of Ptolemais, having been spared by prudently declaring he was a Christian. In the sixth century, a decree of the Council of Auxerre prohibited women, because of the vileness of female nature, from receiving the Eucharist into their naked hands.[61]

The historian William Lecky (1838–1903) recorded the fact, already noted, that 'in the whole feudal legislation [throughout Christian Europe] women were placed in a much lower position than in the Pagan Empire'.[62] Men were urged from the pulpit to beat their wives (compare this with the similar Koranic injunction – see below) and wives to kiss the rod that beat them. Under the word *castigare* in a medieval theological manual, now held in the British Museum, a man is urged to beat his wife 'for her correction'[63] – one of the fruits of pulpit sermons. The authority Eugene Mason noted that 'parents trained their children with blows, and the husbands scattered the like seeds of kindness on their wives'.[64] And any squire could whip women who showed pride or immodesty at his pleasure – with, for example, the French court highly entertained to hear how the Duke of Lorraine and his men 'raided villages, ravishing, torturing and killing every woman, old women included'.[65] The clergy, keen to maintain accord with the lord of the manor, refrained from condemning such excesses and the analogous brutalities perpetrated by humble men. Thus Sir Thomas More reports the fifteenth-century case of the woodsman who chopped off his wife's head because she was a 'scold': when the case came to the bishop the man was completely exonerated.[66] In such a fashion the Christian church created and continued to sustain a centuries-long culture of brutality against women. Uta Ranke-Heinemann, a doctor of Catholic theology, declared:

> All in all, considering the repression, defamation and demonisation of women, the whole of church history adds up to one long arbitrary, narrow-minded masculine despotism over the female sex. And this despotism continues today . . . The subordination of woman to man has remained a postulate of the theologians throughout the history of the Church; and even in today's male Church it goes on being treated as divinely willed dogma.[67]

Much of the woman-hating prejudice and injustice, psychopathology even, that is so discernible in early and medieval Christianity remains manifest today – whether in the opposition to condom use to prevent AIDS,[68] the 'pro-life' fundamentalist opposition to women's rights, the abject born-again submission to Christian husbands,[69] and the clear discrimination and residual polygamy in Mormon communities.[70]

At the same time there are various feminist attempts to redress the balance, as if activist agitation in the modern world can wholly counter the dead weight of accumulated tradition and authority that span two millennia. The female Christian activists – whether labelled feminists,[71] egalitarians[72] or complementarians[73] – seem content to work within the church structures and to avoid bringing any radical disturbance to the foundations. This seems an impossible circle to square. And it often involves the feminists in absurd disputation – for example, in their disagreements over the gender of God.

The complementarians hold that Christian ministers ought to be men since religious language refers to God 'the Father' and Jesus Christ, the 'Son' of God. Here it gets tricky for the feminists since they are forced to acknowledge that whereas man is made directly in the image of God, women only share in this image by being made in the image of man (as stated in 1 Corinthians 11: 7) – a sort of image once removed. This is some feminism! The egalitarians respond by saying that God is not gendered, with terms such as 'Father' and 'Son' to be understood as analogies or metaphors used to communicate God's attributes in patriarchal cultures. It was not theologically necessary for Christ to be male but first-century Jewish culture would not have accepted a female Messiah (perhaps on the second coming Jesus will be a woman). But the feminists cannot agree on this. For example, Wayne Grudem takes exception to such egalitarian arguments, suggesting that Christ's maleness was theologically necessary. In his view any egalitarian attempt to portray God as both 'Father' and 'Mother'[74] represents theological liberalism – to be condemned.

It does seem absurd to regard God as male – does he have a penis and testicles, and what would he do with them? – or female – does she have a vagina and uterus, and what would she do with them? It is all very well to say that man was made in God's image, but surely sexual orientation should be expunged from the divine nature. So it only remains to have an It-God (not to be confused with the film star it-girl Clara Bow, duly worshipped in the 1920s). To see such speculation as ridiculous is a reflection on the nature of gender discussions regarding the Monarch of the Universe and much else in what is euphemistically dubbed theological philosophy.

Hence there are contending sects within Christian feminism, generating disagreements among sects within schisms – the inevitable condition of all world religions. How much simpler it is to sweep the whole archaic baggage away and tackle social problems through reason and compassion. There are still many ethical and political issues to be resolved in society, but it is unhelpful to expect superstition and ignorance to make a useful contribution.

★

Christianity, the misbegotten offspring of Judaism, yielded a new monstrous amalgam, with Islam the next chronological creed to posit a brutal and vindictive sky god with all the accompanying miracles and repressions. The scene was already set, and Islam was not about to abandon the desert traditions of sexism and superstition that had proved so congenial to male believers over the centuries. Allah (God), we are expected to believe, dictated his message to an illiterate Arab, Mohammed, who some later commentators thought might be subject to epileptic fits. Mohammed then allegedly dictated the words to scribes or to others for oral transmission. After much subsequent argument, with parts of the message on palm leaves, shells and other convenient items that were variously lost or newly found, decisions were taken by Muslim authorities as to which version of the Koran should be accepted as the true word of God. It was all a remarkably human process for such a divine communication. It was also remarkable for being partly plagiaristic on the Jewish and Christian traditions. Bits of the Old and New Testaments can be found in the Koran and serve to demonstrate the kinship of the three desert creeds that allegedly derive from Abraham. There are of course various important differences between the three great sky-god religions, but one of the baleful similarities is the attitude to women.

Muslims are expected to accept the whole of the Koran, though in practice many do not, particularly in secular states. Orthodox Muslims 'prove' that all of the book must be true by quoting the text itself: 'Those who are well-grounded in knowledge say: "We believe in it; it is all from our Lord."'[75] (However, they rarely focus on the words preceding this statement: 'No one knows its [the Koran's] meaning except God,' which is scarcely helpful to anyone struggling to make sense of it all.) In the same way some Christians quote the Bible in an attempt to justify its truth – the irony of this circular argument escapes believers intent on buttressing their faith. Despite this manifest handicap, orthodox Muslims, like fundamentalist Christians, are not expected to question or doubt the literal word of God.

One problem is that Allah seems able to speak only Arabic, perhaps not able to master more than one language and thus obliged to read to Mohammed from the divine copy of the Koran laid up in heaven (or had he memorised it all, as some devout Muslims are said to have done?). The problem necessarily impacts on the veracity of translation since, for whatever reason, Allah has seemed reluctant to speak to the *New York Times*, Cliff Richard or the BBC in English. In any event Muslims are expected to accept the literal word, and part of that word is that women are inferior to men and should be kept in their place, if necessary by the most brutal means.

Thus there is one particular verse in the Koran that has caused progressive Muslims (the phrase is not quite an oxymoron) immense difficulties. Surah 4 ('Women'), verse 34 states, unambiguously enough: 'Men have authority over women because God has made the one superior to the other.' The supposed inferiority of women is reinforced by many other texts in the Koran, some of them almost sarcastic in their flavour. Surah 53 ('The Star'), verses 28–9 disparage unbelievers for giving angels the names of females (what could be worse?): 'Of this they have no knowledge'; and Surah 37 ('The Ranks'), verses 150–3 ask rhetorically whether God could have created female angels (people suggesting such a thing are 'liars'): 'Would He [God] choose daughters rather than sons?' We are not expected to answer the question. (In Arabic there is an insulting phrase meaning 'father of daughters'.) The imagined inferiority of women is also indicated in a host of other Koranic verses, namely those dealing with rights and legal status. In Surah 2 ('The Cow'), verse 228, men are said to 'have a status above women'; in verse 282 of the same surah, one male witness is regarded as equal to two female ('if either of them [women] commit an error, the other will remember'); Surah 4: 12 declares that a man's inheritance should be equal to that of two women; and Surah 4: 176 specifies that, according to God's direction, if there are brothers and sisters the males will have twice the share of an inheritance as the females.

It is important to say more about Surah 4: 34, since once the inferiority of women had been established as divine writ, albeit with the expectation that husbands would maintain their wives, various consequences were plain. In particular, wives could be beaten if they were disobedient: 'As for those from whom you fear disobedience, admonish them, forsake them in beds apart, and beat them.'

This piece of Koranic text is sometimes referred to as the *qawwamun* verse, signalling that men are 'in charge of' women because God has made one superior to the other. (The verse seems to be at odds with other divine statements such as Surah 30 ('The Greeks'), verse 20: 'He [God] hath created wives for you of your own species, that ye might dwell with them, and hath put love and tenderness between you.' This discrepancy itself causes further problems because Surah 4: 84 states that there are no contradictions in the divine word.) In any event translators, apologists and believers have struggled to find an interpretation of the *qawwamun* verse that is less offensive to women in the modern age. It is an impossible task.

The feminist Kecia Ali, assistant professor of religion at Boston University, quotes one translation of the text: 'Men are *qawwamun* in relation to women . . . Those women whose *nushuz* [disobedience] you fear, admonish them, and abandon them in bed, and strike them' – and asks whether the injunction 'to strike' women is to be taken literally.[76] This of course is a very familiar religious ploy in the modern age. As soon as a text is found to jar with contemporary sensibilities, because it is either factually incredible or morally repellent, apologists rush to suggest that the words are symbolic or allegorical or figurative, intended to convey an important truth but not in a literal way. Heretics were executed in earlier times for suggesting such a thing. But Ali is hard pressed to find an interpretation of the verse that is more acceptable to Muslim women who are striving to emerge in the modern world (fundamentalists have no such problem – women are inferior, proclaimed so by Allah, and that settles the matter). Fatima Mernissi, quoted by Ali, acknowledges that the Koran refers to *nushuz* to indicate 'the punishment a husband must inflict on the wife in case she rebels',[77] and gives the 'disobedience' a purely sexual connotation. In short, a man should beat his wife if she refuses sexual intercourse. Put another way, Allah authorises Muslim men to rape their wives.

Turning to other translations does not help matters. Ali points out that the Arab verb *daraba* has been variously translated as 'to

strike', 'to beat', 'to hit' and 'to scourge', with two recent translations opting for 'to spank' in an obvious attempt to reduce the
severity of the assault on the wife. Other translations have
preferred 'chastise', 'pet' and 'tap', with the most common version
remaining as 'beat'. I have even seen one translation that uses the
word 'beat' and then adds 'lightly' in parentheses, again struggling
to minimise the harshness of the assault.

One modern translator invited much criticism and even abuse
by expunging the word 'beat' altogether. Laleh Bakhtiar, an
academic based in Chicago, argued that anyone adhering to the
assault element of the verse was denigrating Islam, and that in any
case *daraba* should be interpreted as 'to go away from'.[78] This
suggestion, with other comments, earned Bakhtiar death threats
from orthodox Muslims and she gained little support from other
academics. Neal Robinson, a professor of Islamic studies, said that
the translation of *daraba* as 'hit' was inescapable.[79] Ali summarised
the common view:

> Commentators have broadly agreed . . . that the term [*daraba*] is meant
> literally, not metaphorically, and that the verse gives permission for a
> husband to strike his wife for *nushuz*, although only if admonition and
> abandonment in bed have had no effect . . . Surah 2, verse 228 (the
> 'degree' verse) and Surah 4, verse 34 ('Men are *qawwamun*') [are]
> notoriously difficult verses for exegetes concerned with gender justice
> and equality.[80]

The allegedly divine authorisation of physical abuse against wives
illustrates a general attitude of Islam to violence. And when such
an injunction to beat one's wife is accompanied by authorisation
for polygamy (Surah 4: 3), for changing one wife for another
(Surah 4: 20) and for the sexual abuse of slaves (Surah 4: 24) the
attitude of Koranic law to women is plain. Professor Mona
Siddiqui, a doctor of classical Islamic jurisprudence, has noted that
in a typical version of Islamic marriage the two parties to the
contract are the man and the woman's male guardian: 'The
woman may be viewed as the third party to the contract . . .
Islamic law regulates gender significance by giving a woman
identity primarily through her relationship with a male member of

her family.'[81] This arrangement is supposed to guarantee, from the male perspective, not only a woman's protection but also her 'subjugation'.[82] And again there is emphasis on the wife's duty to obey her husband – to the point that a specific term, *nashiz*, denotes the disobedient wife.[83]

In the same vein Ghada Karmi, a doctor of Islamic medieval medicine, quoted Mernissi, who indicated that Islamic law and customs are used to ensure the 'subjugation' of women in Morocco, in this regard a typical Muslim state.[84] Karmi also cited a conference held in 1993 to highlight the violence that women are subjected to throughout the Arab world.[85] In addition to the widespread problem of domestic violence, women suffer disproportionately from illiteracy and lag behind men in both primary and secondary education and in employment. And in such regards the Koran is a gross impediment to social progress.

Women are equal to men in some regards – for example, in their religious duties and in areas of punishment – but 'there are observations and injunctions about women and their legal position which are hard to reconcile with the concept of equality . . . The Qur'anic regulations over the matters most important to women: marriage, divorce, child custody, unquestionably discriminate against women, when taken at face value.'[86] Karmi also highlights the relative sexual freedom of men, able to have up to four wives and any number of concubines, and to divorce with extraordinary ease. The classical jurist al-Suyuti (c. 1445–1505) recorded that some men in Islamic history married more than eighty wives in their lifetimes, and the theologian al-Ghazali (1058–1111) noted that the prophet's grandson, Hasan, married 200 times, sometimes marrying four women at once.[87] Karmi assesses the situation in moderate terms, suggesting that the development of Islamic law with respect to women 'exemplifies to perfection this process of patriarchal legitimisation'.[88]

In addition to the Koran, the associated schools of Islamic law and the Hadith, containing Mohammed's alleged commentaries on women[89] and everything else, there is also a substantial body of fatwas, the historical and modern injunctions and commands issued by Muslim authorities of various sorts to guide behaviour.

Here it is enough to give a few samples from a typical compilation – namely, the *Islamic Fatawa Regarding Women* compiled by Muhammad bin Abdul-Aziz Al-Musnad and delivered as Sharia rulings by the Grand Mufti of Saudi Arabia.[90] This volume contains 366 commentaries and rules, many of which appear ridiculous, such as the need to blot out pictures in magazines with ink before a woman is allowed to read them and the advisability of not wearing a watch during the mourning period because it resembles jewellery. A few examples convey the flavour of the countless restrictions placed on women by men under the authority of the fatwas. Many are supported by alleged sayings of the prophet:[91]

- Women are not allowed to teach boys since this would be 'filled with evil and harmful consequences . . . the door to this kind of practice must be completely closed'.
- If a woman stays in a mosque after she has started to menstruate, does she commit a sin? She is obliged to leave as quickly as possible because a 'menstruating woman, post-partum bleeding woman and sexually defiled person are not allowed to sit in the mosques' (the question as to whether a menstruating woman can touch a copy of the Koran 'is another controversial issue which cannot be discussed in detail here').
- If a woman whose shins, forearms or hair are uncovered prays, her prayer is 'not valid' and she commits a sin on two counts – for being uncovered and for praying 'in that state'.
- Women can uncover the hands but not the feet while praying.
- A woman cannot be married to an unbeliever. If he converts in order to marry her, it may be a trick and if he later 'apostates' he must be killed for the prophet.
- Similarly, if a Muslim woman knowingly marries a Christian 'she is liable to a legal punishment'. Again, if the man 'apostates' after a conversion, 'his neck must be struck off'.
- Do women have a shortcoming in reasoning and religion? Yes, as a class, men are superior to women in general.
- Women are not allowed to drive because this 'leads to many evils and negative consequences . . . [such as] her mixing with

men without her being on her guard . . . Allah has ordered the wives of the Prophet and the women of the believers to remain in their houses, to wear *hijab* and not to display their adornments to non-*mahram*[92] males as that leads to promiscuity that overruns a society.'

• Wives should accept that their husbands are the 'most knowledgeable' as to whether they should be allowed to go to the marketplace or anywhere else.

• A woman will be rewarded for reading the Koran, whether she understands it or not.

It is plain that Muslim literature, whether allegedly deriving from a jealous and vindictive Allah (see Chapter 2) or from Mohammed and the plethora of superstitious and ignorant imams that followed him, is persistently hostile to women, regarding them as less than human and in consequence deserving fewer rights than men. The inevitable corollary is that the woman-hating words sustain gross patterns of discrimination and abuse throughout the Islamic world.

It should be said at the outset that Muslim apologists typically claim that the patterns of abuse – forced marriages, female circumcision, domestic violence etc. – are merely cultural matters that have nothing to do with Islam. But I suggest that this sophistical separation of religion and culture is completely bogus. Religion is a part of culture, just as particular traditions help to shape the character of religion itself. Many of the abuses are carried out in the name of Islam, and it would be foolish to suggest that Koranic authorisations for wife beating, slave holding and polygamy have no bearing on the treatment of women in Islamic societies. The religious literature, granted a divine imprimatur, is taken at its word and shapes the treatment of women throughout the world. Here I can only give a few examples from a copious file. I readily acknowledge that a list of sexist abuses and crimes could easily be given for non-Muslim societies, but I maintain that the ones provided here are directly linked to the misogynist teachings of Islam.

In Saudi Arabia, according to the Minnesota Lawyers International Rights Committee, the religious police (*mutawwa'in*) carry sticks with which to beat women on the streets if they are

thought to be dressed immodestly. There are recorded cases of
the police hitting women on their upper bodies and faces when
they were judged to be offending the Islamic norms of dress and
behaviour.[93] Men are expected to control their women and may
be punished if their women misbehave, sometimes involving a
prison sentence for fathers or husbands, which in turn consigns
the women to house arrest since they are not allowed to venture
forth without male guardians. The women themselves are often
imprisoned – and tortured – in jail. When fourteen women
drove a short distance in November 1990 to protest the ban on
women drivers, the Saudi civil police surrounded the cars,
pounded on the windows, denounced the women as prostitutes
and sinners, and hauled them off to the police station for
questioning. Male relatives were summoned and made to sign
documents stating that such gross infringements would never
happen again. Then the Saudi authorities distributed 'police
reports' – carrying the women's names, addresses and telephone
numbers – to public buildings and on the streets, with the
injunction 'Do what you believe is appropriate regarding
these women'.

One of the consequences of the US-led invasion of Iraq in
March 2003 was to stimulate an Islamic ascendancy which had
disastrous consequences for women accustomed to living under a
secular regime. It is useful to remember that under Saddam
Hussein women held a number of seats in the Ba'athist National
Assembly, and that discrimination against women was prohibited
in law. For example, labour law no. 71, enacted in 1987,
guaranteed equal pay for men and women for equal work. Other
laws protected women's rights in education, health and social
welfare.[94] In April 2003, soon after the invasion, Christian girls
wearing lipstick and no headscarves were voicing fears that their
freedoms would end if hardline Shi'ite clerics turned the secular
Iraq into an Islamic republic. Their fears were well founded.

The female Iraqi blogger 'Riverbend', a computer science
graduate, said it felt like women had been thrown back fifty years.
She used to dress how she wanted. Now girls wearing jeans risked
being attacked, abducted and abused – killed even – by Islamic
fundamentalists. And she was terrorised into unemployment.

Women were no longer welcome in her former workplace and she was told to go home because no-one could protect her: 'I cried bitterly all the way home – cried for my job, cried for my future and cried for the torn streets, damaged buildings and crumbling people.'[95]

In July 2003 Human Rights Watch reported that Iraqi women were being prevented from participating in public life. Women were being confined to their houses, only allowed to emerge when concealed in Islamic garb and hidden behind husbands and fathers. In some parts of Iraq, wearing a pair of trousers was considered a defiance of Muslim orthodoxy punishable by death. One Basra woman, Dr Kefaya, who worked in a women's and children's hospital, ignored Islamist demands that she abandon her job, until a man walked into the building and murdered her. One witness, Mrs Aziz, spoke of dead friends: 'My friend Sheda and her sister. They were threatened. One day they returned to their house with two other women. They were all shot.'[96] In the same fashion Zeena al-Qushtaini, a divorced woman who owned a Baghdad pharmacy, was abducted and shot twice in the head. Later her body was found dressed in a full-length black *abaya* that she would never have chosen to wear, the headscarf covered in blood.[97]

A 26-year-old university lecturer, Noor, used to go out to a local restaurant with her boyfriend, but then the 'men in black' arrived on her doorstep. They threatened to kidnap her, shave her head and shoot her if she refused to observe Islamic strictures.[98] By now, Shi'ite and Sunni clerics were issuing anti-feminist fatwas. For example, the Sunni cleric Abu Houseifa declared: 'Women cannot drive. Women cannot go out after midday. Women and men are not allowed to go out and walk together.' Shops were being stripped of all women's clothing deemed inappropriate, and Islamic thugs were driving round shooting any women who broke the rules.[99] Elsewhere religious zealots were throwing acid in the faces of women judged not to be wearing Islamic attire. In May 2006 teenage girls in the Amariya district were dragged into houses to have their heads shaved, while the Islamists warned that in future any women not wearing the hijab would be killed.

The Muslim police did not regard female victims as a priority and those women injured by sexual abuse at the hands of religious thugs, even if able to undertake the perilous journey to a functioning hospital, were often refused medical treatment. 'Women and girls live in an atmosphere where, if they are raped . . . they have poor legal recourse and have well-grounded fears of social ostracism, rejection by their families, and even physical violence.'[100] The American activist Fern Holland, who had travelled to Iraq from Oklahoma to champion women's rights, was shot dead at a checkpoint by Iraqi police; and the Iraqi women's rights activist Sundus Abbas Hasan, targeted by the Islamists for execution, was forced to flee the country.

In 1994 Palestinian women, 'daring to challenge male-dominated tradition and culture [sustained by Islam]',[101] supported the creation of a unique battered women's shelter in the Galilee village of Kfar Yassif. Some men reportedly saw the support for the shelter as a 'provocation'.[102] At the same time Suha Arafat, the wife of the PLO chairman, Yasser Arafat, was demanding a women's revolution: 'I have told my husband, if he does not accept the rights of women, I myself will lead the protests outside the offices of the Palestinian interim government.' Previously the activist Palestinian author Raymonda Tawil, Suha Arafat's mother and the author of *My Home, My Prison*, had attacked conservative Palestinian society, which made prisoners of women in their own homes: 'A woman has no rights in the Arab world. Tunisia is the only exception. I want to adapt Tunisian law on the social and political rights of women.'[103] Jihan Sadat, the late Egyptian president's widow, and Queen Noor of Jordan had protested in the same fashion about the suppression of women under Islam – and had both become victims of hate campaigns in which their lives were under threat.

It has been argued that Wafa Idris became in January 2002 the first suicide bomber in the Israeli–Palestinian conflict partly because of the Palestinian repression she suffered in Muslim society. When her marriage ran into problems, her husband Ahmed consulted the local imam, who quoted from the Koran to indicate how a disobedient wife should be punished. A video of the talk showed two men surrounded by blocks of wood in varying sizes, while one of them explained 'which block should be used on the woman for which offence'.[104] (Elsewhere on the video an audience was counselled about sadomasochistic couples who enjoyed the punishments described in the Koran, and therefore were exempt from practising them.)

Idris's close friend, Itimad Abu Lidbeh, indicated why Idris might have welcomed the suicide option: 'When she lost her baby . . . I sensed she had no desire to go on living.'[105] Without a family and oppressed by the Palestinian culture, Idris had no future. A psychiatrist, Iyad Sarraj, commented that 'cultural, religious and nationalistic reasons, combined with her own personal depression, gave Wafa the reason and the courage' to commit suicide.[106] The author Barbara Victor surmises that the thought of martyrdom, rewarded in Islam by everlasting life at Allah's table in Paradise, coupled with oppression of the endless Israeli occupation, might have made suicide a welcome option: 'And what if the idea that women who die as martyrs will finally achieve equality to men were added to the equation?'[107] Another female suicide bomber, Darine, said she would never marry 'because she had no intention of becoming a slave', regarding human relationships as 'a steel form into which we are poured by our family and which don't allow us to liberate ourselves'.[108] Victor says that 'her parents were putting a lot of pressure on her to be an obedient, full-time childbearing and child-rearing spouse in a family where the husband was all-powerful and had absolute authority'.[109] And the plight of the unmarried Palestinian woman was also dire. Any infringement of strict Islamic rules can bring death at the hands of male relatives carrying out an honour killing. According to one Palestinian observer, 'so many young Arab-Israeli women . . . fear for their lives at the hands of their fathers or brothers'.[110] Another Arab, a Palestinian woman, commented hesitantly that if an unmarried girl becomes pregnant there are only three options: she marries her partner, her father hides her in the house or 'her male relatives kill her'.[111]

In March 1990 a Pakistani woman who had entered Britain under false pretences, and who claimed that she had been raped, was given a reprieve from deportation because of how she would have been treated in Pakistan. Experts in Islamic law emphasised that without independent male witnesses or a confession from the accused, rape would be impossible to prove – which meant that the woman could be charged with adultery under Islamic Zina law. If convicted in Pakistan, the woman could have faced forty lashes and ten years in jail.[112]

In Kuwait, where women have traditionally been prohibited from taking part in any local or national elections, there were desultory steps towards reform following the first Gulf War. Women, dubbed 'suffragettes' in the Western press, were demonstrating for equal rights but achieving little.[113] As late as 2003 the all-male parliament was considering a government-sponsored bill giving women the vote and the right to stand in elections. Draft laws, which had to be endorsed by the feudal emir, had been rejected in the past. In May 1999 one such draft was approved by the then emir, Sheikh Jaber al-Ahmad al-Jaber al-Sabah, but in November the extremists managed to stall the new legislation and the parliament voted against it. In January 2001 Kuwait's highest court rejected a demand for women to be given the right to vote, and in July 2003 Islamists swept to victory in all-male parliamentary elections. In March Hidaya Sultan al-Salem, a female journalist working for full political rights for women, was killed by a burst of machine gun fire.

At the same time a Briton was banned from teaching in Kuwait after he composed an imaginary letter from Mohammed to the archangel Gabriel asking him for a job as a prophet, in order to teach writing technique to his students. In January 2000 two female authors and a publisher were jailed for distributing 'blasphemous' books. On 5 April 2006 women voted, in a local by-election, for the first time. Today, while the Kuwaiti monarchy pretends an interest in human rights, women have still to obtain social and political equality, and writers, foreign teachers and others have to watch their step.

In 1997 publicity was given to the harrowing case of two British sisters, having long endured patriarchal cruelty at the hands of their Muslim father, being sold by him in 1980 as teenage brides to Yemen.[114] And forced Muslim marriages are directly linked to honour killing: a desperately unhappy bride will understandably be driven to seek comfort and love elsewhere, whereupon it is likely she will be murdered by her male relatives. The journalist Sue Lloyd-Roberts reported such a case in Jordan. An English teacher, Ahmed, was horrified to learn that his sister had slept with a fellow student at university. Ahmed took her to a doctor to 'reinstate' her virginity, after which she married but left her husband for another man. Ahmed commented that 'her lust got the better of her', and that she would have done it 'a third, a fourth, a hundred times'; and he decided that there was only one solution: 'I had to kill her.' He explained: 'I reminded myself that this act [the murder] had the backing of the whole family . . . As my hands tightened [around his sister's neck], I recited the Koran.' Before she died, Ahmed forced her to recite 'Allah is great and Mohammed is the only prophet', in the hope that this would wipe out all her sins and get her into Paradise.[115]

In October 1998 Pakistan's ruling Muslim League exercised its majority in the national assembly to vote in Sharia law in an effort to promote Islamisation throughout the land. Women were reportedly concerned about the likely clampdown on human rights, with Islamabad gripped by rumours that extremists were patrolling public places in search of women wearing Western dress and injecting HIV into the arms of women who were violating the Islamic dress code.[116] In 1999 it was estimated that about 2,000 women had been murdered by their male relatives in honour killings the previous year. One woman, Shagufta, was killed for shopping without permission, many others for talking to a man who was not a relative.[117]

Other cases on file include a Yemeni woman repeatedly raped by her father and made pregnant by him (he was jailed for twenty years and she was jailed also – for five years); a Turkish state-funded religious foundation saying that men can beat their wives but should avoid the face; female bathers at the popular Moroccan resort of Mehdia being told by preachers to 'forsake not God's law . . . clothe yourself as the faithful' (like the women paddlers covered from head to toe); a Sharia court in northern Nigeria sentencing a seventeen-year-old to 180 lashes for having had pre-marital sex (she would be flogged forty days after giving birth); a woman stoned to death in Iran for acting in 'obscene films', a charge she denied; a leading Egyptian feminist, Nawal al-Saadawi, pressured to divorce for declaring the hajj a vestige of paganism ('a historical fact'); a devout Muslim father in Britain knifing his favourite daughter to death after finding a boyfriend in her bedroom ('according to the law it [the murder] was not right, but according to religion it was right'); a thirty-year-old single mother, Amina Lawal, sentenced to be stoned to death for adultery in northern Nigeria; an Iranian cutting off his seven-year-old daughter's head, thinking she had been raped by her uncle; three Nigerian women killed – one beheaded – after refusing to wear the burqa; a devout Muslim father cutting his daughter's throat for taking a Christian boyfriend; a 23-year-old Muslim woman stoned to death in Marseilles by two Muslim boys; Sania Mirza, a leading female tennis player in India, forced to withdraw from tournaments after fatwas and death threats; Muslim clerics in India ordering women not to work with men; the Somali-born Ayaan Hirsi Ali, a writer, feminist and former Dutch politician, given death threats; women and children in Iran beaten in the name of Islam ('he [the prison guard] said he believed in only two things – Islam and the rule of the clerics'); two Sudanese women sentenced under Sharia law to death by stoning for adultery; hundreds of Iranian women arrested in May 2007 for not observing Islamic dress code (women's lack of equality 'written into law'); a Muslim woman in Malaysia forcibly separated, according to Sharia law, from her Hindu husband and their children; a seventeen-year-old Yezidi girl stoned to death in Kurdistan for having an Arab boyfriend; female TV journalists in Palestine threatened with death if they refused to wear the hijab; the Taliban killing a girl for daring to attend school; Saudi banks ordered to keep female staff away from men; a Kurdish man boasting at the Old Bailey of how he had killed a Kurdish woman by kicking and stamping on her neck 'to get her soul out'; Muslim medical staff breaking anti-MRSA hygiene rules in September 2007 by refusing to bare their arms; according to a detailed report (*Crimes of the Community*) Muslim policemen in Britain turning a blind eye to honour killings (authorities afraid of being seen as 'Islamophobic or racist'); and an American businesswoman in Saudi Arabia arrested, and later abused in prison, for sitting in Starbucks with a man.

In December 2008 Setereh, a lovestruck eighty-year-old woman in Iran, was denied the right to marry Jamshid, her betrothed, since she was unable to obtain her father's permission and could not prove that he was dead. He had abandoned her when she was two, and now Setereh was condemned to live separately from a man who made her 'heart start beating faster'. Campaigners said that this was further evidence of discrimination against women under the laws of Muslim Iran. Another case concerned an eight-year-old Saudi Arabian girl married off by her father to a 58-year-old man. The girl's mother tried to file divorce papers but the judge declared that she did not 'have the right to file', and said that the girl could file the papers when she reached puberty. Here the problems are that the time of puberty is not defined in law and that Saudi judges insist that even adult women speak to them through a male guardian or lawyer – yet more evidence of Muslim discrimination against women.[118]

In December 2008 the Taliban, using announcements in mosques and radio broadcasts, ordered the closure of all girls' schools in the Swat district of Pakistan. If the schools were not closed by 15 January the school buildings would be blown up and the girls attacked. It was emphasised also that women should not leave their homes without wearing the strictest Islamic garb. Shah Dauran, the Muslim leader of the Swat Taliban, commented: 'Female education is against Islamic teachings and spreads vulgarity in society.' Already the Taliban had destroyed 125 girls' schools in the area over the previous year, with Mullah Fazlullah also using radio broadcasts to exhort parents to stop sending their daughters to schools which 'inculcate Western values'. Following such militant threats, the local authorities reported that 50 per cent of girls in the area and many women teachers had stopped attending school. Elsewhere in Pakistan – for example, in Waziristan and other tribal areas – more than 100 schools had been burnt down, leaving tens of thousands of children with no education.[119]

If people complain about such abuses and discrimination, or otherwise upset Muslim orthodoxy, they are likely to be terrorised or even murdered by religious fanatics. The cases of Salman Rushdie, forced to seek police protection, the murdered Theo van Gogh, and Ayaan Hirsi Ali, forced to flee assassination threats for criticising Muslim abuses, are relatively well known but there are many other instances when religious terror is directed at progressive writers. Here one further example will suffice. The award-winning novelist Taslima Nasreen, under death threats from Muslims, was forced to flee her home in Bangladesh, to seek a temporary sanctuary in Delhi and then to find a more permanent refuge in virtual 'solitary confinement' in Paris. After criticising the 'inherent misogyny' of conservative Muslim society, religious fanatics offered a cash reward for her decapitation. Nasreen declared: 'My aim is to raise consciousness, to struggle for justice for women, so I have no alternative but to criticise Islam because Islam oppresses women. I know millions of women have been suffering because of religion, tradition, culture and customs and I feel a responsibility to do something.'[120]

It seems clear that today Islam sustains patterns of discrimination and abuse against women that are discernible in all Muslim countries and in all Muslim communities in the non-Muslim world. To reinforce a point made earlier, it cannot be argued that such patterns are a matter of cultural tradition and bear no relationship to Islam 'properly understood'. The religion emerged in a cultural context, and where some reforms were possible – for example, prohibiting the burying alive of female offspring – the principal misogynistic elements not only survived but were reinforced by texts that were granted divine authority. It is significant that one of the objections of the early Muslims to the supplanted polytheisms was that the pre-Islamic desert communities gave reverence to female divinities. Hence it is possible to argue that Islam helped to undermine the already fragile status of women in Arabia and beyond.

This view of Islam is rehearsed not only among secularists and other non-Muslims in the modern world. Throughout the Islamic world Muslim women are struggling, often in desperate circumstances, to improve their social and political status. Here I need only mention the Kuwaiti 'suffragettes', the Women's Rights Association in Iraq,[121] the Association Marocaine des Droits de la Femme in Morocco,[122] the Union Nationale des Femmes de Tunisie in Tunisia[123] and the Revolutionary Association of the Women of Afghanistan.[124] Many of these movements, but not all, are linked to secularist groups and parties in Muslim countries, themselves under constant harassment and threat. It should be possible for Muslim women to achieve some amelioration of their plight within the context of their faith, but full emancipation will only come following a successful onslaught on the anti-feminist cant and superstition sustained in Muslim literature and mosques around the world.

The manifest discrimination against and abuse of women in Judaism, Christianity and Islam is reflected also in all other religions. The writer Lucy Moore has described the *purdah* (in Urdu 'curtain') tradition that continues to operate under Hinduism in India, whereby in some primitive communities women must be permanently hidden from public view. Purdah, like the repellent caste system, survived through the period of the British Raj. Historically, as in Judeo-Christianity and Islam, the birth of a girl was generally regarded as a disappointing event. Consequently, when a son was born, a Rajput father would organise a musical celebration, with sweets distributed among his friends. The birth of a daughter would be greeted by the announcement that 'nothing' had been born into the family – indicating that since the baby was female she would be nothing in the world, 'and the friends [would] go home grave and quiet'.[125] A female Bengali writer, Surat Kumari, asked the rhetorical question: 'A bride's of value only to keep the lineage alive; for what else does one take on the burden of bringing in an unwanted girl from another family?'[126] In such a context female infanticide was common; in 1870 a report revealed that in one Indian state some 300 children had been 'stolen by wolves' – all were female.[127]

   Again, as with the desert religions of the Middle East, much of the struggle against abuse and discrimination under Hinduism derived from women striving for emancipation. A book, *The Position of Women in Indian Life*, published in London in 1910 and applauded by the young Ramsay MacDonald, heralded grass-roots, women-run schemes such as cooperative credit societies that would emerge almost a century later; and the Women's Indian Association, founded in 1917 and linked to the suffragettes, demanded equal rights for the first time. And again, the struggle of women for emancipation was forced to contend with the misogynistic writings that defined the religious tradition.

In the *Mahabharata*, a sacred text of Hinduism, the question is discussed of women being 'the root of all evil' and 'exceedingly frail'.[128] One of the disputants, a woman, observes: 'There is nothing else that is more sinful than woman. Verily, women are the root of all faults.' The disposition of women is to be ungrateful, envious and sexually promiscuous. ('There is none whom they are incapable of admitting to their favours. They never take into consideration the age . . . ugly or handsome, if only the person happens to belong to the opposite sex.') And this sinfulness of women seems to have no limits: 'They are incapable of being restrained when bent upon transgression . . . Women are never satiated with men . . . when women were created [by 'that eternal Brahman'] these faults that I have enumerated were planted in them!'[129] And it doesn't get any better.

Why do men, the Hindu disputants ask, attach themselves to women when they are 'stained with so many faults'?[130] Women please men but constantly deceive them and are utterly disreputable: 'She is poison. She is a snake. She is fire.'[131] But in a previous creation, we are told, women were all virtuous – until Brahman imbued them with all manner of carnal desires. The Vedas teach that women are 'living lies . . . Men are quite incapable of restraining them within bounds. The Creator Himself is incapable of restraining them within the limits that are proper.'[132]

There is only one possible solution. Men must do the best they can in curtailing the sinful natures of women; in particular, wives should be made to realise that 'the husband is the wife's Highest Deity'. A husband describes in the *Mahabharata* what this actually entails:

> She [his wife] never eats before I eat, and never bathes before I bathe. She rejoices if I rejoice, and becomes sorry when I am sorry. When I am away she becomes cheerless and when I am angry she ceases not to speak sweetly. Ever devoted to her lord and ever relying upon her lord, she was ever employed in doing what was agreeable to and beneficial for her lord . . . Devoted to me and constant in her love, my spouse is exceedingly sweet-tempered and worships me devoutly.[133]

In this context we are not surprised to find that a 'true wife' is one 'who has borne a son'.[134] And other Hindu writers sustain the view that, in effect, the wife should be seen as nothing more than a domestic slave, unstintingly serving her husband and bearing children.

Thus Swami Vivekananda, while elevating the role of women in the home, saw her domestic duties as 'a woman's proper office': 'The happiness of the woman for a woman lies not in catering for carnal passions, not in challenging man in his own field by forgetting her natural course of duties, but in leading the ideal life as taught in the sacred scriptures.'[135] In the same vein Swami Shivananda wrote that to a woman 'there is no higher duty than service to her husband' and that 'she should worship him daily . . . She should perform all actions to please him' – and this applies whatever the behaviour of the husband. It is important that, if necessary, the wife sacrifice herself to her disreputable husband by showing 'intense devotion . . . even if he is lustful, and even if he has no good conduct'.[136] A wife should ignore her husband's 'vicious qualities' and not speak of them to anyone; even if he shows her no love and insults her she should show him warm affection. Above all, the wife should stick tenaciously to her *dharma* (duty), 'even though he may be wicked' and even though 'she is ill-treated' by him. A clearer recipe for domestic abuse would be hard to imagine.

For good measure Shivananda adds that since women talk too much they should observe a vow of silence for two hours daily. Moreover, their other 'evil qualities' should be noted – such as 'jealousy, hatred, pride, hypocrisy, intolerance and crookedness'. And wives do not know how to behave properly towards family members, so they should strive to overcome such characteristic shortcomings. The *Mahabharata* helps by pointing out that 'even if one happens to belong to the inferior order, even if one happens to be a woman', the path of Yoga can improve matters.[137]

And so Hindu doctrine runs on: 'A woman is impure by her very birth' (from the Aranya Kanda); 'Devotion of body, speech and mind to her husband's feet is the only duty, sacred vow and penance of a woman' (Aranya Kanda); 'It is the nature of women . . . to be vicious, fickle and sharp-tongued and to sow seeds of dissension' (Aranya Kanda); 'The husband is the god for a worthy wife' (Ayodha Kanda); and so on and so forth.

Here it is impossible to trace in detail the consequences of this sort of teaching but we need only recall the incidence through history of child marriage (sometimes involving girls as young as five), bride burning (if the dowry is judged to be insufficient), widow burning (sati), witch burning and mass wife burning (dozens burnt at a time). Such practices are sanctioned by scriptural teaching; one example will suffice. The 'Sati Hymn' of the Rig Veda is traditionally recited during the immolation of widows: 'Let those women, whose husbands are worthy, and [when the wives] are living, enter the house with ghee [applied] as corrylium [to their eyes; corrylium is a kind of ritual make-up]. Let these wives first step into the pyre, tearless without any affliction and well adorned.'[138] A more liberal Hindu text gives the widow a more generous option: 'If a woman's husband dies, let her lead a life of chastity, or else mount his pyre.'[139]

There is ample evidence that women are massively abused in modern India and that religious ideologies have helped to create and sustain the social framework in which this is possible. See for example cases of women 'forcibly secluded';[140] a dowry killing in which a husband poured kerosene over his wife, set it alight and told her to die;[141] bride buying;[142] a lower-caste girl being burnt to death after being raped;[143] a case of sati being celebrated by a village.[144]

Buddhism and Jainism have been seen as protest movements against the Vedic system, but they did not lead to any major changes in the status of women. These religions placed emphasis on the importance of asceticism, which meant that women were regarded as hurdles on the path to liberation. The Buddha deserted his wife to attain the enlightened state of nirvana and considered a women a gross impediment to spiritual growth. He is said to have instructed his disciples, like the ascetic saints of Christianity, not to talk to a woman or even to look at her.[145] There is continuing debate within Buddhism as to whether a woman can become a buddha (or a bodhisattva) and attain enlightenment, with some Theravadan thinkers insisting that buddhas have to be men. But women should not abandon hope. They may be reincarnated as a male, whereupon the route to nirvana will be open to them.

The Digambara sect of Jainism holds that nakedness in public is an essential element on the road to liberation – which is seen as more difficult for women and so they are regarded as second-class citizens. The Digambaras, with a reverence for all life, also believe that women are inherently *himsic* (harmful), since menstrual blood is reckoned to kill many micro-organisms that live in the female body. This means that women also offend the Jain doctrine of non-violence, the lethal effects of menstrual blood rendering women less peaceful than men. In addition, as with most religions, women are regarded as inherently impure in one way or another.

Sikhism, while claiming scriptural authority for male–female equality, is characterised in its modern version by many of the superstitious disabilities that inflict other religions. Honour killings are practised in Sikh communities, much as under Islam;[146] and medical treatment may be refused in certain cases – if a woman is likely to be examined by a male doctor, and if she (or a man) is likely to offend against her religion by losing her hair following chemotherapy.[147] And underlying all the specific attitudes is the persistent assumption among many Sikh men that women have fewer rights – as, for example, when Sikh women were prevented on the sole ground of gender from taking part in a religious ceremony in Amritsar ('a blow for Sikh women who have been struggling for equal rights').[148] In the same fashion followers of Zoroastrianism, deriving from ancient Persia, boast scriptural authority for gender equality but still exhibit underlying obvious anti-feminist attitudes. For example, as in Roman Catholicism, women are not allowed to be priests; and the Indian Zoroastrians (Parsis) typically insist that a child must have a Parsi father to be eligible for introduction to the faith.

It is obvious that the world religions have typically depicted women as inferior to men, and that this has led to countless manifestations of social discrimination and the worst excesses of torture, abuse and murder. It is no excuse to say that the examples given indicate cultural and not religious practices. Religion and culture are enmeshed in a symbiotic relationship, with a constant interplay between the two. Moreover, religion has often worked both to overthrow existing elements of female emancipation and to provide scriptural authority for ancient traditions that debase women in the family and the wider community. In such a fashion religion has fought real emancipation and sustained a wide range of anti-feminist domestic and social patterns over the centuries.

5

Sexual
psychopathology

'*Inter faeces et urinam nascimur*' ('Between faeces and urine we
are born')

St Augustine of Hippo (354–430)

What are we to make of the religious contribution to sexual
behaviour? Should we be chaste all our lives, as St Paul suggested?[1]
Or should we make love to our obedient wives whenever we feel
like it, irrespective of their feelings, as Mohammed recommended?[2] It is obvious that the practice of sex is one of the most
problematic topics for *Homo sapiens*: non-human animals and
plants seem to have fewer difficulties, not least because they lack
the complex cultures that shape the behaviour of human beings as
social animals. All societies have viewed sex with a mixture of
trepidation and awe, acknowledging its importance and ever eager
to hedge it round with regulations, laws, taboos and prohibitions.
It is a cruel irony that religion, keen to advertise the uniqueness of
humankind, has generated a range of sexual attitudes over the
centuries that amount to nothing less than a psychopathology.

The earliest societies knew little about the mechanics of sex.
For example, the anthropologist Bronisław Malinowski described
how the primitive beliefs of the Trobrianders shaped their
attitudes to the status of men and women in society.[3] Here it was
thought that it was exclusively the mother who built up the child's
body, the father being in no way responsible for its formation –
'The mother feeds the infant in her body. Then, when it comes
out, she feeds it with her milk'; 'The mother makes the child out
of her blood'; 'Brothers and sisters are of the same flesh, because
they come out of the same mother'. Such convictions, coupled

with certain mythological and animistic beliefs, affirm that there is no bond of physical union between the father and the child whatever, and this in turn influenced the tribal attitudes to kinship, descent, inheritance, succession in rank, chieftainship, hereditary offices, and the role of magic.

The anatomical knowledge of the Trobrianders was primitive. They could distinguish and name the vagina, the clitoris, the penis and the testes; but they had no words to describe the mons veneris, the labia and the ovaries. The eyes were regarded as the seat of desire and lust (*magila kaytu*, literally 'desire of copulation'), the cause of sexual passion. Desire was carried to the brain by means of the *wotuna* (literally 'tendril' or 'creeper'), and thence all over the body. The eyes communicated the sexual impulse to the kidneys, which (in men) in turn cause an erection. It was thought that a man with his eyes closed would have no erection, though the Trobrianders qualified this statement by admitting that the olfactory sense can sometimes replace the eyes, for 'when a woman discards her grass petticoat in the dark, desire may be aroused'.[4] The kidneys, it was thought, were equally responsible for communicating sensual desire to the clitoris.

The Trobrianders had no knowledge of the purpose of the testes, pointing out that a woman too can produce a discharge and she has no testes. In fact this part of the male anatomy, serving a purely decorative function, was only an ornamental appendage: 'Indeed, how ugly would a penis look without the testes. [The testes] serve to make it look proper.'[5] Among the Trobrianders, unlike many primitive tribes, there was no particular dread of menstrual blood, though a husband would refrain from sharing a bed with his wife during her menstruation. At this time women would wash themselves daily in the same large water hole from which the whole village drew its drinking water and in which men occasionally took a bath. Beliefs about spirits and birth were complicated, since a spirit might exist for a lengthy period on the Island of the Dead until, wanting a fresh earthly existence, it leapt back in age, found its way back to the Trobriands and sought out the womb of some earthly woman.[6]

As with most religious believers the Trobrianders, combining a mistaken view of the material world with an imaginative mythology, were keen to preserve the differences between spirits and human bodies but realised that the two categories would have to combine at some stage in one way or another. They had no concept of the fertilising properties of seminal fluid: women bore children without any involvement of a male partner, but only after the vagina had been opened by some means. One important Trobriand myth involves a woman called Mitigis or Bolutukwa, who lost her virginity by exposing her body to falling rain and became the mother of the legendary hero Tudava. One day she fell asleep in her rocky dwelling, reclining under a dripping stalactite. The drops of water pierced her vagina, and so deprived her of her virginity in a purely mechanical fashion.[7]

The researcher George Ryley Scott has pointed out that, granted 'the realisation of some dim notion of sex, the greater the mystery attached to the phenomenon, the more pronounced . . . the degree of reverence accorded to it'.[8] And in those tribes where no connection was perceived between sex and procreation, the emotional rapture associated with sexual experience was sufficient to render the male and female genitals objects of veneration and worship. The early Hebrew god instructed his followers to 'be fruitful, and multiply'[9] – and this injunction accorded well enough with widespread pagan practices. Human fruitfulness was connected in mythology with the fertility of the crops, and so it was common for people to indulge in sexual promiscuity at fertility rites and even on the occasions of planting the seed and harvesting. One authority wrote of the Mayan Indians:

> Whatever the seed to be planted, the tillers of the soil must sleep apart from their wives and concubines for several days, in order that on the night before planting they might indulge their passions to the fullest extent; certain persons are even said to have been appointed to perform the sex act at the very moment when the first seeds were deposited in the ground.[10]

It was one of the most remarkable accomplishments of Judeo-Christianity, ever combating the 'ways of the flesh', to convert the sexual enthusiasm of early primitive tribes into a worldwide psychopathology of disgust and shame.

The early Hebrew attitudes to sex are well illustrated in the Pentateuch. From Genesis we learn that Abraham, keen to save his own life, told Pharaoh that his wife Sarai ('a fair woman to look upon') was his sister and allowed Pharaoh to take her to his royal palace, for which generosity he received in return 'sheep, and oxen, and he asses, and menservants, and maidservants, and she asses, and camels'.[11] Abraham later lent his wife to King Abimelech, for which he received a thousand pieces of silver. Thus it seems that women could be donated to enemies in propitiation. One story tells how a drunken mob demanded that Lot, Abraham's nephew, give up some men, 'that we might know them'. Lot protested that the men were guests, and suggested that his two virgin daughters might suffice: 'I have two daughters which have not known man; let me, I pray you, bring them out unto you, and do ye to them as is good in your eyes: only unto these men do nothing; for therefore came they under the shadow of my roof.'[12]

In Exodus, Leviticus and Deuteronomy we find early Hebrew laws intended to deal with bestiality, sodomy, incest, rape, fornication, adultery, unchastity and castration – already indicating the preoccupation with sexual matters that would come to dominate the Judeo–Christian tradition. Sexual intercourse is depicted as sinful;[13] the magical powers of holy water can be used to expose a wife's infidelity (no similar test is provided for unfaithful husbands);[14] God orders Moses to divide up the booty – including 32,000 women and girls – obtained through conquest,[15] and he threatens women with rape.[16] In Judges we find yet another example of a young woman, a farmer's concubine, being offered to satiate a drunken crowd. The next morning she falls dead, whereupon the farmer cuts up her body and sends pieces to the tribes.[17] And so it ran on.

Wives were frequently seized and carried off during festivities or in battle; King Saul asked for 100 foreskins of Philistines in return for the hand of his daughter Michal (Voltaire supposed they were sent as a necklace to the bride); Amnon raped his sister Tamar; and efforts were made – unsuccessfully, it seems – to revive the old King David with a young virgin. The damsel was 'very fair, and cherished the king . . . but the king knew her not'.[18]

God urged his followers to adopt the rite of circumcision,[19] but Jesus went a step further and recommended castration: 'For there are some eunuchs, that are so born from their mother's womb; and there are some eunuchs which were made eunuchs of men: and there be eunuchs, which have made themselves eunuchs for the kingdom of heaven's sake. He that is able to receive it, let him receive it.'[20] (The third-century theologian Origen, many patriarchs of Constantinople, and members of the Skoptsy religious sect in Russia and Romania managed 'to receive it'.) Jesus recommended celibacy, as did Paul, and, as we have seen, urged his followers to hate their parents, wives and families so that they could properly follow him.[21]

The sexual character of the Bible has disturbed many churchmen, intent on spreading a doctrine of abstinence and chastity. On 30 March 2001 the Catholic theologian Don Bruno Maggioni declared to a conference entitled 'Eroticism in the Old Testament' that scripture was 'full of sex and violence', 'so full of eroticism' that it should not be given to children. The main theme of the conference was a quotation from the Song of Solomon: 'Let him kiss me with the kisses of his mouth: for thy love is better than wine'[22] – words that had scandalised the early church. Maggioni told the Catholic daily *Avvenire* that the Bible was a work for adults, not just for its sexual pages but because of the kind of questions it raises about mankind: 'The Bible uses the word to "know", as in "carnal knowledge", which implies a profound relationship of communion and knowledge between man and woman, which, in turn, is a reflection of God's knowing relationship with mankind.' Adam and Eve, said Maggioni, were naked and 'full of sin and shame', signalling that the threat of disorder was always 'lurking in the joy of sex'. So he saw the Bible as taking a natural attitude to sex but at the same time giving a warning of the 'terrible destructive force which sex can assume outside the framework of God's law'.[23] In 2008 Nathan Abrams compiled *Jews and Sex*, a collection of essays on aspects of Jewish life – for example, Yiddish lesbian poetry – which he thought deserved more attention than they had received.[24] Here it is emphasised that the Old Testament, written by different authors at very different times, was often 'self-contradictory' and seemingly obsessed with sexual matters.

In a review article for the book Andy McSmith highlighted some of the stories that appear in the Old Testament: 'The harlot by the roadside' (Genesis 38), who disguised herself as a prostitute in order to seduce Judah; 'Onan' (Genesis 38), who 'spilled his seed upon the ground'; 'Samson and Delilah' (Judges 16), the archetypal case of sexual betrayal; 'The rape of Tamar' (2 Samuel 13), which led in due course to the murder of the rapist Amnon; 'Ruth and Boaz' (Ruth), a love story that went wrong; 'The rape of Dinah' (Genesis 34), which led to a mass circumcision and massacre; 'King Solomon's concubines' (1 Kings 11), telling of how he 'loved many strange women, together with the daughter of Pharaoh, women of the Moabites, Ammonites, Edomites, Sidonians and Hittites . . . and he had seven hundred wives, princesses and three hundred concubines' – and the Queen of Sheba; 'Lot and his daughters' (Genesis 19), in which Lot's daughters conspired to get their father drunk, seduced him and as a result had two sons; 'David and Bathsheba' (2 Samuel 11), already mentioned, in which King David, wanting Uriah's wife, arranged for him to be killed in battle; and 'The Levite's concubine' (Judges 19), already mentioned, in which a concubine was thrown to a mob to divert their attention and so prevent a homosexual rape.

In early Judaism a husband was expected to divorce his wife if she had borne him no children after ten years, excluding the periods during which sex was impossible due to illness or separation. There was no suggestion here that the fault might lie with the husband. The rabbinical courts insisted that the husband dissolve the marriage even against the wishes of both parties, though this position evolved over the centuries. As late as the Middle Ages there were many instances of royal, civil and rabbinical dispensations allowing Jewish husbands 'to marry another wife or other wives' if the marriage had failed to yield progeny for ten years.[25] Another primitive Judaic notion was that a woman who had survived two husbands should not marry for a third time, as it was assumed that the next husband would be sure to die. This superstition of the 'lethal woman' attributed her husbands' deaths to a deadly venereal disease afflicting her through heredity – which meant that two bereaved sisters had the same lethal propensity. But a man who had lost two wives was invariably free to marry a third.[26]

In its origins the Judeo-Christian tradition exhibited much of the phallic interest evident in other cults: only later did Jewish and Christian philosophers decide to make sex into a problem. The very ark of the covenant, the chest of acacia wood housed in the Holy of Holies in the Temple of Solomon, contained among others things a sacred stone which, according to certain Talmudic scholars, was a representation of the male and female organs in union.[27] This has been compared with features of the Eleusinian mysteries of ancient Greece which included a rite known as *erretophoria*, named from the Greek words meaning 'carrying things not to be mentioned', in which a basket carrying a stone phallus and the 'womb' of the goddess Demeter was conveyed through the town in sacred procession.

Abraham deserted a rival god for the worship of Yahweh, but afterwards attempted to introduce the rites connected with adoration of the old deity. According to George Ryley Scott, 'he [Abraham] continued to worship the phallic principles under the name of Yahweh instead of Baal, erecting pillars and making human sacrifices'.[28] Human sacrifices were offered to Baal-Peor, the phallic god of the Moabites and Midianites, and the priests who attended these sacrificial rites indulged in cannibalistic practices. *Baal* was supposed to signify 'My Lord the opener', and *Peor* denoted 'the opening of the maiden's hymen. Again we can see how Judeo-Christianity was rooted in Middle Eastern paganism; and circumcision, clearly deriving from tribal phallicism, continues to play a part in modern Judaism. In Exodus we read how Zipporah threw at the feet of the angry Yahweh the bloody foreskin of her son as a form of appeasement, and how Yahweh was referred to as 'the opener'. Moses forbade the erection of fresh pillars as a way of denouncing the worship of phallic deities, though Joshua and other followers of Yahweh continued to worship manlike images, all of which carried enormous phalli. It has been suggested that 'pillar' actually denoted a priapic statue of unmistakable character, with the depiction of Yahweh as a post, stone or rock signifying his phallic origins.[29] It is significant that the image of the ark has long served as a symbol for the womb. One writer has suggested that the *Argo* of the Greeks, the *Cybium* of Egypt, and the *argha* or *yoni* of India were all represented by a cup or boat – Osiris standing in a boat, Noah in his ark, and Iswara, 'lord of the boat-shaped vessel', rising from the *yoni*.[30] Some commentators have also noticed that the vessel built by Noah sailed on the waters for a period roughly equal to that of human gestation, namely 284 days, after which life issued from the ark.

Judaism, unlike other world religions, prohibited the castration of men and animals alike, while the seventh-century Christian physician Paul of Aegina claimed that physicians were sometimes compelled by those in authority to perform the operation.[31] The third-century Valesians, like Origen (see above), castrated themselves in large numbers 'thinking thereby to serve God'; in 325 the Council of Nicaea banned 'voluntary castrates' from priestly offices; and in medieval Italy many churchmen emasculated themselves 'because of cupidity', until a prohibition by Pope Clement XIV gradually eroded the practice. Today canon law regards castration as an 'irregularity', though it is unclear whether vasectomy is included.

Orthodox Jews are proud of the survival of ritual circumcision, combining procedural and religious elements, over the centuries. But this is a highly questionable practice, often carried out with little attention paid to normal medical conventions, and in consequence entailing various health risks. The suggestion that circumcision be carried out solely by physicians has been criticised in rabbinical circles since this may deprive the ritual of its distinctively religious character, but today ritual circumcisers are commonly required to obtain medical certificates before being allowed to carry out the operation. Jewish law disqualifies non-Jews and non-conforming Jews from carrying out circumcisions, and if the operation is performed for urgent medical reasons it has no religious validity.

Jewish ritual circumcisions were traditionally carried out by non-medical practitioners who derived their 'remarkable competence from an unbroken tradition in this art extending over nearly four millennia, during which the manner of the operation remained virtually unchanged, combined with their mastery of the rabbinical teachings on the subject'.[32] The lay surgeons had access to legal codes and commentaries which rendered 'any recourse to independent medical advice unnecessary'. In short, rabbinical legal texts are quite sufficient to sort out any medical difficulties. Immanuel Jakobovits includes a description of the approved method of ritual circumcision:

> One excises the foreskin, the entire skin covering the glans, so that the corona is laid bare. Afterwards, one tears with the finger-nail the soft membrane underneath the skin, turning it to the sides until the flesh of the glans appears, Thereafter one sucks the membrum until the blood is extracted from the [more] remote places, so that no danger [to the infant] may ensue, and any circumciser who does not carry out the sucking procedure is to be removed [from his office]. After sucking [the wound], one places on it a compress or some medical powder to stop the bleeding.[33]

The three distinct parts of the operation – the excision of the prepuce, the laceration and retraction of the mucous membrane, and the sucking of the blood from the interior of the wound – are mentioned but not clearly defined in the Talmud. The last two parts of the ritual are specifically Jewish, not known among the Muslims, who simply retain the membrane over the glans or wait until it breaks on its own.

Elements of the ritual circumcision have been the subject of many interpretations and much controversy, and today there are procedural options that were not available to the early Hebrews. The writer Shalom Auslander has introduced us to the commercially advertised SmartKlamp, 'a clear plastic at-home circumcision device that looks like a corkscrew designed by Philippe Starck'.[34] The website is proud to proclaim that this mechanism avoids many of the problems often associated with circumcision, such as 'infection of the circumcised wound . . . postoperative bleeding . . . cutting the glans of the penis . . . part amputation of the penis' and the risk of removing too much, or not enough, of the foreskin. Who says that religion does not move with the times?

Early Judeo-Christianity had intimate connections with fertility and phallic cults, moving gradually to the exact opposite extreme. With Jesus, Paul and the early Christian fathers the anti-sexual trends clearly evident in orthodox Judaism were reinforced, and Christianity became wedded to a negative sexual philosophy which remains one of the most destructive threads in the whole tradition. At the same time the anti-sexuality inherent in the early Judeo-Christian tradition was paralleled by similar elements in pagan philosophy.[35] The first-century philosopher Musonius Rufus, for example, argued strongly that no union of the sexes other than marriage was permissible, and his contemporary Dio Chrysostom wanted prostitution to be suppressed by law. We are told that Pythagoras inculcated his views so successfully that when ten of his disciples, being attacked, might have escaped by crossing a bean-field, they died rather than tread down the beans, which were thought to have a mystical affinity with the male genital organs. Plato favoured a law to the effect that 'no one shall venture to touch any person of the freeborn or noble class except his wedded wife, or sow the unconsecrated or bastard seed among harlots, or in barren or unnatural lusts'. Citizens, he urged, should not be worse than birds and beasts, which live pure and chaste until the adult male has paired with the female, whereupon they 'live the rest of their lives in holiness and innocence, abiding firmly in their original compact'.[36]

The reasons why Christianity developed such a deep and enduring hostility to sex can be debated. What is important is to grasp the extent to which this hostility became embodied in Western culture and the impact it had on such specific areas as law, penology, sexual relations and education. The first Christian emperors legislated to suppress what they thought to be sexual licence, and this launched the Christian campaign against sex which is still being waged today. In instances of seduction, for example, both the man and the consenting woman were put to death; various types of sex criminals in ancient Rome had molten lead poured down their throats; and the innocent offspring of illicit sexual intercourse were punished for their parents' sins with ignominy and loss of certain civic rights. Sexual desire itself, even when unaccompanied by any manifestation, was roundly condemned, and the early church laid down a wide range of punishments for writing or reading lascivious books, singing wanton songs, performing suggestive dances, wearing improper clothing, bathing in mixed company, frequenting the theatre and so on. Underlying such Christian attitudes was a disgust at the human body. In St Augustine's much quoted observation, '*inter faeces et urinam nascimur*' ('between faeces and urine we are born). St Bernard saw man as 'nothing else than fetid sperm, a sack of dung, the food of worms', with woman 'the gate of hell'. And the second-century theologian Marcion thought it inconceivable that God could be the author of 'the disgusting paraphernalia of reproduction and for all the nauseating defilements of the human flesh from birth to final putrescence'.

This was a ubiquitous theme in early Christianity and it came to infect all the sexual attitudes that followed. Purity consisted in abstinence, in avoiding any contact with the 'parts of shame'; in particular; those disreputable anatomical features of Woman that invited Lust and Sin. It was all very perplexing for Augustine and his ilk. Why, the sage mused, did Christ chose to be born in the manner of man at all? Surely a more moral option could have been chosen. After all, Adam appeared on earth without needing to pass down the birth canal.

The virginity of Mary perplexed the early theologians since they found it difficult to believe that Jesus was born in the usual way. Some clerics relied on an appropriate miracle that enabled Christ to appear spontaneously at the right time. Others suggested that Jesus emerged through the breast or navel – anything to avoid contact with the 'parts of shame'! Some religious thinkers were worried that God might have impaired Mary's virginity by impregnating her, and so sought other ruses – for example, that the angel Gabriel might have conveyed the divine sperm from heaven and injected it into Mary through her ear. This all gets very tricky, not least with the suggestion that God preserved a respectable distance from all the messy sex business and that Gabriel functioned as some medical intermediary. One Arab physician referred to 'Nafkhae', the 'air or vapour' which Gabriel blew into Mary's windpipe 'for the purpose of impregnation'. In some early Christian paintings the Holy Ghost descends as a dove with the divine sperm in its bill; and in at least one early carving the seminal essence is shown flowing from God's mouth through a tube which led under Mary's skirts. The simplest, but not the most plausible, option would have been for Jesus simply to appear on earth, like a ghost out of the mist. Since the whole tale is fanciful, why not just rely on a simple miracle? Surely, what was good enough for Adam would have been good enough for Christ. Jesus could have just appeared on earth without having to suffer contact with the elements of sexual defilement, the characteristic features of the Fall.

Christianity was obsessed with sin – while allowing virgins to aspire after an allegedly superior morality. An impulse to religious celibacy can be detected in much pre-Christian religion but it was Christianity that most successfully launched the idea and sustained it through many difficult centuries. Today the struggle goes on but the problems continue to mount. The blandishments of the secular world are just too much for many putative priests and this inevitably impacts on recruitment campaigns. Just how is the Roman Catholic Church expected to maintain a satisfactory flow of celibate priests when the authority of the papacy diminishes by the year and there are so many temptations to what may be taken as a more natural route to religious devotion? Propaganda, no longer sufficient, remained the principal weapon of the clerics, but much of its persuasive power was evaporating over the years.

In 1962 the cleric G. P. Dwyer referred to celibacy as 'a high way of the cross', and in 1963 the Rev. A. Pickering spoke of Mary being 'the model of purity' by virtue of her virginity. The meaning is clear enough. Most women, since they are not virgins, are impure and disreputable, so keeping alive the long tradition that only by avoiding sex can women aspire to virtue. Tertullian was happy to regard woman as 'a temple built over a sewer', and the French physician des Laurens could ask how 'this divine animal, full of reason and judgement, which we call man, [can] be attracted by those obscene parts of woman, defiled with juices and located shamefully at the lowest part of the trunk?' St Jerome allowed a man to love his wife, but not too ardently, less he become an adulterer; and he represented the priestly purpose as 'to cut down with the axe of Virginity the wood of Marriage'. Origen, before castrating himself, depicted matrimony as 'impure and unholy' but saw it as a source of fresh virgins.

The clerics hoped that such virgins would preserve their virtue not by eschewing sex altogether but by focusing their carnal desires on the church in general and Jesus Christ in particular. This was rarely stated openly but the language is unambiguous. St Cyprian pointed out:

> If a husband come and see his wife lying with another man, is he not indignant and maddened? . . . How indignant and angered must Christ our Lord and Judge be when He sees a virgin, dedicated to himself, and consecrated to His holiness, lying with a man . . . She who has been guilty of this crime is an adulteress, not against a husband, but against Christ.

So we are encouraged to perceive Jesus as possessing all the normal human frailties of jealousy and anger, eager to preserve the loyalties of a vast army of devoted virgins. Cardinal James Gibbons, in his *Faith of Our Fathers*, maintained that Jesus selected his disciples on the basis of their virginity and chose in heaven a special band of 140,000 virgin angels.[37]

This is one of the many paradoxes at the heart of Christianity, signalling the perverse attitude that on the one hand sexual indulgence is a disreputable sin and on the other it should be properly directed at the appropriate elements of the faith. Thus the famous virgin Geogonia attempted to protect her piety by resisting even a medical examination by a male physician 'with all her body and members thereof . . . Bruised and broken most grievouslie' she refused to allow a medical inspection since her modesty forbade her from bring touched by a man. It proved to be the best policy since God rewarded her with a miraculous cure. There were not many such women. One pious medieval philosopher is quoted: 'A Good Woman is but like one Ele put in a bag among 500 Snakes, and if a man should have the luck to grope out that one Ele from all the snakes, yet he hath at best but a wet Ele by the Taile.'[38]

★

The principal problem was that the clerics, brainwashed into accepting the inherent sinfulness of women, were unable to ignore the temptations that they posed; with the corollary that their stalwart efforts at repression produced what can only be recognised today as psychopathological mental states. William Lecky related how, when St Pachomius and St Palaemon were conversing together in the desert, a young monk rushed up to them and with sobs declared that a young woman had seduced him and then vanished in the air: hallucination was a common affliction of the desert celibates. Later, it was recorded, the young monk committed suicide by jumping into an open furnace. Another monk, in aiding a fainting woman, was unwise enough to touch her: 'Passions long slumbering and forgotten rushed with impetuous fury through his veins.' He tried to clasp the woman to his heart but 'she vanished from his sight, and a chorus of daemons, with peals of laughter, exulted over his fall'.

Other saints were more successful in avoiding contact with women, real or imaginary. Some clerics refused on principle to speak to a woman under any circumstances; some contrived, if at all possible, not even to see a woman. It was reported that St John of Egypt, truly a pious devotee, had not seen a woman for forty-eight years. On one occasion a young Roman girl made a pilgrimage to Alexandria to obtain the prayers of St Arsenius, and forcing herself into his presence begged for his prayers and to be remembered. The worthy saint cried indignantly: 'Remember you! It shall be the prayer of my life that I may forget you.' The Archbishop of Alexandria comforted her by saying that the hermit would pray for her although trying to forget her face 'as she belonged to the sex by which daemons commonly tempt saints'.

The medieval clerics demonstrated their preoccupations with sexual sin by laying down a complex system of penances (penitentials) for the punishment of offenders. Here every misdeed was described in detail and specific punishments described in every case. In five penitential codes dealing with sexual matters there are twenty-two paragraphs dealing with sodomy and bestiality, twenty-five dealing with masturbation on the part of laymen, more dealing with masturbation on the part of the clergy, and so on. Doubtless some people were deterred by the prospect of clerically imposed punishments, though it is likely that most were unaware of the precise wording of the penitentials.

How many married people knew that the church condemned couples who made love using the wrong positions – for example, '*more canino*' (entry from the rear, held to be unduly pleasurable for the male) – and called for a seven-year penance? And how many spouses realised that the church was trying to cut down the number of days on which love making could take place between a husband and wife? First it was prohibited on Sundays, Wednesdays and Fridays, and then for forty days before Easter, for forty days before Christmas, and the three days before attending holy communion. It was also forbidden from conception until forty days after parturition and during any penance. Two popes, Clement VIII and Paul V, declared that anyone should be denounced to the inquisitors of the faith who believed that kissing, touching and embracing for the sake of sexual pleasure were not grievous sins.[39] This view is echoed in modern Catholic injunctions that consign sexual pleasure to married couples and to them alone. Thus Father Henry Davis, in his *Moral and Pastoral Theology* (1935), commented that 'sexual pleasure has no purpose at all except in reference to the sexual act between man and wife . . . It is grievously sinful in the unmarried deliberately to procure or to accept even the smallest degree of true venereal pleasure.'[40]

These clerics rejoiced in the biblical injunction that childbirth was necessarily painful: 'I will greatly multiply thy sorrow and thy conception; in sorrow thou shalt bring forth children [Genesis 3: 16].' Why in the early days of modern medicine should God's will be frustrated by chloroform and other odious concoctions? And even respectable marriage was unable to sanctify what was otherwise a somewhat disreputably sexual business. For example, Bertrand Russell, writing of his grandmother, noted that she regarded marriage as a puzzling institution. Husbands and wives clearly had a duty to love one another but *not too much*, for 'if sex attraction drew them together there must be something not quite nice about them'.[41] The trick, it seems, was to experience enough sexual attraction to allow for procreation without lapsing into undue carnal pleasure. It would be a mistake to think that 21st-century sexuality, in all its aspects, is purged of the sinful

connotations with which Christianity has plagued it over the
centuries.

There are countless practical difficulties surrounding attitudes to
sexual behaviour, many of them deriving from confusion
surrounding traditional religious beliefs. In early 2008 in Britain
husbands were given the right to claim extra welfare benefits
following a partial recognition of polygamous marriages; that is,
where the marriages had occurred in countries where such
arrangements were legal. This innovation largely affected Muslim
families where men are allowed more than one wife under Sharia
law. One estimate suggested that there are up to a thousand
polygamous marriages in Britain. Hence a guideline from the
Department for Work and Pensions states: 'Where there is a
polygamous marriage the claimant and one spouse will be paid the
couple rate.'[42] In these circumstances a husband with multiple
wives may also be eligible for additional housing benefit and
council tax benefit to reflect the larger property needed for his
family. Critics of the new scheme, including the opposition
Conservative Party, commented that the new scheme was
'completely unjustifiable', a precedent that would lead 'to more
demands for the culture of other countries to be reflected in UK
law and the benefits system'. In addition there were accusations
that the ruling was kept quiet because of its controversial nature.[43]
No mention was made of the fact that such 'liberal' legal
accommodations would reinforce the religious attitude that
regards women as sexual commodities to be disposed of according
to the customary views of patriarchal traditions.

Such disputes inevitably sprang from religious conventions –
for example, Mormonism in the United States – where women's
rights are determined by male cultural hierarchies that remain
hostile to pleas for equality between the sexes. This is turn affects
attitudes to sex in general and to how children are to be educated
regarding sexual experience, censorship, abortion and procreation
– topics that occasionally surfaced during the 2008 presidential
campaign of the Mormon Mitt Romney in the United States.
Elsewhere in the campaign, activists were influenced by the broad
swathe of evangelical attitudes, as indicated by the preacher Jerry

Falwell and others of his ilk eager to denounce progressive egalitarianism in sexual matters: 'Most of these feminists are radical, frustrated lesbians, many of them, and man haters, and failures in their relationships with men, and who have declared war on the male gender. The biblical condemnation of feminism has to do with its radical philosophy and goals. That's the bottom line.'[44] Randall Terry, head of the pro-life Operation Rescue group, commented along similar lines that 'dads' should be 'godly leaders of the family with the women in submission, raising kids for the glory of God'.

Such attitudes belong in a spectrum of discrimination and abuse that is discernible in all the world religions (see Chapter 4), where *in extremis* the torture and murder of women for alleged sexual misbehaviour are commonplace cultural patterns that have survived over the centuries. Sometimes extreme forms of abuse are publicised. Usually they are not. One highly publicised case, raised by Salman Rushdie, concerned the abuse of Mukhtar Mai in 2002, raped for an 'honour crime' by Mastoi villagers in Pakistan – a crime that was in fact committed by someone else.[45] The Human Rights Commission of Pakistan has reported that there were 320 reported rapes in the first nine months of 2004 and 350 gang rapes in the same period, all carried out as a means of resolving tribal disputes. At the same time it is widely assumed in the prevailing culture that the woman's best recourse is to kill herself, for even if she survives the wrath of quasi-legal tribal judgments she can only look forward to a life of ostracism and misery, spurned by her community and with no prospect of marriage.

Rushdie also highlighted the so-called Imrana case, in which a Muslim woman from Deoband in Uttar Pradesh, northern India, was raped by her father-in-law, which in turn brought forth a ruling from the ultra-conservative Darul-Uloom seminary of the Deobandi cult that Imrana must leave her husband because the rape had rendered her *haram* (unclean) for him. One of the presiding clerics declared: 'It does not matter whether it [the rape] was consensual or forced.' Hence the innocent woman would be forced to leave her husband because of someone else's crime. Rushdie asks, perhaps rhetorically, why a 'mere seminary' has the power to make such judgments.[46]

Here Indian women such as Imrana were being excluded from protections offered by civil law and were being consigned to the tender mercies of the mullahs. In the 1980s a divorced woman, Shah Bano, was granted 'maintenance money' by the Indian Supreme Court, but there is no alimony under Islamic law, so orthodox Islamists such as those at Darul-Uloom complained that the ruling infringed Muslim personal law and founded the All-India Muslim Law Board to mount protests. The government responded by passing a bill denying alimony to divorced Muslim women. Typically Mulayam Singh Yadav, the then chief minister of Uttar Pradesh, backed the Darul-Uloom fatwa: 'The decision of the Muslim religious leaders in the Imrana case must have been taken after a lot of thought. The religious leaders are all very learned and they understand the Muslim community and its sentiments.'[47] It is time that Pakistan and India and other so-called secular democracies unified their legal systems and took power away from repressive medieval institutions.

Such issues highlight in particular the Islamic attitude to women. Women are inferior to men, should do as they are told and can expect to be properly beaten if they do not. This is not to say that women are not assigned important rights or that they do not have an important place in heaven (see Surah 9: 72), but it does entail that it is always men who will decide their rights. It is this grossly sexist posture that afflicts the sociopolitical status of women throughout the Islamic world. Specific issues that bear on sexual behaviour are deeply affected by this traditional religious attitude. For example, female circumcision, a cruel mutilation designed in part to expunge sexual feeling and thereby to protect female virtue, is an obvious case in point. Here, as elsewhere, it is argued that circumcision is a cultural rather than a religious norm, that even though it has been practised for centuries it has nothing to do with Islam. In short, there is debate as to whether the practice is an African, Arab or Muslim custom, but certain facts are plain.

Strabo ('The Geographer', c.63 BC–c.24 AD), of Amaseia in the Roman province of Pontos, today part of Turkey, mentions the excision of girls in Arabia centuries before the birth of Mohammed. But it is clear that whatever went on in certain non-Muslim countries, Islam served to reinforce the practice of ritual circumcision in many Arab and non-Arab communities. The researcher J. G. F. Riedel noted in the late nineteenth century the ritual of female circumcision on the Molucca Islands of Indonesia, *especially* by the Muslim population:

> The girls are bathed and placed across a stone and an old woman cuts away a portion of their *glans clitoridis*. It is said this is done to suppress and limit their desires before marriage. Burnt and pulverised sago leaves are applied as a styptic. Then the woman carries the girl in her arms into the hut which she must not leave until her wound is healed . . . The custom is said to be Mohammedan in origin.[48]

In the same vein Professor and Mrs C. G. Seligman described nineteenth-century female circumcision among the Kababish, one of the most powerful of the Arab tribes (with strong Islamic influence) of the Anglo-Egyptian Sudan. Here it was the custom to cut off the entire clitoris and to carve away the whole of the vulva; the screams of the child, typically between the third and sixth year, were drowned by the rejoicing of the celebrants, after which the girl's legs were tied together for two or three weeks. Another authority, F. J. Bieber, described early twentieth-century practices among the Muslim Galla communities of Harai in northern Pakistan. Here girls of eight to ten years of age were infibulated in the 'stitching' (*mutscha durba*) process, where the inner labia were scraped until raw and bleeding, after which they were sewn together with horse-hair and the feet bound together for some days. A French physician, Dr Peney, described elements of the ritual:

> The matron . . . begins by slicing off the tip of the clitoris and the edges of the inner lips. Then the razor shears along the rims of the outer lips . . . In order to drown the shrieks of the girl, the assembled guests and kin raise the loudest and shrillest din conceivable until the process is over . . . When the flowing blood has been staunched, the girl is laid flat on her back, her legs extended and tied firmly together.

Another researcher, Vita Hassan, recorded that female circumcision, practised as part of religious ritual, was customary 'among the Mohammedan tribes of the south from Berber to Senaar, including Khartoum, Metemma, Shendi, Wad, Madani, Haraz and their environs'. It is inevitable that the health of the girls is often adversely affected: the procedures are typically carried out by traditional circumcisers with no medical training. For example, one consequence is that the passage of the baby at birth is often impeded 'so the muscles from groin to reins [kidneys] are severed . . . then this laceration is sewn together like the pre-marital wound and the woman is once more impenetrable'.

The feminist writer Elizabeth Gould Davis noted the Arab enthusiasm for female circumcision, whereby 'son of an uncircumcised mother!' is a particularly offensive epithet for one Arab to hurl at another.[49] One researcher suggested that clitoral size, in addition to requirements of virtue, has encouraged excision: 'We have the proof on record of women with large clitorides who have seduced young girls . . . It is to avoid such unnatural connections that the Asiatic nations, especially the Arabians, are in the habit of removing the clitoris.'[50] The explorer Sir Richard Burton described the circumcision of Muslim women on the Arabian peninsula: 'The prostitutes of Aden all had the labia and clitoris completely excised and the skin showing scars and the traces of coarse sewing.'[51] This indicates the sorts of women with whom Burton had most abundant contact; in fact circumcision was customary in the Arab communities.

It should not be thought that such nineteenth-century commentary is irrelevant to issues in the modern world. In early 1994 Egyptian campaigners intensified their efforts to eradicate female genital mutilation in what was claimed to be a modern secular state. Here the reformers were facing the entrenched belief among many Egyptians, both Muslim and Christian, that the excision of at least part of the clitoris and labia was necessary to preserve hygiene, femininity and sexual virtue.[52] According to the Egyptian National Population Council, in the late 1990s around 97 per cent of women in the country were circumcised, with only the richest and most educated rejecting the practice. Today committed Islamists are trying to ensure that female mutilation becomes one of the defining features of the Muslim state. The conservative Sheikh Youssef Al-Badri has claimed that medical evidence supports the theory that female circumcision improves the complexion and prevents 'sexual upheaval'. When confronted by a female reporter, he commented: 'Women who have the necessary part removed have red complexions . . . with cheeks as red as apples. Not like your yellow ones.' (Meanwhile a Badri supporter shouted at the woman: 'You shut up! I'll cut your tongue out and the tongues of those who gave birth to you!')[53] In June 1997 Badri, supported by eight doctors, managed to overturn a ban on circumcision imposed by the Egyptian health ministry after an eleven-year-old girl bled to death after being circumcised by a village barber. Current restrictions on the operation were not being enforced and girls were continuing to die. There were cheers from the predominantly male audience when the ban on circumcision was overturned in court. Badri commented that the deaths were just bad luck and quoted four Hadith which he insisted showed Mohammed's approval of the practice.[54] He had previously commented: 'It's our religion. We pray, we fast, we do circumcision. For fourteen centuries of Islam, our mothers and grandmothers have performed this operation . . . God be praised, we have won and can apply Islam.'[55] No doubt here about whether female circumcision is an essential part of Islam.

In November 2002 Denmark's secular mainstream was in confrontation with religious activists trying to preserve female circumcision after Imam Mustafa Abdullahi Aden was widely quoted as saying that circumcision was a religious duty: 'It is good for girls to be circumcised. It is a sign they are true Muslims.'[56] And he went so far as to recommend the appropriate details of the operations – the entire clitoris and labia should be cut away. In early 1993 Kenyan-born Poline Nyaga, a leading (circumcised) female councillor in Brent, north London, was campaigning for female circumcision to become available on the National Health Service 'as a right' to all British women: 'The operation is not just a medical one. It is a spiritual act that divides childhood from adulthood.'[57] The move provoked protests from her fellow councillors, the World Health Organization and UNICEF; a Labour councillor, Ann John, declared that 'female circumcision is no more a valid cultural tradition than is cannibalism and . . . neither is acceptable to the people of Brent'.[58]

Domestic violence against Muslim women is unsurprising in view of the Koranic injunction that 'disobedient' wives be beaten (see Chapter 4), and ritual circumcision is part of this abuse. For example, the Saudi authorities deem it prudent not to maintain statistics on the extent of violence against women, but hospital workers report that many women are admitted for injuries caused by spousal violence; foreign women are often abused by their Saudi husbands, who are able to prevent their wives from obtaining exit visas.[59] Female circumcision is given no publicity and is rarely mentioned in foreign campaigns for reform. It remains prevalent. A Saudi princess has recorded that her sister was circumcised when about twelve years old, and that the ritual had been carried out on the three sisters that followed her in age. A Western physician had protested to the father, so saving the youngest six daughters from the barbaric custom: 'Nura [the first sister] added that I was blessed not to have endured such a trauma.'[60]

Nura had been circumcised according to long-standing custom.

> The oldest women gathered round the frightened child. Nura, nude from the waist down, was held by four women on a bedsheet that had been spread on the ground. The oldest of the women raised her hand in the air; with horror Nura saw that she had a razor-like instrument in her hand. Nura screamed as she felt a sharp pain in her genital region. Dizzy with shock . . . she saw blood pouring from her wounds.[61]

Nura's mother, as a pious and caring Muslim, had no doubt that the rite was the will of Allah. Again the perennial question is raised: how much is female circumcision a part of Islam and how much a traditional practice that pre-dates Koranic and other related religious teachings? In short, it is both. Whenever, under secular pressures, reforms are attempted in Muslim countries there is invariably a religious backlash with Islamic scholars queuing up to reinforce the word of the prophet. Sheikh Al-Badri and his ilk are far from alone in insisting that circumcision is an essential part of Islam. It is estimated that around two million young girls are circumcised every year – mostly in Africa, but also in the Middle East, America and Europe among immigrant communities.

The practice persists in both Islamic and Christian communities but is most common in Muslim societies – in particular, according to UNICEF, in Sierra Leone, Mali, Djibouti, Eritrea, Sudan, Burkina Faso, Ethiopia and Somalia.[62] One particular problem facing secular societies trying to ban female circumcision is that immigrant communities are able to send their daughters abroad 'on holiday' to be given the operation: the need for global action – and effective enforcement – is manifest. In 1994 the black supermodel Katoucha Niane launched KPLCE – Katoucha pour la Lutte contre l'Excision (Katoucha for the Fight against Circumcision). Early in 2008 she was found drowned in the Seine; some of her friends believed that her disappearance was linked to her activist campaign.[63]

The question of Islam and customary practice rears its head in many contexts that relate to sexual behaviour, many of which are described in the Koran and the Hadith. One of these focuses on the issue of child brides, condemned in secular Muslim states but still evident in tribal practices used to settle differences between feuding clans in various parts of the Islamic world. In June 2008 Pakistani human rights activists were outraged at reports that a long-running blood feud in western Baluchistan had been resolved by the handing over of fifteen girls, aged been three and ten, for marriage. The ancient feudal practice of *vanni*, in which women are exchanged for marriage, is illegal in Pakistan but the law is often ignored by local police who 'turn a blind eye'. *Dawn*, an English-language newspaper, published an editorial that denounced 'barbarity in the name of tradition . . . [the] medieval mindset that dominates many sections of our society'.[64] Asma Jahangir, a leading human rights campaigner, observed that the government would find 'any excuse'[65] to avoid using its authority to protect women.

The issue of child brides in the Muslim world is not helped by the alleged behaviour of the prophet in this regard. It is recorded in medieval texts that the Byzantine commander of Alexandria sent Mohammed two enslaved sisters as a gift, along with a donkey and other goods, and that the prophet took one of these, Mariyya, before freeing her after she bore him a child. The Koran

frequently expresses the permissibility of men using female slaves
('property of thy right hand') for sexual purposes. Allah decreed
that a man should not take more than four wives, but there was
no restriction on his number of concubines, seen as one of the
legitimate fruits of conquest. (Here in fact it is interesting to note,
from the Byzantine example from the seventh century, that the
Christian and Islamic worlds overlapped in regarding women and
girls as suitable sexual commodities to be given as gifts.)

The other problem posed by Mohammed is that he married
Aisha when she was almost certainly a child. According to *Sahih
al-Bukhari*, seen by Sunni Muslims as an authentic Hadith
compilation, Aisha was six years old when her father, Abu Bakr,
gave her in marriage to Mohammed. In *Sahih Muslim*, the second
most respected compilation, a marriage age of either six or seven
is suggested. The various accounts agree that Aisha was 'a girl of
nine' when the marriage was consummated.[66] Despite such evidence, any suggestion that the prophet was a paedophile in his
relationship with Aisha raises fury in the Islamic world.

The traditional attitude that regards women and girls as sexual
commodities, to be exploited and abused by men, is discernible in
all the world religions – not merely as centuries-long custom but
as scriptural doctrine. Surprisingly, as noted, the attitude coexists
with gross prudery, where any public manifestations of sexual
indulgence will be condemned and vilified by fervent religious
believers: in Western countries and elsewhere fundamentalist
Muslims and Christians unite in invoking secular law to impose
media censorship, the suppression of theatrical productions and
any other indications that sex can be flaunted as an element in
entertainment, news and public behaviour.

In India, Muslims and Hindus support police action in
rounding up young couples kissing on beaches near Bombay.
Here what would be regarded in the West as innocuous behaviour
is roundly condemned. In April 2007 more than 100 young
couples were arrested for kissing in public, behaviour regarded by
the authorities as indulgence in 'objectionable positions'.[67] They
were taken away in vans and fined up to 1,200 rupees (then
£14.30) for indulging in 'obscene' behaviour. Rajana Kumari,

director of the Centre for Social Research in Delhi, said that the '[religious] fundamentalists [were] colliding with modern youth'. Even in Bombay, home of Bollywood, religious bigots were unable to cope with 'the newfound confidence of boys and girls to be openly together'.[68]

The moral clampdown closely followed the sweeping success of Shiv Sena (Army of Shiva), a nationalist party accused of orchestrating violence against Muslims in the 1993 riots, in municipal elections. The party, whose supporters attack people celebrating Valentine's Day, has helped to force a ban on sex education books in state schools. (This is highly reminiscent of a pamphlet issued in the West by the Catholic authorities, and carrying in red print 'FOR PRIVATE CIRCULATION ONLY . . . NOT TO BE DISPLAYED FOR GENERAL SALE'. Published in 1950, it was intended to provide guidance to clergy, parents and teachers. 'You would be appalled to see the anatomy charts of the sexual organs and the growth of the unborn child published for use in schools with boys and girls of thirteen.')[69] An editorial in *The Hindu* commented that at a time when India was trying to project itself as a modern state, events such as these reminded us that the country 'continues to be governed by people who equate modernity with promiscuity'.[70] And Adam Kutty, editor of the lads' magazine *Maxim*, said: 'Stop pretending we don't have sex. We do. Look at our population.'[71]

In Egypt young middle-class couples are circumventing religious strictures on pre-marital sex by buying informal marriage contracts, dubbed *urfi* marriages, to facilitate behaviour normal for married people, such as the hiring of hotel rooms, that would otherwise be difficult. In April 2008 Egyptian legislators, under pressure from senior Muslim clerics, were preparing to outlaw the contracts – which offer the promise of marriage according to God and Mohammed – as immoral and against Islamic teaching. For some the *urfi* marriages are seen as a step towards a more formal commitment; to others they are simply a part of a complex pattern whereby wealthy men from Gulf countries 'take a temporary "wife" for the duration of a holiday in Egypt, then dump her, leaving her in disgrace with her own family'.[72] One celebrated case concerned Hind al-Hinnawi, a costume designer who became pregnant by a television actor and secured a court ruling in her favour. Again the traditional religious practice of regarding women and girls as sexual commodities is discernable in both Islam and Christianity – reinforced by the notion that the sexual instinct, an essential but regrettable part of human nature, is less worthy than the spiritual component.

The relationship between the Catholic Church and attitudes to sexual behaviour has passed through many vicissitudes in its long history. Throughout this period the ecclesiastical authorities have almost invariably represented a radical anti-humanist posture, albeit of a shifting character from century to century: like all influential historical figures, the popes have mirrored their times as well as helping to shape them. At one extreme, by any reckoning, the papal hierarchies have indulged in depravities and immoralities – murders, nepotism, extortion of resources from the poor, turning the Lateran Palace into a brothel, etc. – that are largely ignored in modern commentary but which have forced apologists, looking at the historical record, to speculate on 'the problem of bad popes'. Here, with human vanity and appetite given free rein, there was little focus on the minutiae of doctrine except in so far as papal pronouncements consolidated ambition and the lust for power.[73]

At the other extreme, perhaps a more consistent theme, the Catholic authorities have preserved one of the central tenets of traditional Christian thought, already much noted, that the body is to be despised, a necessary vehicle for the soul but properly regarded as gross and disreputable. The focus on the virtue of sexual virginity, aided by all the excesses of Mariolatry – in which a historical human figure is assigned *de facto* magical powers – flows from this prejudice. This theme is clearly discernible in modern papal edicts, though not necessarily shared by the global Catholic laity. Part of the modern crisis in Christian theology is the tension between the increasingly isolated celibate papal authorities and the efforts of priests working to counsel ordinary people struggling to live their lives in accordance with the faith. We all know, in this context, what the Catholic Church makes of artificial contraception, homosexuality, abortion, non-marital sexual behaviour, conception by donor, abortion and so on. Morality, true to a central theme in the historical Christian tradition, has always meant *sexual* morality.

It is significant that John Paul II, striving to sustain the church's historical moral posture in the world, spent much time on what he saw as the proper route to sexual virtue.[74] This he did, in part, by publishing material on sex and love in four parts during the 1980s. Much of John Paul's contribution, finally published in 1997 as a single volume, *Theology of the Body: Human Love in the Divine Plan*, was the fruit of a series of written addresses read out at weekly general audiences over a period of five years. Here, developing the notion of man and woman as sexual partners, the Pope expounded on the evils of contraception, second marriages, 'illicit' sexual unions of all sorts (including sex outside marriage), masturbation, homosexual indulgence and abortion. Part of his aim was to go beyond the strictures and insights of Paul VI's encyclical *Humanae Vitae*, itself uncompromising in its denunciation of contraception, and to provide an exploration of such themes as human beings as an image of God, the significance of gender differences in Adam and Eve, the meaning of marital love, the significance of sexual intercourse and the nature of the family. In one judgement 'many people, even theologians, found the addresses convoluted, dense and repetitive'.[75]

Here it is enough to emphasise John Paul's prodigious effort to reinforce traditional Catholic teaching in the field of sexual behaviour. The papal vision is essentially patriarchal, with woman no more than a pliant 'helper' largely divorced from the realities of sexual experience. There is no attempt to address what sexual love means to men and women in the world – no references to emotion, the normal stresses of life, children, illness, or the entire fabric of art, literature, social anthropology, etc. that bears on the topic. In 600 pages of turgid prose there is no hint that sex might be enjoyable, but suggestions that the 'ecstasy' of sex should be properly viewed as a quasi-spiritual experience largely divorced from real life. Contraception is 'a violation of the interior order of conjugal union, which is rooted in the very order of the person [and] constitutes the essential evil of the contraceptive act'.[76] And John Paul, as we would expect, is equally hostile to remarriage,

homosexual behaviour and couples employing in-vitro fertil-
isation, these latter guilty of selfishness and disordered behaviour,
'reducing procreation to a merely biological laboratory act when
it must be, by God's will, the fruit of a covenant, a communion
of persons, as expressed in the conjugal embrace of a man and a
woman joined in marriage'.[77] All this is such a distortion of what
may be judged to be normal human sexuality that it amounts to a
psychopathology. This disorder is never more apparent than in the
sexual abuse of children.

The scale of the Christian abuse of children is hard to grasp.
Massive publicity was given to the sexual abuse of children by
Catholic priests in the United States, where over the last sixty
years some 4,400 Catholic priests have been credibly accused of
sexually attacking some 11,000 minors, with 90 per cent of the
attacks being directly genital. By the summer of 2004 some $700
million had been paid to victims' families, and that did not count
legal costs. We can judge that the sexual abuse of children in the
United States has cost the Roman Catholic Church more than $1
billion. And the practice is common in other countries. In recent
years some 120 priests in Britain have been investigated for the
abuse of minors, leading so far to twenty-one convictions; in
France twenty priests have been convicted of rape and molestation
of children; in Ireland 150 priests were convicted; and there were
similar 'cases in Italy, Austria, Spain, Mexico, Australia, Canada
and parts of Africa'.[78]

It is obvious that the Christian abuse of children is widespread
in the modern world, and that there are ample historical
precedents. Karen Liebreich, in a scholarly work, has demonstrated that the sexual abuse of children by Catholic priests in the
seventeenth century was practised routinely by members of the
Piarist Order, dedicated to the education of children of the poor.
José de Calasanz, the founder of the order, knew what was going
on and tried to 'cover up this great shame in order that it does not
come to the notice of our superiors'. He needn't have worried.
Pope Innocent X had no hesitation in appointing a known
paedophile to head the order but was forced to close it down
when the scandals became too great to disguise.[79]

★

Throughout Islam there is endless debate about the minutiae of sexual propriety and we do not have to search for long before we encounter elements of sexual sickness. The overall framework may be clear but the tensions remain unresolved from one society to another. How are the differences between traditionalism and modernity to be resolved? How is the faith to be protected under the mounting pressures of modern secularism? In particular, how are specific issues to be decided in the absence of a central doctrinal authority? There is no modern caliphate, no equivalent to the papal edict. The imam's fatwa does not carry the weight of a papal encyclical.

So, for example, Muslim men and women should show 'modesty' in their dress – an injunction that bears mainly on women – but who is to judge? How many different types of 'modest' garb are there in the Muslim world? In April 2008 the Iranian security forces were threatening to punish women who revealed too much flesh in pictures they posted on blogs, a fresh hazard in the internet age. Some women had become so frightened by the threats that they had removed their profiles themselves, and the conservative pressures were mounting. In Saudi Arabia women-only hotels were being inaugurated as a gesture to the modern world. The few female journalists who attended the opening of one such hotel noted that the ceremony was dominated by men. Also, for the first time, women were being allowed to stay in mixed-gender hotels without being accompanied by a *mihrim* (male guardian), an evident response to secular pressures.

In early 2008 Muslim experts in Sharia law were wondering whether marriage could be contracted over the telephone,[80] and a report suggested that there could be as many as 4,000 forced marriages a year in Britain, with children disappearing from school rolls to be coerced into unwelcome unions.[81] Here it was emphasised that the abuses affected all cultures and religions, but many of the forced marriages were perpetrated by committed Muslims. At the same time Muslim sex offenders were opting out of a prison treatment programme because it was against their religion.[82] The Prison Service's Muslim advisor had commented that there was a 'legitimate Islamic position' that Muslims should not discuss their crimes with others, so prohibiting the sorts of group discussion that take place in the sex offender treatment programme (SOTP). One unnamed Muslim prisoner had written in *Inside Times*, the prison magazine, opposing open discussion: 'I have always insisted that it was against Islamic teachings to discuss your offence to [sic] anyone, let alone act it out within a peer group.'[83] This meant that Muslims would require a special dispensation over the SOTP, which in turn would affect their time of release. If the prison authorities failed to respond to the complaints then the Muslim prisoners could legitimately claim discrimination on religious grounds.

In March 2008 Mehdi Kazemi, a gay Iranian teenager, faced deportation from Britain and, simply because of his sexual orientation, ran the risk of execution in Iran. Lord Alli, addressing the House of Lords, said that the young man's partner had been hanged for being gay. He went on: 'The Home Office's position is that gay people can return to Iran safely providing they are "discreet". Heaven knows what that means.' Kazemi himself declared:

> I did not come to the UK to claim asylum. I came here to study and return to my country. But . . . my situation has changed. The Iranian authorities have found out that I am a homosexual and they are looking for me. I cannot stop my attraction towards men . . . I was born with the feeling and cannot change this fact . . . If I return to Iran I will be arrested and executed.[84]

In this case the campaign for Kazemi was successful. On 13 March Jacqui Smith, the Home Secretary, announced that the case would be reconsidered.[85] According to human rights campaigners, more than 4,000 gay men and lesbians have been executed in Iran since the 1979 revolution. (At the same time the issue of homosexuality was continuing to cause problems for Anglicans and for Jews, with the Anglican communion anticipating schism[86] and gay Orthodox Jews in Israel creating a website to help them cope with persecution.[87])

As with such issues as excessive modesty, forced marriages and homosexuality, honour killings are commonplace in Muslim and other fervently religious communities. Again it is argued that religious commitment should not be confused with traditional culture and that Islam does not support the violent punishment of those who offend against the community's sense of 'honour'. And again it is significant that such punishments – beatings, rape and murder – occur most frequently in Muslim, Sikh and Hindu communities; the imams and other religious leaders in these communities say little about the evil of such practices. In one high-profile case – involving female circumcision, rape and murder – there was little doubt that Islam in Kurdish communities had contributed to the perpetration of appalling crimes: 'The rise of Islam had only made matters worse – nobody was in any doubt that a stricter Islamic faith had contributed to an increase in the incidence of honour killing.'[88] When a fifteen-year-old Pakistani girl was tricked into marriage, conducted by telephone, with a Sheffield man with a mental age of five she struggled to escape but was eventually lured back and forced into prostitution. The girl's marriage was not recognised by the Home Office but was approved by the Islamic Sharia Council in Britain. She was typical of the 'runaway brides' at risk of an honour killing. According to official figures a dozen girls are killed in this way in Britain every year, though the government has been warned that this is a serious underestimate.[89] In Pakistan Shehnaz Akhtar, a 25-year-old woman sold into a forced marriage, begged the courts for help: 'In the days before Islam girls were buried alive, now they are sold like sheep and goats. I have been sold to a man I never wanted to live with. What kind of Islam is this?'[90] Another desperate victim, Razia, was driven to pouring kerosene over her head and setting herself alight: 'I felt that death was better than this life.' Dreadfully scarred, she survived, whereupon her husband quickly divorced her and married again.[91] Stoned in Turkey after becoming pregnant by a married man, 35-year-old Semsiye Allak took seven months to die. In the impoverished south-east of the country girls are shot and drowned and have their throats cut for such crimes as having a boyfriend. Many 'honour crimes' are not reported and the subsequent tortures and murders perpetrated by families and clans are usually ignored by the courts.[92]

Other sources of social tension derive from Anglican anxieties

about the building of new mosques in various parts of Britain.
Alison Ruoff, a member of the Church of England's General
Synod, has declared that there should be no more mosques
in Britain:

> You build a mosque and then what happens? You have Muslim
> people moving into that area, all the shops will then become Islamic,
> all the housing will then become Islamic and, as the Bishop of
> Rochester [Michael Nazir-Ali] has so wisely pointed out, that will be
> a no-go area for anyone else. They will bring in Islamic law. We
> cannot allow that to happen.[93]

It is obvious that any such development would have consequences
for the rights of women and sexual attitudes throughout the
community. There are countless examples around the world of
what a gradual transformation of secular society into an Islamic
alternative would mean. To take one, in 2007 the broadcaster
Funmi Iyanda was stopped by policemen in Nigeria. They
pointed at her knee-length dress and called her a prostitute, a
harlot, a useless woman – at a time when the Senate was
considering passing a bill to criminalise 'indecent' dressing: neck-
lines must be two inches or less from the shoulders, and the waist
of a female over fourteen must not be visible. Even opponents of
the bill, seemingly prepared to accept the repression of women in
Nigerian society, were suggesting that policing should be left to
private organisations. The writer Chimamanda Ngozi Adichie
related how she was asked to leave a church in Nsukka because
her blouse had short sleeves.[94]

At the same time polygamy was prevalent in rural areas, while
in Kyrgyzstan the government was announcing plans to
decriminalise polygamy, outlawed under the Soviets. In France
polygamy, common in Muslim communities, was being blamed
for social tensions; and in Bangladesh men were expected to pay
a polygamy tax as part of a modernisation drive. In Egypt Ragab
al-Suweirky, a businessman who admitted to nineteen marriages,
was sentenced to seven years in jail for having more than the four
wives allowed in Islam.

Polygamy is still permitted throughout much of the Muslim

world (in Malaysia a man was jailed for having ten wives when only four were permitted). In the United States the Mormons were being pressured to abandon polygamy though the practice persisted throughout the country. One estimate by watchdog groups suggested that there could be as many as 100,000 Americans living in polygamy, many of them in Utah.[95] When one young bride refused to sleep with her husband, James Harmston, he promised to 'deal with' her 'in the future eternity' and signed his letters to her 'Your Husband, King and Priest'. Harmston was a self-declared prophet of a polygamist and apocalyptic sect, the True and Living Church of Jesus Christ of Saints of the Last Days. In 2001 the Mormon fundamentalist Tom Green was jailed for five years for bigamy. His five wives and seven of his thirty children watched as he was led away from the courthouse in Provo, Utah, in handcuffs to begin his sentence.[96] All of the wives had pledged fidelity to their husband.

In Italy the Bishop of Viterbo, Lorenzo Chiarinelli, denied a 25-year-old paraplegic a church wedding because he could not have children. The purpose of marriage was not only love but also procreation. Ileana Argentin, an MP who suffers from multiple sclerosis, commented: 'We seem to have gone back a hundred years, even a thousand.'[97] Francisco Chimoio, the Archbishop of Maputo, the capital of Mozambique, accused European condom manufacturers of deliberately infecting their products with HIV 'in order to finish quickly the African people': 'I know that there are two countries in Europe . . . making condoms with the virus, on purpose.' He refused to name the countries. 'They want to finish with the African people. This is the programme. They want to colonise . . . If we are not careful we will finish in one century's time.'[98] These are totally unwarranted accusations, but they maintain the perennial message of anti-sexual clerics: that young people should abstain from sexual relations. Such are the fruits of Christianity. In Iran the mullahs still required tanks to push walls over onto homosexuals, crushing them to death; in Egypt partying homosexuals were beaten by the police, arrested and arraigned before the courts to face up to five years in jail. For the first two weeks in detention they were subjected to whipping and electric shocks.[99] Such are the fruits of Islam.

It is plain that religion has never managed to adjust to the nature of human sexuality. Every aspect of sexual behaviour has been variously interpreted by mainstream religion in ways that at best have contributed to the sum total of unhappiness in society and at worst have generated the grossest forms of abuse and torture. Women have suffered most of all. The underlying assumption that half the human race is inferior, a doctrine underwritten by sacred texts interpreted by ignorant male scholars, has led to all manner of horrors – from witch burnings, still practised in various countries, to ritual mutilations, common in much of the Muslim world but discernible in the name of religious piety far beyond it.

Much mainstream religion, particularly Christianity, has generally disparaged sexuality, insisting over the centuries on the superiority of virginity, chastity and lifelong sexual abstinence; or, at the other extreme, it has demanded that women be regarded as sexual commodities. These postures have inevitably led to a persistent denunciation of all variations of human sexual behaviour – a clerical preoccupation that has distorted the moral teachings of religion throughout all its history and which, in its worst manifestations, has yielded a manifest psychopathology. For example, as in Islam, sexual appetite is to be indulged freely within certain strictures defined by men and sustaining an obvious misogyny. For centuries mainstream religion has protected a multifaceted sexual preoccupation that continues to impact on society.

Charles Darwin also, biologist supreme, was preoccupied with sexual behaviour, not as a route to restricting and tormenting human beings in society but as a means of helping to comprehend the law of evolution. His seminal work *The Descent of Man, and Selection in Relation to Sex*, first published in 1871, went into more than two dozen editions over the course of three decades. Here Darwin concluded that sexual selection 'has played an important part in the history of the organic world' and emphasised that it is the *evidence* adduced for his conclusions that is the important consideration:

> I have given the evidence to the best of my ability. We must acknowledge, as it seems to me, that man with all his noble qualities,

with sympathy which feels for the most debased, with benevolence that extends not only to other men but to the humblest living creature, with his god-like intellect which has penetrated into the movements and constitution of the solar system – with all these exalted powers – man still bears in his bodily frame the indelible stamp of his lowly origin.

The creationists, reeling beneath the vast weight of evidence that today sustains the law of evolution, do not like this conclusion. Darwin presented his material on sexual selection just as he offered his cornucopia of evidence for much of the biological world. In all this he demonstrated in the nineteenth century that facts are vastly more important in helping to extend our knowledge of humankind and its place in the universe than the dogmas of ignorant men who prefer the harsh strictures of superstition and repression. In the twenty-first century this should be an easy choice to make.

Notes

Preface

1. David Pears, *Bertrand Russell and the British Tradition in Philosophy* (London: Collins, 1967), p. 159.

Introduction

1. Quoted in Massoud Anssari, 'Blind seven-year-old beaten to death for failing to learn Koran', *Sunday Telegraph*, 1 June 2008.
2. See Richard Kerbaj, 'Teachers "beat and abuse" children at many Koran classes in Britain', *The Times*, 10 December 2008; 'Ghayasuddin Siddiqui, 'Law to protect the young must cover madrassas as well', *The Times*, 10 December 2008.
3. See 'Nine face stoning to death in Iran', BBC News website, 20 July 2008; 'Iran "adulterer" stoned to death', BBC News website, 10 July 2007; 'EU urges Iran to drop draft on witchcraft and heresy', Reuters, 26 February 2006.
4. See Julian Borger, 'The lost boys, thrown out of US sect so that older men can marry more wives', *Guardian*, 14 June 2005.

Chapter 1: The law of evolution

1. Genesis 1: 5–19.
2. Surah 96: 2; in this chapter and elsewhere I am using the Penguin edition (1990), translated by N. J. Dawood.
3. Surah 15: 26; see also Surah 32: 7.
4. Bertrand Russell, *The Selected Letters of Bertrand Russell: The Public Years 1914–1970*, ed. Nicholas Griffin (London: Routledge, 2001), p. 352. This item appears as a postscript in a letter to William Warder Norton dated 18 August 1937 in which he agrees the contract for the publication of *The History of Western Philosophy*.

Russell notes the need to avoid saying anything obscene, which may be why we were granted a Latin translation to save our sensitivities, but he adds: 'But perhaps when you sell the movie rights you will see that this point is not overlooked.' In fact erections are not uncommon when men suffer traumas, such as hanging, at death. It seems that Mohammed cannot claim a unique gesture of piety in this regard.

5. By 1530 Copernicus had largely completed his book *De revolutionibus orbium coelestrium* (On the Revolutions of the Celestial Spheres) but, perhaps through concern for the likely response of the Roman Catholic Church, delayed publication until 1540. He is said to have received his first bound copy just before his death.

6. Quoted in Bertrand Russell, *The Scientific Outlook*, 2nd ed. (London: George Allen & Unwin, 1954), pp. 27–32.

7. Quoted ibid., p. 31.

8. Quoted ibid.

9. Martin J. Scott, SJ, *Science Helps the Church* (Imprimatur Cardinal Spellman, 1945), p. 8.

10. Stephen C. Meyer, 'The Scientific Status of Intelligent Design: The Methodological Equivalence of Naturalistic and Non-naturalistic Origins Theories', in Michael J. Behe, William A. Dembski and Stephen C. Meyer, *Science and Evidence for Design in the Universe: Papers Presented at a Conference Sponsored by the Wethersfield Institute, New York City, 25 September 1999* (San Francisco: Ignatius Press, 2000), p. 156, citing O. Gingerich, 'The Galileo Affair', *Scientific American*, August 1982, pp. 133–43.

11. See Richard Owen and Sarah Delaney, 'Vatican recants with a statue of Galileo', *The Times*, 4 March 2008.

12. Quoted in Joseph Bernhart, *The Vatican as a World Power*, tr. George N. Schuster (London: Longmans, Green & Co., 1939).

13. Quoted in Paul Blanshard, *Freedom and Catholic Power* (London: Secker & Warburg, 1951), p. 199.

14. According to official Catholic sources, pieces of the True Cross are to be found throughout Europe and elsewhere; for example, in Brussels, Ghent, Rome, Venice, Ragusa, Paris, Limburg and Mount Athos. One of the nails was thrown into the Adriatic to calm a storm.

15. Quoted in David S. Schaff, *Our Father's Faith and Ours* (G. P. Putnam's Sons, 1928), p. 486.

16. Quoted in Blanshard, *Freedom and Catholic Power*, p. 211.

17. *National Catholic Educational Association Bulletin*, 1940.

18. See Esther Kaplan, *With God on Their Side: How Christian Fundamentalists Trampled Science, Policy, and Democracy in George W. Bush's White House* (New York: New Press, 2004), pp. 91–2.

19. Quoted ibid., p. 92.

20. See Kimberly Edds, 'At Grand Canyon Park, a rift over creationist book', *Washington Post*, 20 January 2004. The first amendment of the US constitution, while protecting freedom of expression, prohibits Congress from making laws 'respecting an establishment of religion'.

21. In December 2003 the heads of seven leading national geological associations wrote to Joseph Alston, the Grand Canyon superintendent: 'The National Park Service should be extremely careful about giving the impression that it approves of the anti-science movement known as young Earth creationism or endorses the advancement of religious tenets as science. The [Vail] book aggressively attacks modern science and broadly accepted interpretations of the geologic history of the Grand Canyon.' (Quoted in Kaplan, *With God on Their Side*, p. 93.)

22. Steve A. Austin (ed.), *Grand Canyon: Monument to Catastrophe* (Santee, CA: Institute for Creation Research, 1995).

23. Philip W. Anderson et al., letter to George W. Bush, 18 February 2004, initiated by the Union for Concerned Scientists and available at its website.

24. See for example Hugh Kennedy, *The Court of the Caliphs: The Rise and Fall of Islam's Greatest Dynasty* (London: Weidenfeld & Nicolson, 2004).

25. Osama bin Laden was sufficiently impressed with the Abassid dynasty to propose a new modern caliphate that would embrace the entire Muslim world.

26. See Yoginder Sikand, *Bastions of the Believers: Madrasas and Islamic Education in India* (London: Penguin, 2005), p. xxvi.

27. Ibid.

28. Surah 7: 54; Surah 10: 3; Surah 11: 7.

29. The mother receives one third of the property, the wife a quarter of the property, and the sisters two thirds, which adds up to one and a quarter – more than the total property.

30. Surah 16: 15; Surah 21: 32; Surah 31: 9.

31. Surah 67: 5; see also Surah 37: 6–8.

32. Surah 10: 5.

33. Sikand, *Bastions of the Believers*, passim.

34. Mostafa Mahmoud, *Dialogue with an Atheist*, tr. Mohamed Yehia (London: Dar Al Taqwa, 1994), p. 145.

35. The modern superstition surrounding the rabbit's foot derives from a belief rooted in ancient totemism that humankind descended from animals.

36. B. Thompson, *The History of Evolutionary Thought* (Fort Worth, TX: Star Bible & Tract Corporation, 1981), p. 31.

37. Quoted in Bertrand Russell, *History of Western Philosophy* (London: George Allen & Unwin, 1946), p. 45.

38. See H. F. Osborn, *From the Greeks to Darwin: The Development of The Evolution Idea through Twenty-Four Centuries*, 2nd ed. (New York: Charles Scribner's Sons, 1929), p. 52, ref. 6.

39. Ibid., p. 54.

40. So much for the First Cause argument and the modern Big Bang theory.

41. See Titus Lucretius Carus, *De Rerum Natura* (On the Nature of Things), translated in metrical form by William Ellery Leonard (New York: E. P. Dutton, 1916), Book I.

42. Ibid.

43. Ibid.

44. Ibid.

45. Ibid.

46. Ibid., Book V.

47. Osborn, *From the Greeks to Darwin*, p. 4.

48. David Hume, *Dialogues Concerning Natural Religion*, in *Hume on Religion* (London: Collins, 1963), pp. 99–204.

49. Ibid., p. 100.

50. In what follows I will not trouble to identify the points with particular speakers. All the scepticism plainly belongs to Hume.

51. Hume, *Dialogues Concerning Natural Religion*, p. 117.

52. Ibid., p. 131.

53. Ibid., pp. 140–41.

54. Ibid., p. 142.

55. Immanuel Kant, *Critique of Pure Reason*, tr. J. M. D. Meiklejohn (London: J. M. Dent, 1934), p. 364.

56. See Desmond King-Hele, *Erasmus Darwin* (London: Macmillan / New York: St Martin's Press, 1963), p. 81.

57. See Stephen Jay Gould, *Leonardo's Mountain of Clams and the Diet of Worms: Essays on Natural History* (New York: Harmony, 1989), p. 312.

58. See F. G. Crookshank, *The Mongol in Our Midst: A Study of Man and His Three Faces*, 3rd ed. (London: Kegan Paul, Trench, Trubner, 1931), p. 4.

59. A. Huxley, 'A reappraisal of Charles Darwin', *American Scholar*, Autumn 1959, p. 489, footnote.

60. Ernst Krause, *Erasmus Darwin ... with a Preliminary Notice by Charles Darwin*, tr. W. S. Dallas (London: John Murray, 1879), p. 45.

61. Quoted in Raymond V. Holt, *The Unitarian Contribution to Social Progress in England*, 2nd ed. (London: Lindsey Press, 1952).

62. Quoted in J. Seed, 'Theologies of Power: Unitarianism and Social Relations of Religious Discourse 1800–1850', in R. J. Morris (ed.), *Class Power and Social Structure in British Nineteenth-Century Towns* (Leicester: Leicester University Press, 1986), pp. 108–56.

63. See Adrian Desmond and James Moore, *Darwin* (London: Michael Joseph, 1991), p. 78.

64. Ibid.

65. Quoted ibid., pp. 84–5.

66. Taylor was spreading the gospel of infidelity by word of mouth and doing as much damage to Christianity as his ally Robert Carlile with his numerous and widely circulated publications. In 1827 Taylor was arrested for blasphemy, with the authorities well aware that their prisoner was an extremely able scholar and so particularly dangerous (he happened to be an authority on marine and mercantile law). On 7 February 1828, despite a defence delivered by him with great oratorical impact, Taylor was sentenced to one year in Oakham gaol in Rutland with various recognizances added. On release he organised with Carlile 'an infidel mission through the north of England'.

67. Charles Darwin, *The Origin of Species*, intr. W. R. Thompson (London: J. M. Dent, 1928). There are many editions of the *Origin*, some incorporating changes introduced by Darwin himself. This edition is of interest because Thompson was able to comment: 'I am not satisfied that Darwin proved his point or that his influence in scientific and public thinking has been beneficial.' Today the number of scientists who believe that Darwin failed to 'prove his point' are a tiny and dwindling band. There is still debate on marginal issues but the central tenets of Darwinism are now generally regarded in the scientific community as defining the law of evolution.

68. Quoted in Desmond and Moore, *Darwin*, p. 477. Darwin incorporated Kingsley's comment into the last chapter of future editions.

69. Quoted ibid., p. 478.

70. Captain Robert FitzRoy, *Proceedings of the Second Expedition*

1831–1836, published as vol. 2 of *Narrative of the Surveying Voyages of His Majesty's Ships* Adventure *and* Beagle *between the Years 1826 and 1836 Describing Their Examinations of the Southern Shores of South America and the* Beagle*'s Circumnavigation of the Globe*, 3 vols (London: Henry Colburn, 1839).

71. Quoted in Howard E. Gruber, *Darwin on Man: A Psychological Study of Scientific Creativity* (London: Wildwood House, 1974), p. 131.

72. *Beagle* diary, p. 383, quoted in Gruber, *Darwin on Man*, p. 133.

73. See Gruber, *Darwin on Man*, pp. 135–149.

74. See Richard Dawkins, 'Why Darwin matters: Big enough to undermine creation but simple enough to be stated in a sentence, the theory of natural selection is a masterpiece', *The Guardian*, 9 February 2008. Dawkins, in line with convention, refers to the 'theory', not the 'law', of evolution. More of this later.

75. Ibid.

76. Ibid.

77. Quoted in William Irvine, *Apes, Angels and Victorians: A Joint Biography of Darwin and Huxley* (London: Weidenfeld & Nicolson, 1955), p. 63.

78. Darwin, *The Origin of Species*, p. 80.

79. Ibid., p. 81.

80. Ibid., p. 156.

81. Ibid.

82. Interested readers should consult Chapters 6 and 7 of the *Origin*.

83. These and other such examples can be found in James R. Moore, *The Post-Darwinian Controversies: A Study of the Protestant Struggle to Come to Terms with Darwin in Great Britain and America 1870–1900* (Cambridge: Cambridge University Press, 1979).

84. Ibid.

85. Quoted in Desmond and Moore, *Darwin*, p. 603.

86. Charles Darwin, *Journal of Researches into the Geology and Natural History of the Various Countries Visited by HMS* Beagle (London: Ward, Lock & Bowden, 1894), p. 20; Francis Darwin (ed.), *The Life and Letters of Charles Darwin, Including an Autobiographical Chapter*, 3 vols (London: John Murray, 1887), pp. 21, 57, 78, 85–7, 145; Colp, 'Notes on Charles Darwin's *Autobiography*', quoted in Desmond and Moore, *Darwin*, p. 623.

87. Quoted in Francis Darwin, *The Life of Charles Darwin* (Twickenham: Tiger Books International, [1902] 1995), p. 55.

88. See Desmond and Moore, *Darwin*, p. 627.

89. Charles Darwin, *The Descent of Man, and Selection in Relation to Sex*, 2nd ed. (London: John Murray, 1909), p. 945: 'Hence our natural rate of increase, though leading to many and obvious evils, must not be diminished by any means.'
90. Ibid., p. 926. By April 1909 the *Descent* was in its twenty-seventh printing.
91. Ibid., p. 937.
92. Quoted in Darwin, *The Life of Charles Darwin*, p. 56.
93. Quoted ibid.
94. Here Charles Darwin cites his book *The Variation of Animals and Plants under Domestication*, where he argues: 'There seems to be no more design in the variability of organic beings, and in the action of natural selection, than in the course which the wind blows.'
95. Quoted in Darwin, *The Life of Charles Darwin*, p. 60.
96. Quoted ibid.
97. Adrian Desmond, *Huxley: The Devil's Disciple* (London: Michael Joseph, 1994); *Huxley: Evolution's High Priest* (London: Michael Joseph, 1997).
98. Quoted in Desmond, *Huxley: The Devil's Disciple*, p. 328.
99. Quoted in Irvine, *Apes, Angels and Victorians*, pp. 99–100.
100. Quoted ibid.
101. Quoted ibid., pp. 100–101. Huxley extended this point in metaphor to stress the importance of both physical and moral law: 'The gravitation of sin to sorrow is as certain as that of the earth to the sun, and more so – for experimental proof of that fact is within reach of us all – nay, it is before us all in our own lives, if we had but the eyes to see it.'
102. Here I will refrain from adumbrating on the men and women who have committed appalling sins in the world and yet who appear to be well rewarded in life. The destruction of Iraq provides us with a 'fact' or two that can serve to deflate Huxley's ethical optimism.
103. See Chapter 4.
104. See V. M. Spalding, 'Botany in High School', *Academy* (1890), vol. 5, p. 317; A. Hunter Dupree, *Asa Gray 1810–1888* (Cambridge, MA: Belknap Press, 1959), pp. 362–9; Charles Carpenter, *History of American Schoolbooks* (Philadelphia: University of Philadelphia Press, 1963), p. 223. These sources are cited in Edward J. Larson, *Trial and Error: The American Controversy over Creation and Evolution*, rev. ed. (New York: Oxford University Press, 1989), pp. 9–10, to which I owe much in the following section.

105. For example, first edition: Louis Agassiz and A. A. Gould, *Principles of Zoology* (Boston: Gould, 1848), p. 182; last edition, Louis Agassiz and A. A. Gould, *Principles of Zoology* (Boston: Gould, 1873), p. 214.

106. Bessey to Bryan D. Halsted, 2 December 1908, quoted in Ronald C. Tobey, *Saving the Prairies: The Life Cycle of the Saving School of American Plant Ecology 1895–1955* (Berkeley: University of California Press, 1981), p. 9.

107. Charles Benedict Davenport and Gertrude Crotty Davenport, *Elements of Zoology to Accompany the Field and Laboratory Study of Animals* (New York: Macmillan, 1911), pp. 460–70.

108. George William Hunter, *A Civic Biology: Presented in Problems* (New York: American Book Company, 1914), pp. 183, 194–6.

109. Quoted in Lawrence W. Levine, *Defender of the Faith: William Jennings Bryan, the Last Decade 1915–1925* (New York: Oxford University Press, 1965), p. 277.

110. William Jennings Bryan, *The Bible and Its Enemies* (Chicago: Bible Institute, 1921), p. 34.

111. T. T. Martin, *Hell and the High Schools: Christ or Evolution, Which?* (Kansas City, MO: Western Baptist, 1923), p. 9.

112. George Marsden, *Fundamentalism and American Culture* (New York: Oxford University Press, 2006), p. 141.

113. William Jennings Bryan, *In His Image* (New York: Fleming H. Revell, 1922), p. 24.

114. Quoted in Larson, *Trial and Error*, p. 47.

115. Quoted ibid., p. 54.

116. The 1926 'Tennessee Monkey Trial' was cast as a stage play *Inherit the Wind* and two film versions (these latter starring, respectively, Spencer Tracy and Jason Robards).

117. The state Supreme Court later overturned the conviction while upholding the statute. In 1968 the US Supreme Court ruled a similar statute unconstitutional.

118. Quoted in Larson, *Trial and Error*, p. 77.

119. Quoted ibid., p. 78.

120. Ibid., p. 124.

121. Ibid., p. 183.

122. Quoted in James Bone, 'Scientists protest as school chiefs put Darwin on trial', *The Times*, 7 May 2005.

123. See Ian Sample, 'Fundamentalists "threaten scientific progress"', *The Guardian*, 30 November 2005.

124. See Suzanne Goldenberg, 'US judge bans intelligent design from

science lessons', *The Guardian*, 21 December 2005; Harry Mount, 'Keep the divine out of biology lessons, federal judge rules', *Daily Telegraph*, 21 December 2005.

125. Duncan Campbell, 'Academics fight rise of creationism at universities', *The Guardian*, 21 February 2006; Tony Halpin, 'Creationism to be taught on GCSE science syllabus', *The Times*, 10 March 2006; Harriet Swain, 'How did we get here?', *The Guardian*, 15 August 2006.

126. Quoted in Stephen Bates, 'Archbishop: stop teaching creationism', *The Guardian*, 21 March 2006.

127. See Duncan Campbell and Rebecca Smithers, 'Royal Society attacks teaching of creationism as science', *The Guardian*, 12 April 2006.

128. Quoted in Steve Bird, 'Teach the origins of life based on evidence, scientists demand', *The Times*, 22 June 2006.

129. Quoted in James Randerson, 'Revealed: rise of creationism in UK schools', *The Guardian*, 27 November 2006.

130. See Ken McCleod, 'Refloating the Ark', *Morning Star*, 3 March 2008.

131. See Alec Russell, '"Children kept dinosaurs as pets"', *Daily Telegraph*, 24 June 2006; Tom Baldwin, 'Creationist museum brings dinosaurs on board Noah's Ark', *The Times*, 28 May 2007.

132. The bacterial flagellum was first publicised in Michael J. Behe, *Darwin's Black Box: The Biochemical Challenge to Evolution* (New York: Free Press, 1996).

133. See Michael J. Behe, 'Answering scientific criticisms of intelligent design', in Behe, Dembski and Meyer, *Science and Evidence for Design in the Universe*, pp. 134–5.

134. Thomas Burnet, *The Sacred Theory of the Earth* (Carbondale: Southern Illinois University Press, [1691] 1965), p. 16.

135. Quoted in Richard Dawkins, *The God Delusion* (London: Bantam, 2006), pp. 130–31.

136. See Kenneth R. Miller, *Finding Darwin's God: A Scientist's Search for Common Ground between God and Evolution* (New York: Cliff Street, 1999).

137. Kenneth R. Miller, 'The Flagellum Unspun: The Collapse of "Irreducible Complexity"', in William A. Dembski and Michael Ruse (eds), *Debating Design: From Darwin to DNA* (Cambridge: Cambridge University Press, 2004), pp. 81–97.

138. Ibid.

139. Ibid.

140. Quoted in Dan Jones, 'Engines of Evolution', *New Scientist*, 16 February 2008.
141. Mark J. Pallen and Nicholas J. Matzke, 'From *The Origin of Species* to the Origin of Bacterial Flagella', *Nature Reviews Microbiology* (2006), vol. 4, pp. 784–9.
142. Jones, 'Engines of Evolution'.
143. See Dawkins, *The God Delusion*, pp. 132–3.
144. Richard Dawkins, 'Foreword', in Niall Shanks, *God, the Devil, and Darwin: A Critique of Intelligent Design Theory* (New York: Oxford University Press, 2004), pp. ix–x.
145. Joseph Needham, 'Mechanistic Biology and The Religious Consciousness', in Joseph Needham (ed.), *Science, Religion and Reality* (London: Sheldon Press, 1925).
146. The account of the trial, at Dover, Pennsylvania, is in Andrea Bottaro, Matt A. Inlay and Nicholas J. Matzke, 'Immunology in the Spotlight at the Dover "Intelligent Design" Trial', *Nature Immunology* (2006), vol. 7, pp. 433–5.
147. See William A. Dembski, *Intelligent Design: The Bridge between Science and Theology* (Downers Grove, IL: IVP Academic, 1999).
148. John D. Barrow and Frank J. Tipler, *The Anthropic Cosmological Principle* (Oxford: Clarendon Press, 1985).
149. Paul Davies, *The Goldilocks Enigma: Why Is the Universe Just Right for Life?* (London: Allen Lane, 2006).
150. See for example the *Origin*, the *Descent* and *The Expression of the Emotion in Man and Animals* (1872).
151. J. D. Watson and F. H. C. Crick, 'A Structure for Deoxyribose Nucleic Acid', *Nature* (1953), vol. 171, p. 738. The article was kept intentionally brief in order to establish a speedy priority – a common procedure in 1950s science. It concluded with the statement that full details of the DNA structure would be published elsewhere. In January 1954 they published the 'full details' of their work in *Proceedings of the Royal Society*. Subsequent related articles include: M. H. F. Wilkins, A. R. Stokes and H. R. Wilson, 'Molecular Structure of Deoxypentose Nucleic Acids', *Nature* (1953), vol. 171, pp. 738–40 [showing that the DNA structure exists in biological systems]; R. Franklin and R. G. Gosling, 'Molecular Configuration in Sodium Thymonucleate', *Nature* (1953), vol. 171, pp. 740–41 [providing further evidence of the helical structure of nucleic acids]; and J. D. Watson and F. H. C. Crick, 'Genetical Implications of the Structure of Deoxyribonucleic Acid', *Nature* (1953), vol. 171, pp. 964–7

[describing how the double helix allows replication of DNA].

152. I owe what follows to Sean B. Carroll, *The Making of the Fittest: DNA and the Ultimate Forensic Record of Evolution* (New York: W. W. Norton, 2006).

153. Carroll, *The Making of the Fittest*, p. 119.

154. In 2001 Tom Bethel opined that 'virtually no scientific evidence for evolution exists' ('Hagiography for Moderns', *Christianity Today*, 3 September 2001); the year before, Henry M. Morris wrote in 'The Scientific Case against Evolution' (*Impact*, December 2000) that 'there is no real scientific evidence that evolution is occurring ... or ever occurred ... [It] is not a fact of science ... It is not even a science at all'; and Phil Fernandes wrote in a doctoral dissertation (1997) for the Institute of Biblical Defense that 'evolution is a myth, devoid of *any* scientific evidence [emphasis added]'. These attempts to deny the vast body of scientific knowledge are cited in Carroll, *The Making of the Fittest*, p. 234.

155. See Frans de Waal, 'Morally Evolved: Primate Social Instincts, Human Morality, and the Rise and Fall of "Veneer Theory"', in *Primates and Philosophers: How Morality Evolved*, ed. Stephen Macedo and Josiah Ober (Princeton: Princeton University Press, 2006), p. 29.

156. See Sam Jones, 'Monkeys show sensitivity to unfair reward schemes', *The Guardian*, 24 November 2007.

157. See Frans de Waal, 'The Animal Roots of Human Morality', *New Scientist*, 14 October 2006.

158. Quoted in Lucy Cockcroft, 'Creationists peddle lies about fossil record, says scientist', *Daily Telegraph*, 28 February 2008.

159. J. G. M. Thewissen, E. M. Williams, L. J. Roe and S. T. Hussain, 'Skeletons of Terrestrial Cetaceans and the Relationship of Whales to Artiodactyls', *Nature* (2001), vol. 413, pp. 277–81; J. G. M. Thewissen, S. T. Hussain and M. Arif, 'Fossil Evidence for the Origin of Aquatic Locomotion in Archaeocete Whales', *Science* (1994), vol. 263, pp. 210–12.

160. Barack Obama, *Dreams from My Father: A Story of Race and Inheritance*, new ed. (Edinburgh: Canongate, 2007), p. 163.

161. Suzanne Goldenberg, 'Democratic converts narrow "God gap"', *The Guardian*, 7 November 2008.

162. Barack Obama, *The Audacity of Hope: Thoughts on Reclaiming the American Dream* (Edinburgh: Canongate, 2007), p. 208.

163. Ibid., p. 218.

164. Ibid., p. 226.

165. Kaplan, *With God on Their Side*, subtitle.

166. Nabil Shaath, the Palestinian foreign minister, described a meeting with Bush: 'President Bush said to all of us: "I'm driven with a mission from God. God would tell me: 'George, go and fight those terrorists in Afghanistan.' And I did, and then God would tell me: 'George, go and end the tyranny in Iraq.' ... And I did."' ('God told me to invade Iraq, Bush tells Palestinian ministers', BBC press release, 6 October 2005.)

167. Kaplan, *With God on Their Side*, pp. 95–6.

168. Ibid., p. 99

169. Quoted ibid., pp. 99–100.

170. Ibid., pp. 106–7.

171. Quoted ibid., p. 107.

172. 'Faith-Based Reasoning', *Scientific American*, June 2001.

173. The Christian right managed to get bills passed in several states requiring doctors to warn women of the alleged link. This is a clear example of where pro-life activists are prepared to spread falsehoods to discourage women from having abortions.

174. Union of Concerned Scientists, *Scientific Integrity in Policymaking: An Investigation into the Bush Administration's Misuse of Science* (Cambridge, MA: Union of Concerned Scientists, 2004), pp. 2, 32.

175. See Chapter 3.

176. I owe much of what follows to Ziauddin Sardar, 'Weird science', *New Statesman*, 25 August 2008, pp. 26–7.

177. Consider, for example, Surah 29. 20: 'Roam the earth and see how God has brought the Creation into being'; and Surah 3. 190: 'In the creation of the heavens and the earth, and in the alternation of night and day, there are signs for men of sense.'

178. Sardar, 'Weird science', p. 26.

179. Quoted ibid.

180. Ibid.

181. Ibid., p. 27.

182. Ibid.

183. George Monbiot, 'How these gibbering numbskulls came to dominate Washington', *The Guardian*, 28 October 2008.

184. See Graydon Carter, *What We've Lost* (London: Little Brown, 2004), pp. 321, 322.

185. See Monbiot, 'How these gibbering numbskulls came to dominate Washington'; Susan Jacoby, *The Age of American Unreason* (New York: Pantheon, 2008).

186. See Geoff Simons, 'Preface', in *Iraq Endgame?: Surge, Suffering and the Politics of Denial* (London: Politico's, 2008).

Chapter 2: Superstitious roots

1. In this quotation Hume observes also that there are fewer supernatural events as people learn more about the world: 'The former [prodigies etc.] grow thinner every page ... as we advance nearer the enlightened ages.'

2. The quotation from Hume compares with Albert Einstein's comment on his admirers: 'I am sure it is the mystery of non-understanding that appeals to them ... It impresses them, it has the colour and the appeal of the mysterious.' (Albert Einstein, *A Stubbornly Persistent Illusion: The Essential Scientific Writings of Albert Einstein*, ed. Stephen Hawking (Philadelphia: Running Press, 2008).)

3. A. J. Ayer, *The Problem of Knowledge* (Harmondsworth: Pelican, 1956), pp. 14–19.

4. The ancient Romans developed a system of *augury* (from *avis* 'bird', thus meaning divination studying birds, or soothsaying in general). Throughout the Middle Ages augury had a powerful hold in much of Christian Europe. The *Poema de Mio Cid* narrates how its hero pays attention to the croakings of the crow, and an old collection of Italian *novelle* describes a nobleman who, 'like most of his countrymen', is addicted to augury practices.

5. Haruspicy (from the Assyrian *har* 'liver') originated in Babylonia and was carried to the West by the Etruscan priesthood. Divination from the shoulder-blades or from the 'wishbone' of fowl is still a popular superstition in Europe and elsewhere. With these practices and many others the intimate links between religion and superstition are plain.

6. It is interesting that Christianity did not put a stop to incubation. People simply slept in Christian churches rather than pagan temples. Hence the Christian religion, already infected with a multitude of pagan superstitions, continually added others to its repertoire. Incubation has also been found in many primitive tribes where a person is sometimes given a drug to aid the divine visitation or, in modern terms, the hallucinatory experience.

7. It is hardly necessary to note the widespread appeal of astrology in modern society. But it is of interest that in astrology, like religion, there are many schools of thought, schisms that attract their own disciples. As with religion and unlike science, there are no universally agreed protocols to settle differences of opinion between the various schismatic groups.

8. Necromancy, a precursor of modern spiritualism, was practised in ancient Greece, Arabic lands and various parts of medieval Europe. The oldest known example is the Nekyia of the *Odyssey*. The tale of the Witch of Endor in the Old Testament, Odin's conjuration of the dead *völva* in the Norse *Völuspá*, and a story forming part of the *Hervarar saga ok Heiðreks* show how widespread the doctrine has been. Again it is easy to see, through the survival of 'spirits' and their interest in human affairs, the links with orthodox religion.

9. W. H. Mallock, *Studies of Contemporary Superstition* (London: Ward & Downey, 1895).

10. Bronisław Malinowski, *Sex, Culture and Myth* (London: Rupert Hart-Davis, 1963), p. 256.

11. See Douglas Hill, *Magic and Superstition* (London: Paul Hamlyn, 1968), p. 11.

12. Alexander H. Krappe, *The Science of Folk-Lore* (London: Methuen, 1930), pp. 211–29.

13. See Fawn Brodie, *The Devil Drives: A Life of Sir Richard Burton* (Harmondsworth: Penguin, 1971), pp. 260–61.

14. This case, from Freud's *Psychopathology of Everyday Life*, is discussed by Gustav Jahoda in *The Psychology of Superstition* (London: Allen Lane, 1969).

15. B. F. Skinner, '"Superstition" in the Pigeon', *Journal of Experimental Psychology* (1948), vol. 38, pp. 168–72.

16. B. F. Skinner, *Science and Human Behavior* (New York: Macmillan, 1953).

17. Bertrand Russell, *Sceptical Essays* (London: George Allen & Unwin, 1928), p. 1.

18. See Bertrand Russell, *Human Society in Ethics and Politics* (London: George Allen & Unwin, 1954), pp. 138–44.

19. Syed Kamran Mirza, 'Islam and Superstitions', tr. Abul Kassem, FaithFreedom website, 3 April 2006.

20. Ibid.

21. See Duncan Campbell, 'Life sentences for pair who beat and stabbed faith healer to death', *The Guardian*, 11 March 2008.

22. Ibid.

23. Quoted in Nick Britten, 'New mother who refused blood died for her faith', *Daily Telegraph*, 6 November 2007.

24. Quoted in Jeremy Page, 'Dalai Lama offers his flock a vote on whether he should be reincarnated', *The Times*, 28 November 2007.

25. From 1762 Voltaire, the pseudonym of François-Marie Arouet,

produced a range of anti-religious writings and the *Dictionnaire philosophique* (1764).

26. There are immense complications in all this. One listing of the 'Angels of the Four Cardinal Points' spends half a page listing the names of angels that rule the east, the west, the north and the south. But it is worse than that because the angels seem to work a shift system. For example, after finding that on Tuesday the east is in the care of Friagne, Guael, Damael, Calzas and Aragon, we learn that on Sunday the angels on duty are Samael, Bachiel, Atel, Gabriel and Vionatraba (see Wade Baskin, *The Supernatural Source Book: A Handbook of Precepts and Practices to Dominate the World* (Edison, NJ: Castle, 2006, pp. 33–4)).

27. See Colleen McDannell and Bernhard Lang, *Heaven: A History*, 2nd ed. (New Haven, CT: Yale University Press, 2001), p. xiii.

28. Quoted in Eugen Drewermann, *Über die Unsterblichkeit der Tiere: Hoffnung für die leidende Kreatur* (Olten, Switzerland: Walter, 1990), p. 17.

29. Surah 78: 31–4.

30. Sources cited in McDannall and Lang, *Heaven*, p. 27.

31. Matthew 10: 35.

32. See Luke 14: 26.

33. Sources cited in McDannall and Lang, *Heaven*, p. 342.

34. Ibid., p. 352.

35. Bertrand Russell, 'A Free Man's Worship', in *Philosophical Essays* (London: Longmans, 1910).

36. See Harry E. Wedeck, *A Treasury of Witchcraft* (London: Vision, 1961), p. 85.

37. See Pennethorne Hughes, *Witchcraft* (Harmondsworth: Pelican, 1965), p. 213.

38. H. C. Lea, *Materials towards a History of Witchcraft, vol. 1*, ed. Arthur C. Howland (New York: Thomas Yoseloff, [1939] 1957).

39. Rossell Hope Robbins, *The Encyclopedia of Witchcraft and Demonology* (Feltham: Spring, 1959), p. 127.

40. Ibid.

41. Here I rely on the abridged version: J. G. Frazer, *The Golden Bough* (London: Macmillan, 1957).

42. George W. Gilmore, 'Demon, Demoniac', in *The New Schaff-Herzog Encyclopedia of Religious Knowledge* (New York and London: Funk & Wagnalls, 1908–14), vol. 3, p. 399.

43. See Luke 10: 17, 20.

44. See Isaiah 14: 12–13; Ezekiel 28: 11–19; Revelation 12: 7–10.

45. See Revelation 20: 11–15.
46. E. G. White, *The Great Controversy* (Leicester: Advent, [1911] 2004), p. 378.
47. Daniel, 12: 2.
48. White, *The Great Controversy*, p. 397.
49. Ibid., p. 410.
50. Merrill F. Unger, *Demons in the World Today: A Study of Occultism in the Light of God's Word* (Wheaton, IL: Tyndale House, 1971), p. 2.
51. See Luke 4: 33; Revelation 9: 11.
52. See 1 Timothy 4: 1; Revelation 14: 16.
53. See Ephesians 6: 10–20.
54. See Luke 8: 30; Revelation 9: 11.
55. See Matthew 25: 41.
56. 'I form the light and create darkness: I make peace and create evil: I the Lord do all these things', Isaiah 45:7 (see also Judges 9: 23; 1 Samuel 16: 14; 2 Thessalonians 2: 11).
57. The original *Vision of St Paul* was written in Greek, probably in the third century, with the oldest Latin form dating from the eighth century. By the twelfth century several French vernacular versions had appeared and a number of abbreviated redactions were available.
58. This is a summary of a text produced by Paul Meyer in the periodical *Romania* (1895), vol. 24, pp. 365–75. It is quoted in D. D. R. Owen, *The Vision of Hell: Infernal Journeys in Medieval French Literature* (Edinburgh: Scottish Academic Press, 1970), pp. 3–5.
59. This material, only a part of what is available, is characteristic of much of the Koran. No other Koranic theme is given as much attention as how people are to be tortured after they die.
60. Surah 4: 56.
61. See for example Robert H. Thouless, *An Introduction to the Psychology of Religion* (Cambridge: Cambridge University Press, 1923); William James, *The Varieties of Religious Experience: A Study in Human Nature* (London: Fontana, [1902] 1960). I well remember reading these books decades ago and thinking: 'So it's all psychological. There is no religious truth, only reasons why people believe.' See also Chapter 3 of the present book.
62. See Christine Crowe, 'Possessed by Demons', in Peter Haining (ed.), *A Circle of Witches: An Anthology of Victorian Witchcraft Stories* (London: Robert Hale, 1971), pp. 127–8.
63. Jean Lhermitte, *Diabolical Possession, True and False*, tr. P. J.

Hepburne-Scott (London: Burns & Oates, 1963), pp. 7–8. One chapter is entitled 'Genuine Demoniacal Possession'.

64. I owe most of the information in the following section to an unpublished Ph.D. thesis, 'Religious Beliefs and Religious Delusions' (2000), written and researched by Ronald Siddle for the Faculty of Medicine at Manchester University. I am grateful for access to this document. It was fascinating to explore this material and to note its relevance to many aspects of the psychology and psychiatry of religious belief. The author is not responsible for any polemical tone in this section: that responsibility is mine.

65. See Harold G. Koenig, *Is Religion Good for Your Health?: The Effects of Religion on Physical and Mental Health* (New York: Haworth Pastoral Press, 1997).

66. See S. F. Huq, P. A. Garety and D. R. Hemsley, 'Probabilistic Judgements in Deluded and Non-deluded Subjects', *Quarterly Journal of Experimental Psychology Section A* (1988), vol. 40, pp. 801–12; P. A. Garety, D. R. Hemsley and S. Wessely, 'Reasoning in Deluded Schizophrenic and Paranoid Patients: Biases in Performance on a Probabilistic Inference Task', *Journal of Nervous and Mental Disease* (1991), vol. 179, pp. 194–201.

67. Siddle, 'Religious Beliefs and Religious Delusions', p. 64.

68. Mark Ekblad and Loren J. Chapman, 'Magical Ideation as an Indicator of Schizotypy', *Journal of Consulting and Clinical Psychology* (1983), vol. 51, pp. 215–25.

69. Siddle, 'Religious Beliefs and Religious Delusions', p. 70.

70. See D. Hay, 'Religious Experience amongst a Group of Post-graduate Students: A Qualitative Study', *Journal for the Scientific Study of Religion* (1979), vol. 18, pp. 164–82.

71. See W. P. Wilson, 'Religion and Psychoses', in Harold G. Koenig (ed.), *Handbook of Religion and Mental Health* (San Diego: Academic Press, 1998), pp. 161–73.

72. Siddle, 'Religious Beliefs and Religious Delusions', p. 82.

73. See J. L. Nevius, *Demon Possession*, 8th ed. (Grand Rapids, MI: Kregel, 1968).

74. See Matthew 5: 29.

75. See R. Scanati, M. Madry, A. Wise, H. D. Moore, M. C. Schneider and M. L. Stephens, 'Religious Beliefs and Practices among the Most-dangerous Psychiatric Inmates', *Forensic Reports* (1991), vol. 4, pp. 1–16.

76. See Robbins, *The Encyclopedia of Witchcraft and Demonology*.

77. Exodus 22: 18; Leviticus 19: 26; Leviticus 19: 31; Leviticus 20: 6;

Leviticus 20: 27; Deuteronomy 18: 20; Deuteronomy 19: 10–12; 1 Samuel 15: 23; 2 Kings 9: 22; 2 Kings 21: 6; 2 Kings 23: 24; Isaiah 8: 19; cited in Robbins, *The Encyclopedia of Witchcraft and Demonology*, pp. 46–7.

78. The *Catholic Encyclopedia*, determined to exculpate Pope Innocent VIII, states that the importance attached to the encyclical in the context of the ensuing witch-hunts is 'altogether illusory'. Some scholars have suggested that the bull is essentially political, motivated by jurisdictional disputes between the local German Catholic priests and those of the Inquisition, who answered more directly to the Pope.

79. See Heinrich Kramer and James Sprenger, *Malleus Maleficarum* (Hammer of Witches), tr. Montague Summers (London: Arrow, 1971), pp. 112–25.

80. Ecclesiastes 7: 26–9.

81. Kramer and Sprenger, *Malleus Maleficarum*, p. 116.

82. Ibid., p. 119.

83. King James I, *Daemonologie* (1597), published in a modern edition with *Newes from Scotland Declaring the Damnable Life and Death of Doctor Fian, a Notable Sorcerer Who Was Burned at Edenbrough in January Last (1591)* by Book Tree of San Diego, edited by G. B. Harrison. See also the Ambrosian monk Francesco Maria Guazzo's *Compendium Maleficarum* (1608), a collection of commentaries noting that witchcraft and sorcery had 'spread in all directions', leaving 'no country, town, village, or district, no class of society' free from the practice. The *Compendium*, dealing with diabolical pacts, demons, the practices of witches etc., is published in a modern edition by Dover, New York.

84. Cited in Robbins, *The Encyclopedia of Witchcraft and Demonology*, pp. 113–14.

85. James I, *Daemonologie*, p. xi.

86. Ibid., p. 9.

87. Wilhelm Pressel, *Hexen und Hexenmeister* (1860), quoted in Robbins, *The Encyclopedia of Witchcraft and Demonology*, p. 510.

88. Max Gluckman, *Politics, Law and Ritual in Tribal Society* (Oxford: Blackwell, 1965).

89. G. B. Gardner, 'Foreword', in *Witchcraft Today* (London: Rider, 1954).

90. Quoted in Simon de Bruxelles, 'Mysterious pits shed light on forgotten witches of the west', *The Times*, 10 March 2008.

91. See Ruth Gledhill, 'Girls just want to learn witchcraft', *The Times*,

4 August 2000; Sophie Parkin, 'Just a spell she's going through: Why are so many young women interested in witchcraft?', *The Guardian*, 29 October 2001.

92. See Jonathan Petre, 'Campaign to pardon last witch jailed in Britain', *Daily Telegraph*, 29 February 2008.

93. Quoted in 'Cardinal Medina says new rite of exorcism similar to old', *The Wanderer*, 4 February 1999.

94. Quoted in 'Priestess guilty of manslaughter', *The Guardian*, 26 November 1994.

95. Quoted in 'US jail suspends devil worship services', *The Guardian*, 2 September 2002.

96. Quoted in Jason Burke, 'A "witch" is burnt in rural Pakistan', *The Independent*, 30 January 1999.

97. See Catherine Philp, 'Maori family exorcism kills mother', *The Times*, 27 November 2007. *Makutu* curses are interpreted as a way of enforcing *tapu*, the laws of Maori society, through the fear of transgression. They can be cast in secret by *tohunga makutu*, specially trained members of the community, on those who fail to observe *tapu* and bring misfortune or death.

98. Quoted in Helen Carter, 'Witch drowns after beach ceremony', *The Guardian*, 24 November 2000.

99. See Christopher Noble, 'Legal bill exonerates the last of the Salem witches', *The Independent*,1 November 2001.

100. Almost every village in India boasts a tantric, who can be called upon to settle any problem, including possession by spirits. Advertisements in newspapers and on billboards carry details of tantrics specialising in particular problems, such as infertility. Tantrism is an amalgam of mystical and occult practices that were born of early Hinduism, but today it is linked also to Buddhist incarnation and is synonymous with yoga and spiritual sexual experiences.

101. See Catherine Philp, 'Witch doctors cause rise in child sacrifices', *The Times*, 3 March 2004.

102. See Sonia Verma, 'King urged to spare "witchcraft" woman's life', *The Times*, 16 February 2008.

103. See 'Mother "heard Devil"', *The Times*, 25 October 2007.

104. Quoted in Mike Pflanz, 'Tribal queens "ruling by witchcraft"', *Daily Telegraph*, 8 October 2007.

105. See Andrew Norfolk, 'Father put pins through his sons' tongues "to save them from the Devil"', *The Times*, 14 November 2007.

106. See Surah 2: 222.

107. See 'Born of fire: jinn', *The Economist*, 23 December 2006.

108. See Leo Lewis, 'Killing for the cult', *The Times*, 14 November 2007.

109. Ibid.

110. See Simon de Bruxelles, 'Sheep are mutilated "in Satanic rituals"', *The Times*, 22 September 2006.

111. See John Hooper, 'Blood-drinking devil worshippers face life for ritual Satanic killing', *The Guardian*, 1 February 2002.

112. George D. Chryssides and Margaret Z. Wilkins, A *Reader in New Religious Movements* (London: Continuum, 2006). Here, descriptions are given of such 'new religions' as Brahma Kumaris, the Church of Scientology, the Church Universal and Triumphant, the Family Federation for World Peace and Unification (formerly the Unification Church), Friends of the Western Buddhist Order, the International Society for Krishna Consciousness, Osho (formerly Rajneesh), the Raelian Movement, Soka Gakkai International and The Family (formerly the Children of God).

113. For example, Tom Cruise and John Travolta are active supporters of Scientology; Nancy Cartwright, the voice of Bart Simpson, donated $10 million in 2007. In September of that year a Belgian prosecutor recommended that Scientology should be tried for fraud and extortion.

114. See Barbara McMahon, 'Accused family killer was "denied treatment by Scientologist parents"', *The Guardian*, 10 July 2007.

115. At the time of her death Tate was married to the film director Roman Polanski, who wrote in his autobiography: 'In moments of unbearable personal tragedy some people find solace in religion. In my case the opposite happened. Any religious faith I had was shattered by Sharon's murder. It reinforced my faith in the absurd.' (Roman Polanski, *Roman* (New York: William Morrow, 1984), p. 449.)

116. These and other cult examples are given in Peter Haining, *The World's Most Evil Cults: Real-Life Stories of Depraved and Violent Organizations* (Bath: Parragon, 2006).

117. Ibid.

118. See Helen Carter, 'Jehovah's Witness died after refusing transfusion', *The Guardian*, 20 January 2000. In June 2000 the church elders were debating whether members could have blood transfusions in critical circumstances, providing that they repented afterwards (see Stephen Bates, 'Transfusion row rocks Jehovah's Witnesses', *The Guardian*, 15 June 2000).

119. See M. Galanter, R. Rabkin, J. Rabkin and A. Deutsch, 'The "Moonies": A Psychological Study of Conversion and Membership in a Contemporary Religious Sect', *American Journal of Psychiatry* (1979), vol. 136, pp. 165–70.

Chapter 3: What do you mean?

1. John 1: 1.
2. I owe the following examples to James George Frazer, *The Golden Bough*, abridged ed. (London: Macmillan, 1957), Chapter 22.
3. Ibid., pp. 244–5.
4. Quoted ibid., p. 247.
5. Ibid., pp. 260–61.
6. See for example Giulio C. Lepschy, *A Survey of Structural Linguistics*, 2nd ed. (London: Andre Deutsch, 1982).
7. Pete Tobias, a rabbi at the Liberal Synagogue, Elstree, Hertfordshire, asked whether it mattered if Moses was hallucinating when he encountered the burning bush. In one explanation of the experience Moses was under the influence of an extract from an acacia tree that altered his perceptions – so perhaps he was 'high on drugs ... hot, weary and stoned'. According to Tobias the important consideration is that the injustice of slavery was recognised and a group of enslaved people gained their freedom. So another miracle bites the dust (see Pete Tobias, 'Face to faith', *The Guardian*, 8 March 2008).
8. A. C. Bouquet, *Sacred Books of the World* (Harmondsworth: Penguin, 1954), p. 19.
9. The question of translation is considered further in connection with the Koranic injunction that disobedient wives should be beaten (see Chapter 4).
10. Bouquet considers ancient literary fragments that show 'something at least of the worship practised by our early forefathers'; specimens of more highly developed temple hymns belonging to polytheisms; 'the golden age of creative religious development' from the Upanishads to the close of the New Testament canon; and 'post-biblical' materials, especially the Koran but including also such writings as the Japanese Sect Shinto texts (*Sacred Books of the World*, passim).
11. See Alister Hardy, *The Biology of God: A Scientist's Study of Man the Religious Animal* (London: Jonathan Cape, 1975).
12. Chandradhar Sharma, *A Critical Survey of Indian Philosophy* (London: Rider, 1960), p. 27.

13. Ibid., p. 165. The Sankhya school also included a theory of evolution, predating Darwin by well over a millennium but having no connection with the scientific categories understood by nineteenth-century biologists (ibid., pp. 157–63).

14. Hans Küng, *Does God Exist? An Answer for Today*, tr. Edward Quinn (London: Collins, 1980).

15. Ibid., p. 701.

16. A. R. Peacocke, *Science and the Christian Experiment* (London: Oxford University Press, 1971).

17. Ibid.

18. A. J. Ayer, *Language, Truth and Logic*, 2nd ed. (London: Victor Gollancz, [1946] 1960), p. 116.

19. Merrill F. Unger, *Demons in the World Today: A Study of Occultism in the Light of God's Word* (Wheaton, IL: Tyndale House, 1971).

20. Surah 56. 1–55; Surah 69. 14–39.

21. Bertrand Russell, *The Scientific Outlook* (London: George Allen & Unwin, 1931), p. 136.

22. Ibid.

23. Quoted in E. P. Thompson, *The Making of the English Working Class*, rev. ed. (Harmondsworth: Penguin, 1968), p. 412.

24. See Leviticus 27: 28–9; Judges 11: 29–40; 2 Samuel 21.

25. John A. T. Robinson, *Honest to God* (London: SCM Press, 1963); John A. T. Robinson and D. L. Edwards (eds), *The Honest to God Debate* (London: SCM Press, 1963), including a new chapter by John Robinson.

26. Paul Tillich, *The Shaking of the Foundations* (New York: Charles Scribner's Sons, 1948), ch. 7.

27. John A. T. Robinson, *The New Reformation?* (London: SCM Press, 1965).

28. Ibid., pp. 106–22.

29. Ibid., p. 111.

30. Quoted in Marjorie Proops, 'For these girls, it's all happening', *Daily Mirror*, 5 March 1964.

31. Robinson, *The New Reformation?*, p. 113.

32. Ibid., p. 121.

33. Peter Donovan, *Religious Language* (London: Sheldon Press, 1976), pp. 15–24.

34. Ibid., p. 23.

35. A. Ingraham, 'Nine Uses of Language', in *Swain School Lectures* (London: Kegan Paul, 1903), pp. 121–82, quoted in C. K. Ogden and I. A. Richards, *The Meaning of Meaning: A Study of the Influence*

of Language upon Thought and of the Science of Symbolism, 10th ed. (London: Routledge & Kegan Paul, 1972), pp. 46–7. The Ingraham quotation was used also by Dr Brian Robinson in a criticism of attempts to elevate theology to the status of a real academic subject (Letters, *The Guardian*, 13 September 2007).

36. Ezekiel 3: 1-3.
37. See Karen Armstrong, *The Bible: The Biography* (London: Atlantic, 2007), p. 11. In the same vein Thomas L. Thompson (*The Bible in History: How Writers Create a Past* (London: Jonathan Cape, 1999)) indicates how the Bible evolved, signalling above all that it is not a work of history.
38. See Exodus 24: 3; Exodus 24: 4–8; cited in Armstrong, *The Bible*, p. 23.
39. Exodus 24: 12.
40. Armstrong, *The Bible*, pp. 21–2.
41. Ibid., pp. 22–3.
42. Ibid., p. 227.
43. Gerald L. Bruns, 'Midrash and Allegory: The Beginnings of Scriptural Interpretation', in Robert Alter and Frank Kermode (eds), *The Literary Guide to the Bible* (London: Collins, 1987), pp. 641–2, quoted in Armstrong, *The Bible*, p. 227.
44. Quoted in Armstrong, *The Bible*, p. 227.
45. Ibid., p. 229.
46. Quoted in J. F. Bethune-Baker, *An Introduction to the Early History of Christian Doctrine to the Time of the Council of Chalcedon* (London: Methuen, 1903), pp. 168–9.
47. Ibid., pp. 172–3.
48. See a detailed account of these controversies ibid., pp. 239–326.
49. Robert M. Grant and David Noel Freedman, *The Secret Sayings of Jesus (According to the Gospel of Thomas)* (London: Fontana, 1960), pp. 185–6. The Gospel of Thomas belonged to a collection of thirteen volumes of gnostic papyri discovered near the modern village of Nag Hammadi, Egypt, in 1945. The first complete translation of the gospel appeared in 1958. It is partly derivative from the canonical gospels but contains other material.
50. Matthew 10: 34.
51. See Luke 22: 36.
52. Matthew 12: 32.
53. See Luke 14: 26.
54. See Matthew 10: 34–5.
55. See Mark 11: 13–14, 20–21.

56. Mark 7: 5–19.

57. Matthew 23: 33.

58. Robertson's findings were popularised by Robert Blatchford in
    God and My Neighbour (1903) and Philip Vivian in *The Churches and
    Modern Thought* (1906). L. G. Rylands, in *Did Jesus Ever Live?*
    (1935), provided a brief statement of the Christ-myth hypothesis;
    and Thomas Whittaker, in *The Origins of Christianity* (1904),
    combined the work of Robertson with the critical analysis offered
    by the Dutch professor W. C. van Manen on the same theme.
    Some writers have suggested that true religion should be protected
    by divesting it of the mythical aspects of the Christ story.

59. It has long been a doctrine of Catholicism that the blood and wine
    do not merely *represent* the body and blood of Christ in
    communion but are actually *converted into* these by the magic that
    the priest is able to perform.

60. See Jonathan Wynne-Jones, 'Why the BBC thinks Christ did not
    die this way', *Sunday Telegraph*, 16 March 2008.

61. See Surah 4. 157.

62. H. G. Wood, *Did Christ Really Live?* (London: Student Christian
    Movement Press, 1938).

63. Ibid., pp. 159–85.

64. Ibid., p. 161.

65. Ibid. The Pakistani secularist Ibn Warraq, in his book *Why I Am
    Not a Muslim* (Amherst, NY: Prometheus, 1995), emphasises that
    there are many scholars who doubt the historical reality of Jesus
    Christ, including Robertson, Bruno Bauer (1809-82), Arthur
    Drews (1865–1935), Henri van den Bergh van Eysinga
    (1868–1920) and Albert Kalchoff; in recent years Guy Fau (*Le Fable
    de Jesus Christ*, 2nd ed. (Paris: Union Rationaliste, 1964)), Prosper
    Alfaric (*Origines sociales du christianisme* (Paris: Union Rationaliste,
    1959)), W. B. Smith (*The Birth of the Gospel* (New York:
    Philosophical Library, 1957)) and Professor G. A. Wells of
    Birkbeck College, University of London, have all developed the
    Christ-myth theory.

66. Quoted in Warraq, *Why I Am Not a Muslim*, p. 152.

67. It is interesting to note how a wide range of Christian thinkers,
    busy in the twentieth century, helped to prepare the ground for a
    resurgence of full-blooded atheism in the twenty-first. We have
    encountered such writers as Tillich, Robinson, Bonhoeffer and
    Küng. Note also the significant volumes published by Constable in
    the 1960s: D. M. Mackinnon et al., *Objections to Christian Belief*

(1963) and Michael de la Bedoyere (ed.), *Objections to Roman Catholicism* (1964). What is remarkable is that all the essays in these two books were written by Christians. Two decades later Gerald Priestland, the BBC's religious correspondent, keen to give publicity to anti-Christian arguments, published *The Case against God* (London: Collins, 1984), giving scope to the likes of A. J. Ayer, John Mortimer and Iris Murdoch to challenge the alleged reasons for believing in God. In January 2006 an Italian judge ordered a priest, Father Enrico Righi, to appear in court to prove that Jesus existed. The case came to court three years after the priest had denounced a retired agronomist in a Viterbo parish newsletter for questioning Christ's historical existence (See Richard Owen, 'Prove Christ exists, judge orders priest', *The Times*, 3 January 2006).

68. Tariq Ali, *The Clash of Fundamentalisms: Crusades, Jihads and Modernity* (London: Verso, 2002), pp. 49–50.

69. Ibid., p. 50.

70. Ibid.

71. The Hadith acquired their supposed authority only because Mohammed was assumed to be the prophet of God. If there had not been any divine 'recital' then his sayings would not have been significant. God, through Gabriel, allegedly induced Mohammed to 'hear voices' – a well-recognised psychiatric symptom – and so the prophet was supposedly selected for a divinely ordained mission. Hence his utterances were very important to believers.

72. See for example the discussion in W. Montgomery Watt, *Muhammad at Mecca* (London: Oxford University Press, 1953), pp. 60–63.

73. Albert Hourani, *A History of the Arab Peoples* (London: Faber & Faber, 1991), p. 15.

74. Ibid.

75. The glory days of the Abbasid dynasty were yet to come.

76. Jeffrey (1892–1959) was professor of Semitic languages at the School of Oriental and African Studies. His works include *The Foreign Vocabulary of the Qur'an* (Baroda, Indonesia: Oriental Institute, 1938).

77. See Warraq, *Why I Am Not a Muslim*, p. 108.

78. Ibid.

79. Ibid., p. 109.

80. Quoted ibid.

81. Ibid., pp. 112–14.

82. Ibid., p. 127.
83. In another essay Ibn Warraq describes in detail the totalitarian nature of Islam, in *Why I Am Not a Muslim*, pp. 163–71.
84. Yoginder Sikand, *Bastions of the Believers: Madrasas and Islamic Education in India* (New Delhi: Penguin Books India, 2005).
85. See Ian Traynor, 'Turkey strives for 21st century form of Islam', *The Guardian*, 27 February 2008; Suna Erdem, 'Morality, justice and women's rights: a portrait of Islam for the 21st century', *The Times*, 28 February 2008.
86. Quoted in Traynor, 'Turkey strives for 21st century form of Islam'.
87. Quoted ibid.
88. Quoted in Erdem, 'Morality, justice and women's rights'.
89. See Ruth Gledhill, 'Jewish regret at Pope's "missed opportunity" in rewritten prayer', *The Times*, 6 February 2008.
90. The seven deadly sins are lust (punished by being smothered in fire and brimstone), gluttony (forced to eat rats, toads and snakes), avarice (put in cauldrons of boiling oil), sloth (thrown in snake pits), anger (dismembered alive), envy (put in freezing water) and pride (broken on the wheel). The seven 'holy virtues' are generally regarded as chastity, abstinence, temperance, diligence, patience, kindness and humility.
91. See Richard Owen, 'Seven deadly sins: are you guilty?', *The Times*, 10 March 2008.
92. See Owen Bowcott and Riazat Butt, 'Ex-Islamists start moderate thinktank', *The Guardian*, 1 March 2008.
93. See letters in *The Times*, 30 November 2007.
94. Fiona Govan, 'Iran envoy defends amputation "of the hand that steals"', *Daily Telegraph*, 9 February 2008.
95. Carole Sarler, 'The silence of the imams… while another child dies', *The Observer*, 7 February 1999.
96. See Ashling O'Connor, 'Hindus up in arms as god clashes with government', *The Times*, 14 September 2007.
97. D. J. West, *Eleven Lourdes Miracles* (London: Gerald Duckworth, 1957).
98. The book also included a chapter on psychosomatic and hysterical elements in illness, and instanced some remarkable recoveries due to normal factors.
99. William Dalrymple, 'In a state about Israel', *Sunday Times*, 21 January 1996.
100. See Peter Watson, 'Holy Moses: biblical doubt over "Promised Land"', *The Observer*, 11 February 1996.

101. Quoted in Robert Uhlig, 'Creation is put on trial as geologist contests discovery of Noah's ark', *Daily Telegraph*, 28 November 1996. Justice Ronald Sackville ruled in a federal court that creationist Allen Roberts had made false representations on a national lecture tour when he claimed to have found Noah's ark in eastern Turkey. In November 1997 the CIA had reportedly been using satellite surveillance in a hunt for the ark. Some of tens of thousands of previously classified photographs had focused on a boat-shaped mark (dubbed by the scientists the 'Ararat anomaly') on the slopes of Mount Ararat.

102. See Jonathan Leake, 'Earth tremor visited hellfire on Sodom', *Sunday Times*, 11 January 1998.

103. See Robert Matthews, 'Science solves the 10 plagues of Egypt', *Sunday Telegraph*, 16 August 1998.

104. Quoted in Alan Philps, 'Was bad sight Goliath's problem?', *Daily Telegraph*, 18 February 2000; Phil Reeves, 'David was just a blur to a myopic Goliath, says study', *The Independent*, 18 February 2000.

105. Richard Owen, 'Would you Adam and Eve it? There was no apple in Eden', *The Times*, 26 October 2002.

106. Quoted ibid.

107. Colin J. Humphreys, *The Miracles of Exodus: A Scientist's Discovery of the Extraordinary Natural Causes of the Biblical Stories* (London: Continuum, 2003).

108. See Roger Highfield, 'Mount Sinai was volcano in Saudi Arabia, says scientist', *Daily Telegraph*, 13 June 2003.

109. Quoted in Owen, 'Would you Adam and Eve it?'.

110. See Jonathan Petre, 'Biblical plagues and parting of Red Sea "caused by volcano"', *Daily Telegraph*, 11 November 2002.

111. See Carl Ruck, 'Was there a whiff of cannabis about Jesus?', *Sunday Times*, 12 January 2003. Ruck suggests that Jesus may have used cannabis-based oils to cure eye and skin diseases, and that his very name – Christ – derives from being anointed with cannabis-enriched oil. In 1935 a Slovakian linguist identified the plant known as 'fragrant cane' in the Bible as flowering cannabis, a link accepted by some Jewish authorities. Chris Bennett, the host of 'Burning Shiva', a show on Canada's Pot-TV, suggested that Jesus acquired the title *messiah* when he was anointed with cannabis oil by John the Baptist.

112. See Julian Borger, 'Jesus walking on thin ice, claim scientists', *The Guardian*, 6 April 2006.

113. See Richard Jinman, 'Was Jesus first victim of DVT?', *The Guardian*, 9 June 2005.
114. See Dalya Alberge, 'Judas did as Jesus asked – "gospel" reveals the other face of a traitor', *The Times*, 7 April 2006.
115. Conal Urquhart, 'Forgers "tried to rewrite biblical history"', *The Guardian*, 31 December 2004.

Chapter 4: Less than human

1. The suggestion that women were not really human beings is analogous to how nineteenth-century anthropologists debated whether blacks were human beings or whether they occupied a place somewhere between apes and *Homo sapiens*, and analogous also to how the Nazis depicted Jews as less than human, *Untermenschen*.
2. See for example Theresa M. Kenney (ed.), '*Women Are Not Human': An Anonymous Treatise and Responses* (New York: Crossroad, 1998). In 1999 the feminist Catharine MacKinnon contributed an essay, 'Are Women Human?' to *Reflections on the Universal Declaration of Human Rights* (ed. Barend van der Haijden and Bahia Tahzib-Lie, The Hague: Martinus Nijhoff). She later published a collection of essays under a similar title (*Are Women Human? and Other International Dialogues* (Cambridge, MA: Belknap Press, 2006)) and in 2007 gave a lecture, 'Women Are Not Human', at Harvard's Radcliffe Gymnasium. Also in 2007 the peace activist Bruce Kent was rhetorically charged with implying that women are not human by opposing their right to abortion (http://jesurgislac.greatestjournal.com).
3. Edward Westermarck, *Christianity and Morals* (London: Kegan Paul, Trench, Trubner, 1939), p. 129.
4. This supreme Sumerian being had tangled locks, a 'lap of honey', a vulva like 'a boat of heaven', a womb that poured forth natural bounty (with every lettuce honoured as 'the Lady's pubic hair'), and dreadful power that destroyed 'by fire and flood' and 'filled rivers with blood'. See Rosalind Miles, *The Women's History of the World* (London: Michael Joseph, 1988), pp. 18–19; Paul Friedrich, *The Meaning of Aphrodite* (Chicago and London: University of Chicago Press, 1978), pp. 13–15, cited by Miles with many other sources.
5. Sir Arthur Evans, *The Palace of Minos: A Comparative Account of the Successive Stages of the Early Cretan Civilization as Illustrated by the Discoveries at Knossos*, 4 vols (London: Macmillan, 1921–36), passim.

6. See Erich Neumann, *The Great Mother: An Analysis of the Archetype*, tr. Ralph Manheim (New York: Pantheon / London: Routledge & Kegan Paul, 1955), p. 94.
7. Miles, *The Women's History of the World*, p. 20.
8. The Celts are believed to have derived from an area encompassing part of France and southern Germany. By the fifth century BC they had reached Spain, the British Isles, the Balkan region and Asia Minor. In the fourth century they invaded and sacked Rome.
9. See T. G. E. Powell, *The Celts* (New York: F. A. Praeger, 1958), p. 52.
10. Quoted in Elizabeth Gould Davis, *The First Sex* (J. M. Dent, 1973), p. 210.
11 Quoted ibid., pp. 210–11.
12. The Celtic queen Tomyris slew Cyrus the Great, king of Persia, on the battlefield; and Queen Cartismandua led the Celtic Brigantes against the Roman legions. Better known is Boudica of the Iceni, who captured the Roman cities of London, Colchester and St Albans, slaying 70,000 Romans in the process, before being defeated by the reinforced legions of Suetonius Paulinus.
13. Davis, *The First Sex*, p. 209.
14. See Lee Alexander Stone, *The Story of Phallicism* (Chicago: Pascal Covici, 1927); George Ryley Scott, *Phallic Worship: A History of Sex and Sex Rites in Relation to the Religions of All Races from Antiquity to the Present Day* (London: Panther, [1941] 1970).
15. Cited in Miles, *The Women's History of the World*, p. 43.
16. Scott, *Phallic Worship*, p. 18.
17. See Phyllis Bird, 'Images of Women in the Old Testament', in Rosemary Radford Ruether (ed.), *Religion and Sexism: Images of Woman in the Jewish and Christian Traditions* (New York: Simon & Schuster, 1974), pp. 41–88.
18. Ibid., p. 48.
19. Ibid., p. 50–71.
20. There are various apologists, sometimes Jewish women, who have struggled to explain away this manifestly discriminatory and abusive prayer. For example, Judith Hauptman cites Rabbi Judah, writing in the Tosefta, who explains that the blessing expresses a man's gratitude 'for being created male, and therefore for having more opportunities to fulfil divine commandments than do women, who are exempted from a good many' (Judith Hauptman, 'Images of Women in the Talmud', in Ruether (ed.), *Religion and Sexism*, p. 196) – as if the diminished religious status of women constitutes

some mitigation for the prayer. Or perhaps the blessing 'is simply expressing the joy any man feels at being exactly who he is … the ancient Greek used to express his thanks for being born a man and not an animal, male and not female, a Hellene and not a barbarian … This understanding of the blessing, too, is not inflammatory, because nothing negative is being said about women, only something positive about men.' (Ibid.) It may be judged that such apologetics failed to remove 'the pernicious content' that Hauptman acknowledges is currently read into the prayer.

21. Hauptman, 'Images of Women in the Talmud', p. 205.
22. Ibid., p. 197.
23. Ibid., p. 210, citing Erich Fromm, *The Art of Loving* (New York: Harper & Brothers, 1956), p. 12.
24. See Israel Shahak and Norton Mezvinsky, *Jewish Fundamentalism in Israel* (London: Pluto Press, 1999), p. 37.
25. See *Talmudic Encyclopedia*, vol. 2, pp. 255–7.
26. Maimonides, *Talmud Torah Laws*, Chapter 1, Rule 13, cited in Shahak and Mezvinsky, *Jewish Fundamentalism in Israel*, p. 39.
27. *Kitzur Shulchan Aruch*, Chapter 3, Rule 8.
28. Kadid Leper, 'Woman is a sack full of excrement', *Hai'r*, 18 April 1997.
29. Israel Shahak, 'Israel's Discriminatory Practices Are Rooted in Jewish Religious Law', *Washington Report on Middle East Affairs*, July/August 1995, pp. 18–19 (an abridged translation of an article that appeared in the Israeli newspaper *Davar* on 15 March 1995). Shahak draws attention to the case given in halacha. A woman can testify that one dish or a few dishes are kosher. But if she testifies about a large number of dishes prepared for a big reception her testimony is invalid on the assumption that her laziness and resultant reluctance to make a major effort could induce her to lie if they were in fact non-kosher.
30. This ruling appears in the English translation of the *Talmudic Encyclopedia*, but it cannot be found in any of the books dealing with Judaism in English or other languages.
31. See Shahak, 'Israel's Discriminatory Practices Are Rooted in Jewish Religious Law'. Other details are provided in the same article to demonstrate the racist character of Jewish religious law.
32. Quoted in Sarah Hall, 'Jewish law sees divorced wife "chained" for 40 years', *The Guardian*, 14 August 2001.
33. See David Sharrock, 'Israel's rabbis put curfew on women', *The Guardian*, 25 February 1998.

34. John Stuart Mill, *On Liberty* (New York: Liberal Arts Press, [1859] 1956), p. 59.
35. Davis, *The First Sex*, p. 229.
36. Powell, *The Celts*, p. 84.
37. 1 Corinthians 11: 9.
38. 1 Corinthians 14: 34–5. This injunction, among others, ensured over centuries that women would not be allowed to open their mouths in church: 'The virgins should silently pray the Psalms or read ... When they pray they are to move their lips, but their voices should not be heard' – as St Cyril of Jerusalem emphasised (*Introductory Catechism*, Chapter 14). Women have always been forbidden from singing in Catholic church choirs – a ban reiterated by Pope Pius X in the twentieth century. Pius XII cautiously permitted women's singing, but only 'outside the presbyterium or the altar rail'.
39. Ephesians 5: 22–4.
40. 1 Timothy 2: 11–12.
41. 1 Peter 3: 1–2.
42. See Note 1.
43. Clement of Alexandria, *Pedagogus*, II, 33, 2; quoted in James Cleugh, *Love Locked Out: A Survey of Love, Licence and Restriction in the Middle Ages* (London: Anthony Blond, 1963), p. 265.
44. Alexander Roberts and Sir James Donaldson (eds), *Ante-Nicene Christian Library, vol. 4: The Writings of Clement of Alexandria, vol. 1*, tr. W. Wilson, (Edinburgh: T. & T. Clark, 1867), p. 209.
45. Constantine also murdered his son Crispus and his brother-in-law Licinius. Then he had Licinius's son, Licinianus, whipped to death.
46. Pierre de Bourdeille, Abbé de Brantome, *The Lives of Gallant Ladies* (London: Elek, [1901] 1961), p. 21.
47. See H. M. Gwatkin (ed.), *Cambridge Medieval History, vol. 2: The Rise of the Saracens and the Foundation of the Western Empire* (London: Cambridge University Press, 1913), p. 106.
48. Quoted in Will and Mary Durant, *The Story of Civilization, vol. 4: The Age of Faith* (New York: Simon & Schuster, 1950), p. 826.
49. Thomas Aquinas, *Summa Theologiae*, Part I, Question 92, Article 1, Objection 1.
50. Ibid., Question 92, Article 1.
51. Ibid., Question 92, Article 3.
52. Heinrich Kramer and James Sprenger, *Malleus Maleficarum* (Hammer of Witches), tr. Montague Summers (London: Arrow, 1971), pp. 112–23.

53. Ibid.
54. By contrast the supposed beauty of bishops was constantly celebrated upon their tombs, as remarked by Edmond Le Blant, *Inscriptions chrétiennes de la Gaule*, pp. xcvii–xcviii, cited by William Lecky, *History of European Morals: From Augustus to Charlemagne*, 10th ed. (London: Longmans, Green, 1892), vol. 2, p. 338.
55. St Ambrose, *On Penance*, Part I, Chapter 16.
56. See Uta Ranke-Heinemann, *Eunuchs for the Kingdom of Heaven: The Catholic Church and Sexuality*, tr. Peter Heinegg (New York: Penguin, 1991), p. 130.
57. Clement of Alexandria, quoted ibid.
58. Chrysostom wrote in his *Homilies on Timothy*: 'The woman taught once, and ruined all. On this account … let her not teach … The whole female race transgressed … Let her not, however, grieve. God hath given her no small consolation, that of childbearing … Women will have no small reward on their account, because they have trained up wrestlers for the service of Christ [Homily IX, on 1 Timothy 2: 11– 15].'
59. Tertullian, *De Cultu Feminarum*, Book I, Chapter 1.
60. Arthur Findlay, *The Curse of Ignorance: A History of Mankind from Primitive Times to the End of the Second World War* (London: Psychic Press, 1947), vol. 1, pp. 658–9.
61. See Lecky, *History of European Morals*, p. 338.
62. Ibid., pp. 338–9.
63. G. G. Coulton (ed.), *Life in the Middle Ages* (Cambridge: Cambridge University Press, 1910), vol. 3, p. 119.
64. Eugene Mason, 'Introduction', in Marie de France, *The Lays of Marie de France* (London: J. M. Dent, 1911), pp. x, xv. Wife-beating became so widespread and excessive that in 1427 even a churchman, Bernadino of Sienna, suggested in a sermon that 'not for *every* cause is it right to beat her' (quoted in Coulton (ed.), *Life in the Middle Ages*, vol. 1, p. 224). Only, presumably, for some.
65. Jules Michelet, *Satanism and Witchcraft: A Study in Medieval Superstition*, tr. A. R. Allinson (New York: Citadel, 1939), p. 35.
66. See Thomas More, *Dialogues*, cited in Coulton (ed.), *Life in the Middle Ages*, vol. 3, pp. 166–7.
67. Ranke-Heinemann, *Eunuchs for the Kingdom of Heaven*, p. 135. Ranke-Heinemann holds a degree in Catholic theology. In 1970 she became a professor at the University of Essen but lost her academic chair in New Testament and ancient church history for interpreting Mary's alleged virgin birth theologically and not

biologically. Since late 1987 she has held the chair in history of religion at Essen.

68. See for example Esther Kaplan, *With God on Their Side: How Christian Fundamentalists Trampled Science, Policy, and Democracy in George W. Bush's White House* (New York: New Press, 2004), pp. 167–93.

69. See Elizabeth Nickson, 'This woman promises to honour, obey and submit to her husband', *Sunday Times Magazine*, 21 February 1999.

70. There are many statements supporting polygamy in Mormon literature (from such men as Joseph Smith, Brigham Young, Wilford Woodruff etc.). See for example Todd M. Compton, 'The Four Major Periods of Mormon Polygamy', Signature Books library website. The apostle Bruce R. McConkie in his book *Mormon Doctrine* (Salt Lake City: Bookcraft, 1958) looked forward to the time when 'the holy practice' of polygamy would be implemented once again. Today Mormon women, in common with their Catholic counterparts, cannot exercise priesthood: they are not 'ordained' but only 'set apart' to church positions. Mormon leaders assert that female priesthood is 'contrary to the Lord's plan' and that today's church 'follows the pattern the Lord has set'.

71. See the Christians for Biblical Equality website.

72. See Ronald W. Pierce and Rebecca Merrill Groothuis (eds), *Discovering Biblical Equality: Complementarity without Hierarchy* (Downers Grove, IL: Inter-Varsity Press, 2004), p. 17.

73. See Wayne A. Grudem, 'Should We Move beyond the New Testament to a Better Ethic?', *Journal of the Evangelical Theological Society*, (2004), vol. 47, pp. 299–346.

74. Is this a sort of hermaphrodite deity? Divine hermaphrodism and an attendant host of androgyny cults were numerous in the ancient pagan world.

75. Surah 3. 5. Translations vary but the gist is preserved.

76. See Kecia Ali, *Sexual Ethics and Islam: Feminist Reflections on Qur'an, Hadith, and Jurisprudence* (Oxford: Oneworld, 2006), p. 118.

77. Islam Online.net, 'Addressing Misconceptions about Prophet's Marriage to Aisha,' quoted ibid., p. 121.

78. See Sean O'Neill, 'Wife-beating rejected in "new" Koran', *The Times*, 31 March 2007.

79. Ibid.

80. Ali, *Sexual Ethics and Islam*, pp. 122, 123.

81. Mona Siddiqui, 'Law and the Desire for Social Control: An Insight

into the Hanafi Concept of *Kafa'a* with Reference to the Fatawa
Alamgiri (1664–1672)', in Mai Yamani (ed.), *Feminism and Islam:
Legal and Literary Perspectives* (Reading: Garnet, 1996), p. 52.

82. Ibid.

83. Ibid., p. 54.

84. Fatima Mernissi, *Beyond the Veil: Male–Female Dynamics in a Modern
Muslim Society* (Cambridge, MA: Shenkman, 1975), pp. ix–x, 82,
quoted by Ghada Karmi, 'Women, Islam and Patriarchalism', in
Yamani (ed.), *Feminism and Islam*, p. 69.

85. See Karmi, 'Women, Islam and Patriarchalism'.

86. Karmi, 'Women, Islam and Patriarchalism', p. 75.

87. See Abu Hamid Al-Ghazali, *Ihya'ulum al-din*, cited in Mernissi,
Beyond the Veil, p. 18.

88. Karmi, 'Women, Islam and Patriarchalism', p. 83.

89. There are abundant misogynistic statements and injunctions in the
Hadith, many of which are being recast or removed by the Turkish
government as it struggles to drag Islam into the twenty-first
century (see Chapter 3).

90. Muhammad bin Abdul-Aziz Al-Musnad (compiler), *Islamic Fatawa
Regarding Women*, tr. Jamaal Al-Din Zarabozo (Houston:
Darussalam, 1996). *Fatawa* is the Arabic plural of *fatwa*.

91. Ibid. The page numbers identify the examples respectively: 62,
85–7, 103, 105, 185, 187, 305–7, 310, 339, 362.

92. A *mahram* is an unmarriageable kin with whom sexual relations
would be considered incestuous.

93. See *Shame in the House of Saud: Contempt for Human Rights in the
Kingdom of Saudi Arabia* (Minneapolis: Minnesota Lawyers
International Rights Committee, 1992), p. 80. The report includes
extensive documentation, which I have not repeated here, to
source all the reported cases.

94. At the same time the Ba'athist regime was deeply repressive in
many ways, even, according to some claims, sanctioning official
rape. See Fran Hazelton (ed.), *Iraq since the Gulf War: Prospects for
Democracy* (London: Zed, 1994), pp. 63–4, 66.

95. 'Riverbend', *Baghdad Burning: Girl Blog from Iraq* (London: Marion
Boyars, 2005), pp. 16–19, 23–5.

96. Quoted in Terri Judd, 'For the women of Iraq the war is just
beginning', *The Independent*, 8 June 2006.

97. See Hala Jaber, 'Rebels kill Iraqi women as "betrayers" of Islam',
Sunday Times, 20 March 2005. With the progressive secularisation
of Iraq prior to the 2003 invasion more and more women were

choosing not to wear the traditional all-enveloping *abaya* and were being encouraged in their choice by their menfolk. See Nadje Sadig al-Ali, *Iraqi Women: Untold Stories from 1948 to the Present* (London: Zed, 2007), pp. 96–7. After the invasion the trend was thrown into reverse and women wearing Western dress could not be seen in public.

98. See Marie Colvin and Widiane Moussa, 'Men in black terrorise Iraq's women', *Sunday Times*, 4 June 2006.
99. Ibid.
100. 'Climate of Fear: Sexual Violence and Abduction of Women and Girls in Baghdad', *Human Rights Watch* (2003), vol. 15, no. 7 (E), p. 1.
101. Ibid.
102. Shyam Bhatia, 'Arab refuge lifts veil on battered wives', *The Observer*, 20 February 1994.
103. Quoted in Shyam Bhatia, '"We have no rights in the Arab world"', *The Observer*, 19 September 1993.
104. Barbara Victor, *Army of Roses: Inside the World of Palestinian Suicide Bombers* (London: Constable & Robinson, 2004), p. 45.
105. Quoted ibid., p. 45.
106. Quoted ibid., p. 46.
107. Ibid., p. 46.
108. Quoted ibid., p. 105.
109. Ibid.
110. Quoted ibid., p. 195.
111. Quoted ibid., p. 196.
112. See Heather Mills, 'Reprieve for woman who faces Islamic punishment', *The Independent*, 8 March 1990.
113. See Andrew Malone, 'War heroines of Kuwait turn suffragettes', *Sunday Times*, 10 March 1996; Raymond Whittaker, 'Parliament victory in sight for Kuwait's suffragettes', *Independent on Sunday*, 14 November 1999.
114. See Nicci Gerrard, 'For the sake of the children', *The Observer*, 9 March 1997.
115. See Sue Lloyd-Roberts, 'Killing honour', *Sunday Telegraph Magazine*, 12 April 1998.
116. See Suzanne Goldenberg, 'Women fear Islamic clampdown', *The Guardian*, 3 October 1998.
117. See Julian West, 'Shopping without permission costs Sindh wife her life', *Sunday Telegraph*, 14 March 1999.
118. See Ian Black, 'Saudi girl, eight, married off to 58-year-old is denied divorce', *The Guardian*, 23 December 2008.

119. See Zahid Hussain, 'Islamic militants threaten to blow up girls' schools if they refuse to close', *The Times*, 26 December 2008.

120. Quoted in Angelique Chrisafis, 'Paris opens door to author fleeing Islamist threats', *The Guardian*, 5 January 2009.

121. See Geoff Simons, *Iraq Endgame? Surge, Suffering and the Politics of Denial* (London: Politico's, 2008).

122. See Laurie A. Brand, *Women, the State, and Political Liberalization: Middle Eastern and North African Experiences* (New York: Columbia University Press, 1998).

123. Ibid.

124. See Anne E. Brodsky, *With All Our Strength: The Revolutionary Association of the Women of Afghanistan* (New York: Routledge, 2003).

125. Quoted in Lucy Moore, *Maharanis: The Extraordinary Tale of Four Indian Queens and Their Journey from Purdah to Parliament* (New York: Viking, 2005), p. 73.

126. Quoted ibid.

127. Ibid., p. 74.

128. *Mahabharata*, Anusasan Parva, Section 38. The *Mahabharata*, with 110,000 couplets and dating to the first millennium BC, is the world's longest literary epic. It was orally transmitted and not printed until the nineteenth century. The central plot is the familiar one of a supernatural conflict between the forces of Good and Evil. The passages I quote are taken from the translation by K. M. Ganguli published between 1883 and 1896.

129. Ibid.

130. Ibid., Section 39. Elsewhere, a contradictory minority view, that 'women can commit no fault' is expressed in the *Mahabharata*, Santi Parva, Section 266.

131. *Mahabharata*, Anusasan Parva, Section 40.

132. *Mahabharata*, Santi Parva, Section 144. The Veda collection, dating to around 1500 BC, in part defines the sacred knowledge of the Hindus. In addition there are three other collections: the Brahmanas, the Aranyakas and the Upanishads.

133. Quoted in 'The Husband is the wife's Highest Deity', *Mahabharata*, Santi Parva, Section 144. Elsewhere the text says that women too should be worshipped, but they are weak and should be protected

134. *Mahabharata*, Adi Parva, Section 74.

135. Ibid.

136. Manu, 'Duties of Women', quoted in Swami Shivananda (1887–1963), *Duties of Women* (Rishikesh: Divine Life Society).

Manu's *Code of Laws* is a grossly anti-feminist document. 'Slaves and women' were prohibited from reading the Vedas, a woman could not strive to attain heaven, she could not worship or sacrifice by herself, she could only reach paradise by implicit obedience to her husband, even if he was devoid of all virtues.

137. *Mahabharata*, Santi Parva, Section 240.
138. Rig Veda X. 18. 7; quoted in M. P. V. Kane, *History of Dharmasashtra* (Poona: Bhandarkar Oriental Research Institute, 1953), vol. 4.
139. Vishnusmirti, xxv, 14, quoted in A. C. Clayton, *The Rig Veda and Vedic Religion* (Varanasi: Bharati Prakashan, [1913] 1980).
140. R. Ilangovan, 'Women still suffer "forced seclusion" here', *The Hindu*, 17 May 2002.
141. See Lucy Ash, 'Killing in the name of dowry', *The Times*, 21 July 2003.
142. See Rahul Bedi, 'Brides are a scarce commodity in India', *Daily Telegraph*, 7 March 2003.
143. See 'India rape row woman burned', *The Guardian*, 13 March 2003.
144. See Catharine Philp, 'Widow's suttee sacrifice divides India', *The Times*, 12 August 2002; Suzanne Goldenberg, 'Fanning the flames of a love for death', *The Guardian*, 5 December 1996.
145. See N. N. Bhattacharya, *History of Indian Erotic Literature* (New Delhi: Munshiram Manoharlal, 1975).
146. See for example David Ward, 'Sikh wife's affair sparked honour killing by husband and his mother, Old Bailey told', *The Guardian*, 3 May 2007.
147. See David Charter, 'Minorities refuse cancer treatment because of beliefs', *The Times*, 26 June 2001.
148. See 'Women's seva sinks lower', *Sikh Sentinel*, 31 July 2003.

Chapter 5: Sexual psychopathology

1. See 1 Corinthians 7: 8–9.
2. See Surah 2. 223.
3. See Bronisław Malinowski, *The Sexual Life of Savages in North-Western Melanesia: An Ethnographic Account of Courtship, Marriage, and Family Life among the Natives of the Trobriand Islands, British New Guinea*, 3rd ed. (London: Routledge & Kegan Paul, 1932), p. 3.
4. Ibid., p. 142.
5. Ibid., p. 144.
6. Ibid., pp. 145–52.

7. Ibid., pp. 155–6. Her second name, Bolutukwa, is derived from *litukwa* 'dripping water' plus *bo-*, the female prefix.
8. George Ryley Scott, *Phallic Worship: A History of Sex and Sex Rites in Relation to the Religions of All Races from Antiquity to the Present Day* (London: Panther, [1941] 1970), p. 56.
9. Genesis 1: 28.
10. Hubert Howe Bancroft, *The Native Races of the Pacific States of North America* (New York: D. Appleton, 1874), vol. 1, p. 720.
11. Genesis 12: 11–19.
12. Genesis 19: 1–8.
13. See Psalms 51: 5.
14. See Numbers 5: 21, 22, 27.
15. See Numbers 31: 17, 18, 35, 40.
16. See Deuteronomy 28: 30; 2 Samuel 12: 11; Isaiah 13: 16; Jeremiah 6: 12, 8: 10.
17. See Judges 19: 22–30.
18. 1 Kings 1: 1–4.
19. See Genesis 17: 10–14, 23–7; Leviticus 12: 3.
20. Matthew 19: 12.
21. Luke 14: 26; Matthew 10: 34–5, 37.
22. Song of Solomon 1: 2. In 2 Samuel we find how King David had an affair with Bathsheba, wife of Uriah, a Hittite mercenary in his army, and then put her husband in the front line so that he would be killed. They married and their second son was Solomon, author of the Song of Solomon, sometimes dubbed the Song of Songs.
23. Richard Owen, 'Erotic Bible "for adults only"', *The Times*, 29 March 2001.
24. Nathan Abrams, *Jews and Sex* (Nottingham: Five Leaves, 2008). On 13 March 2008 the book was formally launched when the Jewish Museum hosted a panel discussion in north London.
25. Sources given in Immanuel Jakobovits, *Jewish Medical Ethics: A Comparative and Historical Study of the Jewish Religious Attitude to Medicine and Its Practice* (New York: Bloch, 1959), pp. 156–7.
26. Sources ibid.
27. See Benjamin Walker, *Sex and the Supernatural: Sexuality in Religion and Magic* (London: Macdonald, 1970), p. 15.
28. Scott, *Phallic Worship*, p. 123.
29. See Deuteronomy 32: 4, 18; Psalms 18: 2 ('The Lord is my Rock').
30. See Edward Sellon, 'On the Phallic Worship of India', *Memoirs of the Anthropological Society* (1865), vol. 1.
31. Paul of Aegina, *On Castration*, vi, 28, quoted by Savas Nittis,

'Hippocratic Ethics and Present-Day Trends in Medicine', *Bulletin of the History of Medicine* (1942), vol. 12, p. 380.

32. See Jakobovits, *Jewish Medical Ethics*, pp. 192–8.
33. Ibid., pp. 193–4.
34. Shalom Auslander, *Foreskin's Lament: A Memoir* (New York: Riverhead, 2007), p. 285.
35. These examples are given with sources in Edward Westermarck, *Christianity and Morals* (London: Kegan Paul, Trench, Trubner, 1939), p. 362.
36. Plato's faith in the sexual virtue of animals would not have survived the modern knowledge that non-human creatures are capable of rape, infidelity, prostitution, group assault, bestiality etc.
37. See Paul Blanshard, *Freedom and Catholic Power* (London: Secker & Warburg, 1951), p. 125.
38. Quoted in G. Rattray Taylor, *Sex in History: Society's Changing Attitudes to Sex throughout the Ages* (New York: Ballantine, 1954), p. 64.
39. See Blanshard, *Freedom and Catholic Power*, p. 124.
40. Quoted ibid.
41. Bertrand Russell, *The Autobiography of Bertrand Russell, vol. 1: 1872–1914* (London: George Allen & Unwin, 1967), p. 21.
42. Quoted in Jonathan Wynne-Jones, 'Multiple wives will mean multiple benefits', *Daily Telegraph*, 3 February 2008.
43. Ibid.
44. Jerry Falwell, 'Trends in Christian Higher Education', speech at Regent University, Virginia Beach, VA, 22 September 1993.
45. Salman Rushdie, 'Where is the honour in this vile code that condemns women to die in shame?', *The Times*, 18 July 2005. The acquittals of the men for rape were later suspended by the Pakistan Supreme Court, suggesting that Mukhtar Mai may gain some measure of redress for her violation.
46. This case and others highlight the problems of allowing two legal systems to run in parallel in the same society – a difficulty that achieved some publicity when in February 2008 the Archbishop of Canterbury suggested that some accommodations should be made in English civil law to Sharia.
47. Quoted in Rushdie, 'Where is the honour in this vile code that condemns women to die in shame?'.
48. This and subsequent sources are cited in Hermann Heinrich Ploss, Max Bartels and Paul Bartels, *Woman: An Historical, Gynaecological and Anthropological Compendium* (London: Heinemann, 1935).

49. Elizabeth Gould Davis, *The First Sex* (London: J. M. Dent, 1973), p. 154.

50. Thomas Bell, *Kalogynomia, or the Laws of Female Beauty* (London: Stockdale, 1821), p. 177, quoted ibid., p. 156.

51. Richard Burton, *Love, War and Fancy: The Customs and Manners of the East from Writings on the Arabian Nights*, ed. Kenneth Walker (London: William Kimber, 1964), p. 108.

52. See Deborah Pugh, 'Egypt to end genital mutilation', *The Guardian*, 28 March 1994.

53. Quoted in Shyam Bhatia, 'Women battle for mutilation in name of God', *The Observer*, 30 July 1995.

54. See Jocasta Shakespeare, 'Muslims back the ritual of pain', *Daily Telegraph*, 20 August 1997.

55. Quoted in Kathy Evans, 'Egypt court backs female circumcision', *The Guardian*, 25 June 1997; 'Circumcision approved', *Daily Telegraph*, 25 June 1997.

56. Quoted in Julian Isherwood, 'Denmark demands end to female circumcision', *Daily Telegraph*, 14 November 2002.

57. Quoted in Alison Boulton, 'Calls for female circumcision on NHS sparks storm', *The Observer*, 14 February 1993.

58. Quoted ibid.

59. *Human Rights Report: Saudi Arabia* (Washington, DC: State Department, 1996), p. 10.

60. Quoted in Jean P. Sasson, *Princess* (London: Bantam, 1993), pp. 159–62.

61. Quoted ibid., p. 160.

62. See 'Women at risk', *The Observer*, 10 September 1995.

63. See Alasdair Sandford, 'Pioneering model found dead in Seine', *The Guardian*, 1 March 2008.

64. Quoted in Declan Walsh, '15 child brides used to settle Pakistan feud', *The Guardian*, 5 June 2008.

65. Quoted ibid.

66. Sources cited in Kecia Ali, *Sexual Ethics and Islam: Feminist Reflections on Qur'an, Hadith, and Jurisprudence* (Oxford: Oneworld, 2006), p. 135.

67. Ashling O'Connor, 'City where the kissing has to stop', *The Times*, 7 April 2007.

68. Quoted ibid.

69. Aidan Pickering, *Sex Instruction in the Home* (London: Catholic Truth Society, 1950).

70. Quoted in O' Connor, 'City where the kissing has to stop'.

71. Quoted ibid.
72. Carolynne Wheeler, 'Egypt cracks down on the £5 "licence to live in sin"', *Sunday Telegraph*, 27 April 2008.
73. See for example Peter De Rosa, *Vicars of Christ: The Dark Side of the Papacy* (London: Bantam, 1988); William Lecky, *History of European Morals: From Augustus to Charlemagne* (London: Longmans, 1869 and subsequent editions); Henry Lea, *History of Sacerdotal Celibacy in the Christian Church* (London: Williams & Norgate, 1907 and subsequent editions).
74. See for example John Cornwell, *The Pope in Winter: The Dark Face of John Paul II's Papacy* (London: Viking, 2004).
75. Ibid., p. 135.
76. Quoted ibid., p. 136.
77. Quoted ibid., p. 137.
78. See Cornwell, *The Pope in Winter*, pp. 218–33.
79. See Karen Liebreich, *Fallen Order: Intrigue, Heresy, and Scandal in the Rome of Galileo and Caravaggio* (New York: Grove Press, 2004).
80. See 'Sharia marriage by phone was illegal', *Daily Telegraph*, 20 March 2008.
81. See Matthew Taylor, 'Victims of forced marriages could total 4,000, says study', *The Guardian*, 11 March 2008.
82. See Ben Farmer, 'Sex offender treatment is against our religion, say Muslims', *Daily Telegraph*, 9 April 2008.
83. Quoted ibid.
84. Quoted in Rajeev Syal, 'Gay teenager is facing gallows as his asylum bid is rejected', *The Times*, 12 March 2008.
85. See Richard Ford, 'Reprieve for gay Iranian who fears he will be killed', *The Times*, 14 March 2008.
86. See Jonathan Wynne-Jones, 'Carey and Tutu wade into Anglican conflict over gays', *Daily Telegraph*, 16 November 2007.
87. See 'Orthodox gays get online help', *The Times*, 15 February 2008.
88. David James Smith, 'In a suburban McDonald's a father begged his wayward daughter to come home ... so he and the men of her family could have her beaten, raped and murdered. Fearing violence, but moved by his tears, she relented – and died', *Sunday Times Magazine*, 11 November 2007.
89. See Abul Taher, 'Family of teen Muslim invited men to rape her', *Sunday Times*, 3 February 2008.
90. Quoted in Rory McCarthy, '"I was sold to a man. Is this Islam?"', *The Guardian*, 29 January 2001.
91. Ibid.

92. See Suna Erdem, 'Stoned to death by her own family', *The Times*, 2 July 2003.

93. Quoted in Ruth Gledhill, '"No more mosques" says Synod member', Times Online, 1 April 2008.

94. See Chimamanda Ngozi Adichie, 'Nigeria's immorality is about hypocrisy, not miniskirts', *The Guardian*, 2 April 2008.

95. See Julian Borger, 'Hellfire and sexual coercion: the dark side of American polygamist sects', *The Guardian*, 30 June 2005.

96. See Duncan Campbell, 'Man with five wives gets five years for bigamy', *The Guardian*, 25 August 2001.

97. Quoted in 'Disabled man denied wedding', *The Times*, 10 June 2008.

98. Quoted in Chris McGreal, 'HIV-infected condoms sent to kill Africans, claims archbishop', *The Guardian*, 27 September 2007.

99. See Khaled Dawoud, '50 Egyptian gays in court for "fomenting strife"', *The Guardian*, 18 July 2001.

Bibliography

The books listed here are a selection from my own library; many more titles could be included. To these should be added the invaluable contribution of the quality press. Taken together, the sources combine to show that all religions and cults are predominantly outdated, irrational and dangerous. The alternative – brave compassion guided by cautious reason – is the only route to a better world.

Ahmed, Qanta A., *In the Land of Invisible Women: A Female Doctor's Journey in the Saudi Kingdom* (Naperville, IL: Sourcebooks, 2008).

Al-Musnad, Muhammad bin Abdul-Aziz (compiler), *Islamic Fatawa Regarding Women*, tr. Jamaal Al-Din Zarabozo (Houston: Darussalam, 1996).

Ali, Kecia, *Sexual Ethics and Islam: Feminist Reflections on Qur'an, Hadith, and Jurisprudence* (Oxford: Oneworld, 2006).

Ali, Tariq, *The Clash of Fundamentalisms: Crusades, Jihads and Modernity* (London: Verso, 2002).

Alireza, Marianne, *At the Drop of a Veil* (London: Robert Hale, 1971).

Allen, Charles, *God's Terrorists: The Wahhabi Cult and the Hidden Roots of Modern Jihad* (London: Little, Brown, 2006).

Altizer, Thomas J. J. and William Hamilton, *Radical Theology and the Death of God* (Harmondsworth: Pelican, 1968).

Arjomand, Said Amir, *The Turban for the Crown: The Islamic Revolution in Iran* (Oxford: Oxford University Press, 1989).

Armstrong, Karen, *The Battle for God: Fundamentalism in Judaism, Christianity and Islam* (London: HarperCollins, 2000).

Armstrong, Karen, *The Bible: The Biography* (London: Atlantic, 2007).

Armstrong, Karen, *A History of God* (London: Heinemann, 1993).

Armstrong, Karen, *Muhammad: A Biography of the Prophet* (London: Victor Gollancz, 1991).

Averroes, *Faith and Reason in Islam: Averroes' Exposition of Religious Arguments*, tr. Ibrahim Y. Najjar (Oxford: Oneworld, 2001).

Ayer, A. J., *The Problem of Knowledge* (Harmondsworth: Pelican, 1956).

Balmer, Randall, *Mine Eyes Have Seen the Glory: A Journey into the Evangelical Subculture in America* (New York: Oxford University Press, 1989).

Behe, Michael J., William A. Dembski and Stephen C. Meyer, *Science and Evidence for Design in the Universe: Papers Presented at a Conference Sponsored by the Wethersfield Institute, New York City, 25 September 1999* (San Francisco: Ignatius Press, 2000).

Berman, David, *A History of Atheism in Britain: From Hobbes to Russell* (London: Croom Helm, 1988).

Bethune-Baker, J. F., *An Introduction to the Early History of Christian Doctrine to the Time of the Council of Chalcedon* (London: Methuen, 1903).

Blackham, H. J. (ed.), *Objections to Humanism* (London: Constable, 1963).

Blanshard, Paul, *Freedom and Catholic Power* (London: Secker & Warburg, 1951).

Bouquet, A. C., *Sacred Books of the World* (Harmondsworth: Pelican, 1954).

Budd, Susan, *Varieties of Unbelief: Atheists and Agnostics in English Society 1850–1960* (London: Heinemann, 1977).

Burman, Edward, *The Inquisition: The Hammer of Heresy* (Stroud: Sutton, [1984] 2004).

Capra, Fritjof, *The Tao of Physics: An Exploration of the Parallels between Modern Physics and Eastern Mysticism* (London: Fontana, 1976).

Carroll, Sean B., *The Making of the Fittest: DNA and the Ultimate Forensic Record of Evolution* (New York: W. W. Norton, 2006).

Chadwick, Owen, *The Secularization of the European Mind in the Nineteenth Century* (Cambridge: Cambridge University Press, 1975).

Chryssides, George D. and Margaret Z. Wilkins, *A Reader in New Religious Movements* (London: Continuum, 2006).

Cornwell, John, *The Pope in Winter: The Dark Face of John Paul II's Papacy* (London: Viking, 2004).

Crow, W. B., *A History of Magic, Witchcraft and Occultism* (London: Aquarian Press, 1968).

Cutner, H., *Robert Taylor: The Devil's Chaplain* (London: Pioneer Press, undated).

Darwin, Charles, *The Descent of Man, and Selection in Relation to Sex*, 2nd ed. (London: John Murray, 1909).

Darwin, Charles, *The Expression of the Emotion in Man and Animals* (London: John Murray, [1872] 1921).

Darwin, Charles, *The Origin of Species* (London: J. M. Dent, [1859] 1928).

Darwin, Charles, *The Voyage of the Beagle* (London: Heron, [1845] 1968).

Darwin, Francis, *The Life of Charles Darwin* (London: John Murray, 1902).

Dawkins, Richard, *The Ancestor's Tale: A Pilgrimage to the Dawn of Life* (London: Phoenix, 2005).

Dawkins, Richard, *The Blind Watchmaker* (Harlow: Longman Scientific & Technical, 1986).

Dawkins, Richard, *Climbing Mount Improbable* (London: Penguin, 1997).

Dawkins, Richard, *A Devil's Chaplain: Selected Essays* (London: Phoenix, 2004).

Dawkins, Richard, *The God Delusion* (London: Bantam, 2006).

Dawkins, Richard, *The Selfish Gene* (Oxford: Oxford University Press, 1976).

Dawson, Christopher, *Religion and the Rise of Western Culture* (New York: Image, [1950] 1958). de la Bedoyere, Michael (ed.), *Objections to Roman Catholicism* (London: Constable, 1964).

De Rosa, Peter, *Vicars of Christ: The Dark Side of the Papacy* (London: Corgi, 1989).

Dembski, William A., *Intelligent Design: The Bridge Between Science and Theology* (Downers Grove, IL: IVP Academic, 1999).

Dennett, Daniel C., *Breaking the Spell: Religion as a Natural Phenomenon* (London: Allen Lane, 2006).

Dennett, Daniel C., *Consciousness Explained* (London: Allen Lane, 1991).

Desmond, Adrian and James Moore, *Darwin* (London: Michael Joseph, 1991).

Donovan, Peter, *Religious Language* (London: Sheldon Press, 1976).

Edwards, David L., *Religion and Change* (London: Hodder & Stoughton, 1969).

Ellerbe, Helen, *The Dark Side of Christian History* (Windermere, FL: Morningstar & Lark, 1995).

Ferguson, Kitty, *The Fire in the Equations: Science, Religion and the Search for God* (London: Bantam, 1994).

Flew, Antony, *Darwinian Evolution* (London: Paladin, 1984).

Foakes Jackson, F. J., *The History of the Christian Church: From the Earliest Times to AD 461* (London: George Allen & Unwin, [1891] 1957).

Frazer, James George, *The Golden Bough*, abridged ed. (London: Macmillan, 1957).

Grant, Robert M. and David Noel Freedman, *The Secret Sayings of Jesus (According to the Gospel of Thomas)* (London: Fontana, 1954).

Graves, Robert, *The White Goddess*, rev. ed. (London: Faber & Faber, 1961).

Gruber, Paul H., *Darwin on Man: A Psychological Study of Creativity* (London: Wildwood House, 1974).

Guazzo, Francesco Maria, *Compendium Maleficarum: The Montague Summers Edition*, tr. E. A. Ashwin (New York: Dover, 1988, first published 1608).

Haining, Peter, *The World's Most Evil Cults: Real-Life Stories of Depraved and Violent Organizations* (Bath: Parragon, 2006).

Harding, Nick, *How to Be a Good Atheist* (Harpenden: Oldcastle, 2007).

Harris, Sam, *The End of Faith: Religion, Terror, and the Future of Reason* (London: Free Press, 2005).

Hick, John (ed.), *The Existence of God* (London: Collier Macmillan, 1964).

Hirsi Ali, Ayaan, *The Caged Virgin: An Emancipation Proclamation for Women and Islam* (New York: Free Press, 2006).

Hirsi Ali, Ayaan, *Infidel: My Life* (London: Free Press, 2007).

Hitchens, Christopher, *God Is Not Great: The Case against Religion* (London: Atlantic, 2007).

Hitchens, Christopher (ed.), *The Portable Atheist: Essential Readings for the Nonbeliever* (Cambridge, MA: Da Capo Press, 2007).

Holloway, Richard, *Godless Morality: Keeping Religion out of Ethics* (Edinburgh: Canongate, 2004).

Holy Bible: Today's New International Version (London: Hodder & Stoughton, 2004).

The Holy Bible Containing the Old and New Testaments; Translated out of the Original Tongues and with the Former Translations Diligently Compared and Revised by His Majesty's Special Command A.D. 1611 (London: British & Foreign Bible Society, undated).

Huberman, Jack, *The Quotable Atheist: Ammunition for Nonbelievers, Political Junkies, Gadflies, and Those Generally Hell-bound* (New York: Nation, 2007).

Hume, David, *Hume on Religion*, ed. Richard Wollheim (London: Fontana, 1963).

Humphreys, Christmas, *A Popular Dictionary of Buddhism*, 2nd ed. (London: Curzon Press, 1976).

Index Librorum Prohibitorum (Index of Forbidden Books) (1559–1948).

Irvine, William, *Apes, Angels and Victorians: A Joint Biography of Darwin and Huxley* (London: Weidenfeld & Nicolson, 1955).

Jakobovits, Immanuel, *Jewish Medical Ethics: A Comparative and Historical Study of the Jewish Religious Attitude to Medicine and Its Practice* (New York: Bloch, 1959).

James, E. O., *A History of Christianity in England* (London: Hutchinson, 1948).

James, William, *The Varieties of Religious Experience: A Study in Human Nature* (London: Fontana, [1902] 1960).

James I, *Demonology: Includes 'News from Scotland, on the Death of a Notable Sorcerer'* (San Diego: Book Tree, 2002).

Johnson, Nels, *Islam and the Politics of Meaning in Palestinian Nationalism* (London: Kegan Paul International, 1982).

Kahl, Joachim, *The Misery of Christianity; or, A Plea for a Humanity without God*, tr. N. D. Smith (Harmondsworth: Pelican, 1971).

Kant, Immanuel, *Critique of Pure Reason*, tr. J. M. D. Meiklejohn (London: J. M. Dent, 1934).

Kaplan, Esther, *With God on Their Side: How Christian Fundamentalists Trampled Science, Policy, and Democracy in George W. Bush's White House* (New York: New Press, 2004).

Kenny, Anthony, *The God of the Philosophers* (Oxford: Clarendon Press, 1979).

Kenny, Anthony, *The Unknown God: Agnostic Essays* (London: Continuum, 2004).

Kertzer, David I., *Unholy War: The Vatican's Role in the Rise of Modern Anti-Semitism* (London: Macmillan, 2001).

Kitcher, Philip, *Living with Darwin: Evolution, Design, and the Future of Faith* (New York: Oxford University Press, 2007).

The Koran, tr. N. J. Dawood (Harmondsworth: Penguin, [1956] 1990).

Kramer, Heinrich and James Sprenger, *Malleus Maleficarum* (Hammer of Witches), tr. Montague Summers (London: Arrow, 1971).

Küng, Hans, *Christianity and the World Religions: Paths of Dialogue with Islam, Hinduism and Buddhism*, tr. Peter Heinegg (London: Collins, 1987).

Küng, Hans, *Does God Exist? An Answer for Today*, tr. Edward Quinn (London: Collins, 1980).

Küng, Hans, *Islam: Past, Present and Future*, tr. John Bowden (Oxford: Oneworld, 2007).

Kurtz, Paul (ed.), *A Skeptic's Handbook of Parapsychology* (Buffalo, NY: Prometheus, 1985).

Lamont, Stewart, *Church and State: Uneasy Alliances* (London: Bodley Head, 1989).

Lane Fox, Robin, *Pagans and Christians* (London: Viking, 1986).

Lane Fox, Robin, *The Unauthorized Version: Truth and Fiction in the Bible* (London: Viking, 1991).

Larson, Edward J., *Trial and Error: The American Controversy over Creation and Evolution* (Oxford: Oxford University Press, 1985).

Lea, Henry, *History of Sacerdotal Celibacy in the Christian Church*, 4th ed. (London: Watts, 1932).

Lecky, William, *History of European Morals: From Augustus to Charlemagne*, 10th ed. (London: Longmans, Green, 1892).

Lepschy, Giulio C., *A Survey of Structural Linguistics* (London: Faber & Faber, 1970).

Liebreich, Karen, *Fallen Order: Intrigue, Heresy, and Scandal in the Rome of Galileo and Caravaggio* (New York: Grove Press, 2004).

Lofmark, Carl, *Does God Exist?* (London: Rationalist Press Association, 1990).

Lucretius, *De Rerum Natura* (On the Nature of Things), tr. H. A. J. Munro, 4th ed. (Cambridge: Deighton Bell, 1886).

McDannell, Colleen and Bernhard Lang, *Heaven: A History*, 2nd ed. (New Haven, CT: Yale University Press, 2001).

McGrath, Alister, *The Twilight of Atheism: The Rise and Fall of Disbelief in the Modern World* (New York: Doubleday, 2004).

McGrath, Alister and Joanna Collicutt McGrath, *The Dawkins Delusion? Atheist Fundamentalism and the Denial of the Divine* (London: Society for Promoting Christian Knowledge, 2007).

Mack, Carol K. and Dinah Mack, *A Field Guide to Demons, Fairies, Fallen Angels, and Other Subversive Spirits* (New York: Arcade, 1998).

Mackinnon, D. M., H. A. Williams, A. R. Vidler and J. S. Bezzant, *Objections to Christian Belief* (London: Constable, 1963).

McTernan, Oliver, *Violence in God's Name: Religion in an Age of Conflict* (London: Darton, Longman & Todd, 2003).

Malinowski, Bronisław, *Sex, Culture and Myth* (London: Rupert Hart-Davis, 1963).

Malinowski, Bronisław, *The Sexual Life of Savages in North-western Melanesia: An Ethnographic Account of Courtship, Marriage and Family Life among the Natives of Trobriand Islands, British New Guinea* (London: George Routledge & Sons, 1929).

Mottahedeh, Roy, *The Mantle of the Prophet: Learning and Power in Modern Iran* (London: Chatto & Windus, 1986).

Nasr, Vali, *The Shia Revival: How Conflicts within Islam Will Shape the Future* (New York: W. W. Norton, 2006).

Norman, Edward, *Christianity and the World Order* (Oxford: Oxford University Press, 1979).

Obelkevich, Jim, Lyndal Roper and Raphael Samuel (eds), *Disciplines of Faith: Studies in Religion, Politics and Patriarchy* (London: Routledge & Kegan Paul, 1987).

O'Faolain, Julia and Lauro Martines (eds), *Not in God's Image* (London: Maurice Temple Smith, 1973).

Ogden, C. K. and I. A. Richards, *The Meaning of Meaning: A Study of the Influence of Language upon Thought and of the Science of Symbolism*, 10th ed. (London: Routledge & Kegan Paul, 1972).

O'Hear, Anthony, *Experience, Explanation and Faith: An Introduction to the Philosophy of Religion* (London: Routledge & Kegan Paul, 1984).

Owen, D. D. R., *The Vision of Hell: Infernal Journeys in Medieval French Literature* (Edinburgh: Scottish Academic Press, 1970).

Pelz, Werner and Lotte Pelz, *God Is No More* (London: Victor Gollancz, 1963).

Piscatori, James P. (ed.), *Islam in the Political Process* (Cambridge: Cambridge University Press, 1983).

Priestland, Gerald, *The Case against God* (London: Collins, 1984).

Ranke, Leopold, *The History of the Popes, Their Church and State, and Especially of Their Conflicts with Protestantism in the Sixteenth and Seventeenth Centuries*, 3 vols (London: George Bell & Sons, 1891).

Ranke-Heinemann, Uta, *Eunuchs for the Kingdom of Heaven: The Catholic Church and Sexuality*, tr. Peter Heinegg (New York: Penguin, 1991).

Reichenbach, Hans, *The Rise of Scientific Philosophy* (Berkeley: University of California Press, 1951).

Rhodes, Anthony, *The Power of Rome in the Twentieth Century: The Vatican in the Age of Liberal Democracies 1870–1922* (London: Sidgwick & Jackson, 1983).

Robbins, Rossell Hope, *The Encyclopedia of Witchcraft and Demonology* (Feltham: Spring, 1959).

Robertson, Archibald, *Jesus: Myth or History?* (London: Watts, 1946).

Robertson, Roland (ed.), *Sociology of Religion: Selected Readings* (Harmondsworth: Penguin, 1969).

Robinson, John A. T., *Honest to God* (London: SCM Press, 1963).

Robinson, John A. T., *The New Reformation?* (London: SCM Press, 1965).

Robinson, John A. T. and David L. Edwards (eds), *The Honest to God Debate* (London: SCM Press, 1963).

Ross, Anne, *Pagan Celtic Britain: Studies in Iconography and Tradition* (London: Cardinal, 1974).

Roy, Olivier, *Globalised Islam: The Search for a New Ummah* (London: Hurst, 2004).

Ruether, Rosemary Radford (ed.), *Religion and Sexism: Images of Woman in the Jewish and Christian Traditions* (New York: Simon & Schuster, 1974).

Russell, Bertrand, *Bertrand Russell on God and Religion*, ed. Al Seckel (Buffalo, NY: Prometheus, 1986).

Russell, Bertrand, *'Mysticism and Logic' and Other Essays* (London: George Allen & Unwin, 1917).

Russell, Bertrand, *Religion and Science* (London: Thornton Butterworth, 1935).

Russell, Bertrand, *The Scientific Outlook* (London: George Allen & Unwin, 1931).

Russell, Bertrand, *Why I Am Not a Christian* (London: Watts, 1927).

Sampson, Geoffrey, *The Form of Language* (London: Weidenfeld & Nicolson, 1975).

Sanghera, Jasvinder, *Daughters of Shame* (London: Hodder & Stoughton, 2009).

Sardar, Ziauddin, *Desperately Seeking Paradise: Journeys of a Sceptical Muslim* (London: Granta, 2004).

Scott, Dukinfield Henry, *The Evolution of Plants* (London: Williams & Norgate, undated).

Scott, George Ryley, *Phallic Worship: A History of Sex and Sex Rites in Relation to the Religions of All Races from Antiquity to the Present Day* (London: Panther, [1941] 1970).

Shahak, Israel and Norton Mezvinsky, *Jewish Fundamentalism in Israel* (London: Pluto Press, 1999).

Shanks, Niall, *God, the Devil, and Darwin: A Critique of Intelligent Design Theory* (New York: Oxford University Press, 2004).

Sharma, Chandradhar, *A Critical Survey of Indian Philosophy* (London: Rider, 1960).

Sikand, Yoginder, *Bastions of the Believers: Madrasas and Islamic Education in India* (New Delhi: Penguin Books India, 2005).

Simons, Geoff, 'The Atheist Alternative' (1964, unpublished).

Simons, Geoff, *Is God a Programmer? Religion in the Computer Age* (Brighton: Harvester Press, 1988).

Simons, Geoff, *Is Man a Robot?* (London: Wiley, 1986).

Smart, Ninian, *Philosophers and Religious Truth* (London: SCM Press, 1964).

Smith, George H., *Atheism: The Case against God* (Buffalo, NY: Prometheus, 1979).

Starbird, Margaret, *The Goddess in the Gospels: Reclaiming the Sacred Feminine* (Santa Fe, NM: Bear, 1998).

Taylor, G. Rattray, *Sex in History: Society's Changing Attitudes to Sex throughout the Ages* (New York: Ballantine, 1954).

Thiering, Barbara, *Jesus the Man* (London: Doubleday, 1992).

Thouless, Robert H., *An Introduction to the Psychology of Religion* (Cambridge: Cambridge University Press, 1961).

Tribe, David, *100 Years of Freethought* (London: Elek, 1967).

Unger, Merrill F., *Demons in the World Today: A Study of Occultism in the Light of God's Word* (Wheaton, IL: Tyndale House, 1971).

Valiente, Doreen, *An ABC of Witchcraft Past and Present* (London: Robert Hale, 1973).

Victor, Barbara, *The Last Crusade: Religion and the Politics of Misdirection* (London: Constable, 2005).

Visscher, Maurice B. (ed.), *Humanistic Perspectives in Medical Ethics* (Buffalo, NY: Prometheus, 1972).

Waal, Frans de, *Primates and Philosophers: How Morality Evolved*, ed. Stephen Macedo and Josiah Ober (Princeton: Princeton University Press, 2006).

Wallis, Jim, *God's Politics: Why the American Right Gets It Wrong and the Left Doesn't Get It* (Oxford: Lion, 2005).

Ward, Keith, *Is Religion Dangerous?* (Oxford: Lion, 2006).

Watt, W. Montgomery, *Muhammad at Mecca* (London: Oxford University Press, 1953).

Watt, W. Montgomery, *Muhammad at Medina* (Oxford: Clarendon Press, 1956).

West, D. J., *Eleven Lourdes Miracles: An Examination of the Medical Documents Relating to Eleven 'Miraculous' Cures at Lourdes 1937–1950* (London: Gerald Duckworth, 1957).

Westermarck, Edward, *Christianity and Morals* (London: Kegan Paul, Trench, Trubner, 1939).

Wood, H. G., *Did Christ Really Live?* (London: Student Christian Movement Press, 1938).

Yamani, Mai (ed.), *Feminism and Islam: Legal and Literary Perspectives* (Reading: Garnet, 1996).

Index